RISE AND PROGRESS

OF THE

INDIAN MUTINY

RISE AND PROGRESS
OF THE
INDIAN MUTINY.

BY R. MONTGOMERY MARTIN

GYAN

Published by

Gyan Publishing House
5, Ansari Road
Daryaganj, New Delhi-110002
Phone: 011-47034999, 9811692060
E-mail: books@gyanbooks.com

Distribution Network
gyanbooks.com
India, USA, Canada, UK, Australia, France

ISBN: 978-93-6280-236-1 (PB)

First Published, 1859

2nd Impression 2023

Printed at: Gyan Press, Delhi.

RISE AND PROGRESS OF THE INDIAN MUTINY

Author: R. MONTGOMERY MARTIN

VIEW OF LUCKNOW.

THE LONDON PRINTING AND PUBLISHING COMPANY, LIMITED

RISE AND PROGRESS

OF THE

INDIAN MUTINY.

A FULL EXAMINATION OF THE

ALLEGED CAUSES OF THE INSURRECTION;

AND AN

ADDRESS TO LORD STANLEY

ON THE

CONDITION OF OUR EASTERN EMPIRE.

BY R. MONTGOMERY MARTIN,

AUTHOR OF THE "HISTORY OF THE BRITISH COLONIES."

LONDON:
THE LONDON PRINTING AND PUBLISHING COMPANY, LIMITED,
26, PATERNOSTER ROW: AND ALL BOOKSELLERS.

MDCCCLIX.

TO THE RIGHT HON. LORD STANLEY.

My Lord,

To you, with equal regard to your public position as President of the Council of India, and to your private character as a man capable of analysing and comparing the opinions of others, I beg to offer the following Summary of the "Alleged Causes of the Indian Mutiny."

It was commenced with the object of presenting, in one brief and impartial view, the various reasons which, in England and in India, are adduced (whether by Europeans or Natives) as having more or less directly—generally throughout India, or locally and partially, in certain districts and among certain classes—contributed to produce mutiny among the Sepoys, and insurrection among the people. I had thought to frame a short introductory chapter to a narrative of the rebellion, withholding my own opinions, and leaving the reader to draw conclusions from the course of events, regarding the confirmatory or contradictory evidence thereby afforded.

But brevity and impartiality are both difficult in a case like this. It was not sufficient to state the convictions of living authorities: the warnings of statesmen of a former age, who had thought deeply and spoken plainly, could not be passed over in silence. Without the clue afforded by their too nearly fulfilled prophecies, we might still grope darkly in the labyrinth of the existing system, and prove incapable of initiating a policy free from the errors which have produced our present calamity. The attempt at brevity has therefore been greatly neutralised by a desire to furnish a fair exposition of many varied views, and to preserve, as far as possible, the very words in which the men who formed, saw fit to express, them.

The attempt to refrain from comment has also broken down, because it was not possible to treat with indifference a subject on which one had dwelt anxiously and continuously for above a quarter of a century. I have ever regarded the notion of holding India on a purely military tenure, as much in the light of a blunder as of a crime. Yet the notion prevailed widely; and as late as June, 1857, the Calcutta correspondent of the *Times* boasted that the English had accomplished in India the feat that Prince Schwartzenberg pronounced impossible—"We do sit on bayonets." Before this vaunt reached England, the utterer had probably discovered, that although a seat upon bayonets may be temporarily so well cushioned as to answer the purpose of civil and military officials, it is somewhat dangerous even for them; and for a Christian government in the nineteenth century, the position is, in the highest degree, unsafe, uneasy, and unseemly.

Even supposing it possible for England, at the present time, to prostrate, or keep prostrate, the energies of the swarming millions of Hindoostan, and to rivet round their necks the iron yoke of a military despotism, the task of forging the chains is one in which no British statesman could engage, who rightly understands the nature, and values the privileges, of the constitution for which his fathers struggled and suffered. No true patriot would assist in furthering a policy which must needs react unfavourably on the liberties of England, and drag her down from her high position as the champion of political and religious freedom—recognised as such throughout the world. Heretofore, in India, we have greatly erred by relying too much on the power of the sword, and heeding too little the responsibilities of the sceptre. Crying evils have been suffered to remain for years and years without redress. The administration of justice has been notoriously costly, inefficient, and corrupt (by reason of ill-paid native underlings); the tenure of land has been oppressive and pauperising; public works have been either wholly neglected or miserably disproportioned to the revenues of the country and the wants of the people. The exclusion of the natives from positions of rank and emolument, has been rigidly maintained; and the injustice of the system has been aggravated by the rapid absorption and extinction of Independent, Allied, and Subsidiary States, resulting from avidity for territorial aggrandisement and for European patronage; and also from the act of despotism committed by the British government, in setting aside the ancient Hindoo law of Adoption, which, both in a legal and religious point of view, as a *right* and a *rite*, had been sanctioned and confirmed from the first dawn of British supremacy, down to the administration of Lord Dalhousie.

The question of Adoption is very little understood in Europe. In Hindoostan, "write this man down childless" involves a reproach as regards social position, and a heavy misfortune in a religious point of view. Yet polygamy and barrenness are frequent concomitants. Hence the custom of adopting sons to fill the void of natural issue has been practised from time immemorial, and has become inseparably connected with all arrangements for the transmission of hereditary honours and property.

Swift and sure has been the extinction of Native Dynasties, and the downfall of ancient families, under the combined operation of our Anti-Adoption policy and Resumption commissions. The mass of the people are at the same time sinking year by year deeper in abject poverty, but the government does not grow rich on the spoils; on the contrary, Indian Finance is still, as usual, a perfect slough of despond; for the utmost amount which the revenue screw can extract, is barely sufficient to meet the ordinary peace expenses; and every war increases the burden of the millstone of debt, which is oppressive not in proportion to its intrinsic weight, but because of the paralysed condition—the unnatural depression of the State which bears it.

In no conquered or annexed country of which history presents any record, have the high-born, the intelligent, the wealthy classes of a community, been so sedulously subjugated, so completely deprived of political self-government, and so utterly degraded beneath the level of the "ruling class," as the millions of men who, in the course of a century, have been brought within the control of the East India Company, and of the Executive Administration of Britain; and this, despite Acts of Parliament and solemn public declarations renouncing all desire for extension of territory*—proclaiming to princes and nobles of ancient lineage, that aristocratic England delighted in maintaining their hereditary dignity; announcing that, *de jure* and *de facto*, the fee-simple of the soil did not belong to the Government, but to the native proprietors of the land; and assuring Indians of all Classes, Castes, and Creeds, that they, as free-born British subjects, should be placed on an equality with Europeans in filling the civil and military offices of the State.†

Every one of these engagements has been ruthlessly broken, or contemptuously set aside, by the representatives of a Nation which acknowledges the force of moral responsibility—deems adherence to treaties an imperative duty—believes itself entrusted with a Mission for the diffusion of the Gospel of Peace among the Heathen—and holds forth freedom as the inherent right of man.

It is not surprising that the Sepoys felt for and with their countrymen; besides which they had their own grievances; and there is reason to believe, that the Anti-Caste policy lately pursued, the General Service Order, and the new Invaliding Regulations, appeared like initiatory measures for the destruction of Caste, as a conventionality which occasioned the British government too much inconvenience to be borne with any longer.

The Cartridges were, I firmly believe, the immediate though secondary cause of the Mutiny; but they became so because of the foregone conclusion at which the Bengal army had arrived. Had India been wisely and unselfishly governed, the Sepoys would either have continued faithful, or been as easily dealt with as if they had been bands of Pindarries or Dacoits. But the grievances of the people insured them shelter, support, and even to a considerable extent, co-operation.

A new era has now commenced. The *raj* of the Company has expired. The princes and people of India have been long accustomed to believe that their appeal in extreme cases lay to the Queen and Parliament of England, on whom the entire responsibility of their ordinary welfare has now devolved. They anticipate great things from the change: a munificent, fostering policy is,

* "Schemes of conquest and extension of dominion in India are measures repugnant to the wish, the honour, and the policy of this Nation."—Act 33rd Geo. III., c. 52. A.D. 1793.

† "No Native of the said territories, nor any natural born subject of His Majesty, resident therein, shall, by reason only of his religion, place of birth, descent, colour, or any of them, be disabled from holding any place, office, or employment under the said Company."—Act of Parliament passed 28th of August, 1833, for the "better government of His Majesty's Indian territories." Clause 57.

in their eyes, associated with the royal might of England. A limited monarchy is a thing of which an Asiatic is capable of forming but a very faint idea; and the Indian princes and people now look to the Crown to establish a government of manifest justice and generosity. All India is waiting anxiously to see how the priceless services rendered by the Nizam of Hyderabad, of Sindia and Holcar, of the Rajahs of Putteeala, Jheend, Bhurtpoor, and others, are to be rewarded.

Every hour is precious; every move of incalculable importance; every needless delay is to the last degree impolitic. To resort to the old system, especially as pursued in the North-West Provinces, would be to tempt Providence, and sow seeds for another rebellion to bear fruit at no distant day, of which what we have now gathered may be but as a foretaste. *But unless radical reforms are forthwith decided upon, they will be practically decided against*, and we shall once again find ourselves in the same old groove, out of which nothing but a Revolution can lift us.

Are we to keep India, or are we to abandon her, and sink, none can tell how deeply, in the scale of nations? The old assertion of the indolent and the cowardly—that the present state of things will last our time, will not serve us now. Our path is encircled with difficulties; we cannot stand still; it may be dangerous to advance on heretofore untrodden ground; it is certainly dangerous and ignoble to retreat. Maritime supremacy and vast commerce are closely connected with sound Indian policy; nay, our general well-being is far more immediately affected by the relations with our Dependencies and Colonies, than it is agreeable to the self-reliant national character to acknowledge.

The Comte de Montalembert has truly said, that the real perils which menace England are from without, not from within; and quoting the words of a critic only less kindly than himself (M. de Maistre), he points out the repellant effect of indulging, without restraint, "des préjugés nationaux insupportables et un orgueil sans mesure et sans prudence qui révolte les autres nations."

Pride, prejudice, and blind selfishness, have been our bane in India; to them may be traced most of the evils with which the newly-constituted Council are called upon to grapple. The task is a very arduous, but also a very noble one. Those who best understand the responsibilities which oppress, and the difficulties which surround you, My Lord, are not the least hopeful of the issue. Many who hear the general inquiry—"What will be done for India?" desire to address to you and to your colleagues, as I also cannot refrain from doing, the emphatic words—"Be just, and fear not!"

R. MONTGOMERY MARTIN.

Campden Hill, Kensington, January, 1859.

THE

INDIAN EMPIRE.

HISTORY OF

THE MUTINY OF THE SEPOY TROOPS.

INTRODUCTORY CHAPTER.

ALLEGED CAUSES OF DISCONTENT—OPPRESSIVE AND PAUPERISING TENURE OF LAND—INEFFICIENT ADMINISTRATION OF JUSTICE—EXCLUSION OF NATIVES FROM ALL SHARE IN THE GOVERNMENT—IGNORANCE OF THE LANGUAGES, AND AVERSION EVINCED TOWARDS THE NATIVES—EDUCATION, RELIGION, AND MISSIONARY OPERATIONS—CASTE—FREE PRESS—DEFECTIVE CURRENCY—OPIUM MONOPOLY—NEGLECT OF PUBLIC WORKS—REPRESSION OF BRITISH ENTERPRISE—RECENT ANNEXATIONS—INFRACTION OF THE HINDOO LAW OF INHERITANCE—EXTINCTION OF NATIVE STATES—SATTARA, NAGPOOR, CARNATIC, TANJORE, JHANSI, OUDE, Etc.—STATE OF THE BENGAL ARMY; RELAXED DISCIPLINE; REMOVAL OF REGIMENTAL OFFICERS TO STAFF AND CIVIL EMPLOYMENTS; PAUCITY OF EUROPEAN TROOPS; SEPOY GRIEVANCES; GREASED CARTRIDGES—MOHAMMEDAN CONSPIRACY—FOREIGN INTRIGUES; PERSIAN AND RUSSIAN.

Never, perhaps, was the condition of British India deemed more fair and promising than at the conclusion of 1856. The new governor-general, Lord Canning, who arrived in the spring of that year, had seen no reason to question the parting declaration of his predecessor, Lord Dalhousie—that India was "in peace without and within," and that there appeared to be "no quarter from which formidable war could reasonably be expected at present."*

The British and Anglo-Indian press, adopting the same tone, declared "the whole of India" to be "profoundly tranquil."† The conviction seems to have been general amid all ranks and classes, from the viceregal palace at Calcutta, to the smallest and most distant English post; and thus it happened that the vessel of the state pursued her course with all sail set, in the full tide of prosperity, till a series of shocks, slight at first, but rapidly increasing in strength and frequency, taught a terrible lesson of the necessity for careful steering amid the sunken rocks, the shoals, and quicksands, heretofore so feebly and faintly traced in those famous charts and log-books—the voluminous minutes and correspondence of the East India Company.

The sky had been carefully watched for any indication of the storms of foreign invasion; but the calm waters of our "strong internal administration," and the full current of our "unparalleled native army," had so long borne the stately ship in triumph on their bosom, that few attempts were made to sound their depths. Those few excited little attention, and were, for the most part, decidedly discouraged by the authorities both in England and in India. The consequence has been, that at every step of the revolt, we have encountered fresh proofs of our ignorance of the first conditions on which rested the general security of the empire, and the individual safety of every European in India.

Our heaviest calamities, and our greatest advantages, have come on us by surprise: we have been met by foulest treachery in the very class we deemed bound to us by every tie of gratitude and self-interest, and we have found help and fidelity among those whom we most distrusted. We have failed where we confidently looked for

* Minute by the Marquis of Dalhousie, 28th February, 1856.—Parliamentary Papers (Commons), 16th June. 1856; pp. 6—8.

† The *Times*, 9th December, 1856.

triumph; we have succeeded where we anticipated failure. Dangers we never dreamed of, have risen suddenly to paralyse our arms; and obstacles which seemed well-nigh insurmountable, have vanished into thin air before us. Our trusted weapons have proved worthless; or worse—been turned against us; and, at the outset of the struggle, we were like men whose pistols had been stolen from their holsters, and swords from their scabbards, while they lay sleeping; and who, starting up amazed and bewildered, seized the first missiles that came to hand to defend themselves against a foe whose numbers and power, whose objects and character, were alike involved in midnight darkness.

Very marvellous was the presence of mind, the self-reliance, the enduring courage displayed by English men and women, and many native adherents, in their terrible and unlooked-for trial; and very comforting the instances of Christian heroism which adorn this sad and thrilling page of Anglo-Indian history: yet none will venture to deny, that it was the absence of efficient leaders on the part of the mutineers, and not our energy and foresight, which, under Providence, was the means of enabling us to surmount the first overwhelming tide of disaster. Nothing can be more contradictory than the opinions held by public men regarding the immediate object of the mutineers. Some deny that the sepoys acted on any "prearranged plan;" and declare, that "their primary and prevailing motive was a panic-terror for their religion."* Others regard the revolt as the issue of a systematic plot, which must have taken months, if not years, to organise; and compare the outbreak to the springing of a mine, for which the ground must have been hollowed, the barrels filled, the train laid, and the match fired, before the explosion.† A third party assert, that our own impolicy had gathered together masses of combustibles, and that our heedlessness (in the matter of the greased cartridges) set them on fire.

It is quite certain that the people of India labour under many political and social evils, resulting from inefficient administration. Human governments are, at best, fallible and weak instruments. In Christian England, after so many centuries of freedom, kept and strengthened by unceasing effort, we all acknowledge how far the condition of the masses falls short, in reality, of what in theory we might have hoped for. How, then, can we doubt, that there must be in India much greater scope for oppression, much greater need for watchfulness. We have seen, in Ireland, a notable example of the effects of absentee proprietorship; but here is a case of absentee sovereigntyship, in which the whole agency is systematically vested in the foreign delegates of a foreign power, few of whom have ever acquired any satisfactory insight into the habits, customs, or languages of the people they were sent to govern.

It is easier to account for the errors committed by the Company than for the culpable neglect of Parliament. We know that an Indian question continued to be the "dinner-bell" of the House of Commons, notwithstanding the revelations of the Torture Committee at Madras, until the massacres of Meerut and Cawnpoor showed that the government of India was a subject which affected not only the welfare of the dark-coloured millions from whom we exacted tribute, but also the lives of Englishmen, and the honour of Englishwomen—the friends or relatives, it might be, of the heretofore ignorant and listless legislators.

A right understanding of the causes of the revolt would materially assist all engaged in framing measures for the restoration of tranquillity, and for a sounder system of administration. The following enumeration of the various causes, distant and proximate, which are asserted by different authorities to have been concerned in bringing about the present state of affairs, is therefore offered, with a view of enabling the reader to judge, in the course of the narrative, how far events have tended to confirm or nullify these allegations.

Land-tenure.—The irregular, oppressive, and generally pauperising tenure of land, has been set forth in a preceding section: and since every sepoy looks forward to the time when he shall retire on his pension to live in his own cottage, under his own fig-tree, the question is one in which he has a clear and personal interest. Irrespective of this, the manner in which the proprietary rights of the inhabitants of the Ceded and Conquered provinces have been dealt with,

* See Indophilus' (Sir Charles Trevelyan's) Letters to the *Times*. Republished by Longman as a pamphlet: p. 37.

† See Sir E. Bulwer Lytton's speech at the Herts Agricultural Society, October, 1857.

is a matter of history with which the landowners in native independent states are sure to make themselves acquainted; and the talookdars and hereditary chiefs of Oude, could not but have remembered with alarm, the grievous breach of faith committed against the proprietors of the soil in the North-Western Provinces.

A general allusion to this disgraceful procedure has been already made;* but the following detail is given on the authority of various papers drawn up by Mr. Henry St. George Tucker. The views of Mr. Tucker were, it should be premised, utterly opposed to any system "founded on the assumption of the government being the universal landlord;" which sweeping assumption he regarded "as a virtual annihilation of all private rights."

The Ryotwar Settlement made by Munro, in Madras, he thought tended to the impoverishment of the country, the people, and the government itself; and was, in fact, a continuation of the policy of Tippoo Sultan, who drove away and exterminated the proprietors; his object being to engross the rents as well as revenues of the country.

The landowners of the North-Western Provinces—including Delhi, Agra, Bareilly, and the cessions from Oude in 1801—have, however, peculiar and positive grievances to complain of. In 1803, under the administration of the Marquis Wellesley, a regulation was passed, by which the government pledged themselves, "that a permanent settlement of the Ceded provinces would be concluded at the end of ten years;" and proclaimed "the proprietary rights of all zemindars, talookdars, and other descriptions of landholders possessing a right of property in the lands comprising their zemindaries, talooks, or other tenures, to be confirmed and established under the authority of the British government, in conformity to the laws and usages of the country." In 1805, a regulation was passed by the same government, in nearly corresponding terms, declaring that a permanent settlement would be concluded with the zemindars and other landholders in the Conquered provinces, at the expiration of the decennial leases. But, in 1807, the supreme government being anxious to extend to the landowners of our newly-acquired territory those advantages which had been conferred on the zemindars of the Lower Provinces, by fixing the land-tax in perpetuity, a new regulation was enacted, appointing commissioners for superintending the settlement of the Ceded and Conquered provinces; and notifying "to the zemindars, and other actual proprietors of land in those provinces, that the jumma which may be assessed on their estates in the last year of the settlement immediately ensuing the present settlement, shall remain fixed for ever, in case the zemindars shall now be willing to engage for the payment of the public revenue on those terms in perpetuity, and the arrangement shall receive the sanction of the Hon. Court of Directors."† Far from objecting to the pledge given to the landholders in those regulations; far from contending against the principle of a fixed assessment, either on the ground of policy or of justice, the Court expressed their approbation of the measure contemplated, and gave it their unreserved sanction. To as late a period as 1813, not even a doubt was expressed in the way of discouragement; and the government of India had every reason to presume that they were proceeding in this great work with the full concurrence and approbation of the controlling authorities in this country. Mr. Edmonstone, in his able and instructive letters to the Court (of 31st July, 1821), has shown most conclusively, that the plans and proceedings of the government abroad received an ample confirmation. "Unhappily," says Mr. Tucker, "different views were adopted at a subsequent period; and since 1813,‡ the whole tenor of the Court's correspondence with the supreme government, has not only discountenanced the idea of a permanent settlement of the lands in the Ceded and Conquered provinces, but peremptory injunctions have been issued to that government, prohibiting the formation of such settlement at any future period." The pledge so formally given to the landholders in 1803, and 1805, and 1807, has accordingly remained unredeemed to the present day; temporary settlements have been concluded, in various ways, with different classes of persons; some of the principal talookdars have been set aside, and deprived of the management of their estates; and the great object seems to have been, to introduce the system of revenue administration§ which obtains in

* *Indian Empire*, vol. i., p. 579.

† Calcutta Records—Regulation X. of 1807; sec. 5.

‡ See Letter of Court of Directors to Bengal, 16th March, 1813.

§ The Ryotwar: see *Indian Empire*, vol. i., p. 575.

the territory of Fort St. George. I (in 1827) was a party to the introduction of leases for thirty years in the Western Provinces, by way of compromise for violating the pledge which had been given to the landholders in 1803 and 1805, to confirm the settlement then made with them in perpetuity. "I trust that this long term will operate as some compensation for their disappointment, and that it will, in a great degree, answer the ends proposed by a permanent settlement; but, as a principle, I still maintain, that permanency of tenure, and a limitation of the public demand upon the land, were boons bestowed under the dictates of a just and enlightened policy, and that Lord Cornwallis is to be regarded as the greatest benefactor of India."*

The measure referred to by Mr. Tucker, which I had myself the satisfaction of assisting to procure, was, however, partial in its extent, as well as temporary in its operation. It can hardly be called a compromise; it was simply a sop thrown by the stronger party who broke the bargain, to certain members of the weaker party, who had no resource but to accept it. The public pledge of a permanent settlement with the whole Conquered and Ceded, or, as they are now styled, North-Western Provinces, remains unredeemed. Moreover, even supposing the landholders could forget the manner in which that great boon was freely promised and arbitrarily withheld, they would still have reason to complain of the irregular and often oppressive assessments to which they were and are subjected. There is abundant evidence on this head; but none of greater authority than that of Colonel Sleeman, the resident at Lucknow; who, being commissioned by Governor-general Dalhousie to inquire into the state of Oude, became incidentally acquainted with the results of our fifty years' government of the half of Oude, ceded to us by the treaty of 1801.

"The country was then divided into equal shares, according to the rent-roll at the time. The half made over to the British government has been ever since yielding more revenue to us; while that retained by the sovereign of Oude has been yielding less and less to him: and ours now yields, in land revenue, stamp-duty, and the tax on spirits, two crore and twelve lacs [of rupees] a-year; while the reserved half now yields to Oude only about one crore and thirty-three lacs. Under good management, the Oude share might, in a few years, be made equal to ours, and perhaps better; for the greater part of the lands in our share have been a good deal impoverished by over-cropping; while those of the Oude share have been improved by long fallows." Colonel Sleeman would seem to attribute the greater revenue raised from our territories, to that obtained by the native government, simply to our "good management;" for he adds, that "lands of the same natural quality in Oude, under good tillage, now pay a much higher rent than they do in our half of the estate."† Yet, in another portion of his Diary, when describing the decided aversion to British rule entertained by the landed aristocracy of Oude, he dwells on our excessive assessments, as co-operating with the cost and uncertainty of the law in civil cases, in causing the gradual decay of all the ancient families. "A less and less proportion of the annual produce of their lands is left to them in our periodical settlements of the land revenue; while family pride makes them expend the same sums in the marriage of their children, in religious and other festivals, personal servants, and hereditary retainers. They fall into balance, incur heavy debts, and estate after estate is put up to auction, and the proprietors are reduced to poverty. They say, that four times more of these families have gone to decay in the half of the territory made over to us in 1801, than in the half reserved by the Oude sovereign; and this is, I fear, true. They named the families—I cannot remember them."‡

To Mr. Colvin, Lieutenant-governor of the N.W. Provinces, the Colonel writes, that on the division of Oude in 1801, the landed aristocracy were equal in both portions. "Now (28th Dec., 1853) hardly a family of this class remains in our half; while in Oude it remains unimpaired. Everybody in Oude believes those families to have been systematically crushed."§

The correspondence in the public journals, regarding the progress of the mutiny, affords frequent evidence of the heavy rate of assessment in the North-West Provinces. For instance, the special correspondent of the *Times* (Mr. Russell), writing from the

* See *Memorials of Indian Government;* a selection from the papers of H. St. G. Tucker, edited by J. W. Kaye; pp. 106—137.

† *Journey through Oude, in* 1849-'50, by Colonel Sir W. Sleeman; vol. i., p. 169.

‡ *Ibid.*, vol. i., p. 169.

§ *Ibid.*, vol. ii., p. 415.

camp at Bareilly, speaks of the "indigent population" of Rohilcund; and asserts, on the authority of Mr. Donalds, a settler and planter there, that the Company's land-tax on certain districts was not less than sixty-six per cent.*

It is to be hoped that a searching and unprejudiced inquiry will be instituted wherever decided and general disaffection has been manifested—wherever such statements are made as that from Allahabad; in which it is asserted, that "one, and only one, of the zemindars has behaved well to us during the disturbances here."†

An exposition of the working of the "model system" in Southern India, is given by Mr. Bourdillon, secretary to the government at Madras, in the revenue department, in a pamphlet published in 1852, in which he showed that, in the year 1848-'9, out of a total of 1,071,588 leases (excluding joint holdings in the fourteen principal ryotwarree districts), no fewer than 589,932 were each under twenty shillings per annum; averaging, in fact, only a small fraction above eight shillings each: 201,065 were for amounts ranging from twenty to forty shillings; averaging less than 28*s.* 6*d.* each: and 97,891 ranged between forty and sixty shillings; averaging 49*s.* 6*d.* each. Thus, out of 1,100,000 leases, 900,000 were for amounts under sixty shillings each, the average being less than 19*s.* 6*d.* each per annum. Mr. Bourdillon thus describes the condition of several million‡ of people subject to the Crown of England, and under its complete jurisdiction in some parts for more than half a century:—"Now it may certainly be said of almost the whole of the ryots paying even the highest of these sums, and even of many holding to a much larger amount, that they are always in poverty, and generally in debt. Perhaps one of this class obtains a small amount out of the government advances for cultivation; but even if he does, the trouble he has to take, and the time he loses in getting it, as well as the deduction to which he is liable, render this a questionable gain. For the rest of his wants he is dependent on the bazaar-man. To him his crops are generally hypothecated before they are reaped; and it is he who redeems them from the possession of the village watcher, by pledging himself for the payment of the kist (rent claimed by government.) These transactions pass without any written engagements or memoranda between the parties; and the only evidence is the chetty's (bazaar-man) own accounts. In general, there is an adjustment of the accounts once a year; but sometimes not for several years. In all these accounts interest is charged on the advances made to the ryot, on the balance against him. The rate of interest varies with the circumstances of the case and the necessities of the borrower: it is probably seldom, or never, less than twelve per cent. per annum, and not often above twenty-four per cent. Of course the poorest and most necessitous ryots have to pay the highest. A ryot of this class of course lives from hand to mouth; he rarely sees money, except that obtained from the chetty to pay his kist: the exchanges in the out-villages are very few, and they are usually conducted by barter. His ploughing cattle are wretched animals, not worth more than seven to twelve shillings each; and all the rest of his few agricultural implements are equally primitive and inefficient. His dwelling is a hut of mud walls and thatched roof, far ruder, smaller, and more dilapidated than those of the better classes of ryots above spoken of, and still more destitute, if possible, of anything that can be called furniture. His food, and that of his family, is partly thin porridge, made of the meal of grain boiled in water, and partly boiled rice with a little condiment; and generally, the only vessels for cooking and eating from, are of the coarsest earthenware, much inferior in grain to a good tile or brick in England, and unglazed. Brass vessels, though not wholly unknown among this class, are rare. As to anything like education or mental culture, they are wholly destitute of it."

Mr. Mead, who resided several years at Madras, and who visited other parts of India, declares, that by the system which the British government have pursued, "the native aristocracy have been extinguished, and their revenues lost equally to the rulers and the multitude. The native manufacturers are ruined; and no corresponding increase has taken place in the consumption of foreign goods. Not a fourth of the land is taken up for tillage; and yet 200,000 men annually leave these shores, to seek employment on a foreign soil. The taxation of all kinds, and the landlord's rent,

* The *Times*, July 6th, 1858.

† Parl. Papers, 4th February, 1858.

‡ According to Mr. Mead, "18,000,000 souls, in Madras, have only a penny a-week each to subsist on."—(p. 3.)

amount to but 5*s.* per head; and yet the surplus production of 23,000,000 is but 2*s.* 7*d.*, and the imports but 1*s.* 6*d.*, each person."*

The people of the North-West Provinces are being rapidly reduced to the condition of those of Southern India; and it is asserted, that they would rejoice at any change which promises relief from a "system" calculated to weigh down, with unceasing pressure, the energies of every man who derives his subsistence from the cultivation of the soil.

The Inefficient Administration of Justice is an admitted evil; the costliness, the procrastination, above all, the perjury and corruption for which our civil and criminal, our Sudder and Adawlut courts, are notorious. Shortly before the outbreak of the mutiny, Mr. Halliday, the lieutenant-governor of Bengal, urged, in the strongest language, the necessity for measures of police reform, which should extend to "our criminal judicatories as well as to the magistracy and constabulary organisation." He adds, after referring to the evidence brought forward in Mr. Dampier's elaborate reports—"I have myself made much personal inquiry into this matter during my tours. Whether right or wrong, the general native opinion is certainly that the administration of criminal justice is little better than a lottery, in which, however, the best chances are with the criminals; and I think this, also, is very much the opinion of the European mofussil [country] community. * * * Often have I heard natives express, on this point, their inability to understand the principles on which the courts are so constituted, or so conducted, as to make it appear in their eyes as if the object were rather to favour the acquittal, than to insure the conviction and punishment of offenders; and often have I been assured by them, that their anxious desire to avoid appearing as prosecutors, arose in a great measure from their belief that prosecution was very likely to end in acquittal, even, as they imagined, in the teeth of the best evidence; while the acquittal of a revengeful and unscrupulous ruffian, was known by experience to have repeatedly ended in the most unhappy consequences to his ill-advised and imprudent prosecutor. That this very general opinion is not ill-founded, may, I think, be proved from our own records."†

The youth and inexperience of the magistrates, which contributes so largely to the inefficiency of the courts over which they preside, arises out of the numerical inadequacy of the covenanted service to supply the number of officers required by the existing system. The Hon. A. Kinnaird stated, in the House of Commons, June 11th, 1857, that in Bengal, there were but seventy covenanted and uncovenanted magistrates, or one to 460,000 persons; and that there were three or four cases of a single magistrate to more than a million souls. It is terrible to think of the power such a state of things must throw into the hands of the native police, and this in a country where experience has taught us, that power, thus delegated, has invariably been employed as a means of extorting money. No wonder, then, that "from one end of Bengal to the other," the earnest desire and aim of those who have suffered from thieves or dacoits, should be, "to keep the matter secret from the police, whose corruption and extortion is so great, as to cause it to be popularly said, that dacoity is bad enough, but the subsequent police inquiry very much worse."

The frequent change, from place to place, and office to office, is urged as another reason for the inefficiency of our system. In the district of Dacca, for instance, the average time of continuance in the magistrate's office, has been, for the last twenty years, not ten months. The extent of the evil may be understood by looking over the register of civil servants, and their appointments. The *Friend of India* quotes the case of a well-known name among Indian officials—Henry Lushington—who arrived in India on the 14th of October, 1821, and, by the 9th of May, 1842, had filled no less than twenty-one offices—a change every year. But during this time he returned to Europe twice, and was absent from India four years and a quarter: his occupancy of each office, therefore, averages scarcely nine months. The journalist adds—"Thousands of miles of country, inhabited by millions of people, would have neither justice nor protection, were it not for the illegally assumed power of the planter and zemindar. There are districts in which the magistrate's court is sixty miles away; and in one case, I know of a judge having to go 140 miles to try a case of murder—so wide does his jurisdiction extend. This very district contains upwards of two millions of people; yet to

* Mead's *Sepoy Revolt;* p. 313. (Routledge, 1858.)

† Minute to Council of India, 30th April, 1856.

govern it there are just two Europeans; and one of these spends a considerable portion of his time in sporting, shooting wild animals, and hunting deer."*

The diminished numbers and impaired efficiency of the rural police, or village chowkeedars, during the last twenty years, is another reason why "our magistracy is losing credit and character, and our administration growing perceptibly weaker." They are, says lieutenant-governor Halliday, so inadequately and uncertainly paid, as to be kept in a permanent state of starvation; and though, in former days, magistrates battled for them with unwilling zemindars and villagers, and were encouraged by government to do so, they are now declared to have no legal right to remuneration for service, and have themselves become too often the colleagues of thieves and robbers. The measures suggested by Mr. Halliday as indispensable to the effectual improvement of the Bengal police, were—the improvement of the character and position of the village chowkeedars, or watchmen; the payment of adequate salaries, and the holding forth of fair prospects of advancement to the stipendiary police; the appointment of more experienced officers as covenanted zillah magistrates; a considerable increase in the number of the uncovenanted or deputy magistrates; an improvement in our criminal courts of justice; and, lastly, the establishment of sufficient means of communication with the interior of districts: because no system could work well while the police-stations and the large towns and marts in the interior continued to be cut off from the chief zillah stations, and from one another, by the almost entire absence of roads, or even (during a large part of the year) of the smallest bridle-roads or footpaths.

The proposer of the above reforms added, that they would involve an increased expenditure of £100,000 a-year on the magistracy and police of Bengal; and this statement, perhaps, furnishes an explanation of the little attention excited by a document full of important but most unpalatable assertions. The onus cannot, however, be allowed to rest solely on the local authorities. The consideration of the House of Commons has been urgently solicited, by one of its own members,† to the report of the lieutenant-governor; and the fact of such flagrant evils being alleged, by a leading functionary, to exist in the districts under the immediate eye of the supreme government, is surely a sufficient warning, not merely of the necessity of promptly redressing the wrongs under which the Bengalees laboured, but also of investigating the internal administration of the distant provinces. It is unaccountable that the judicial part of the subject should have been so long neglected, after the unreserved condemnation of the system, pronounced by Lord Campbell in the House of Lords in 1853. In reply to the complaint of the Duke of Argyll regarding the strong expressions used in a petition for relief, presented on behalf of the people of Madras, his lordship adverted to the mode in which "ingenuous youths" were dispatched from the college at Haileybury, with, at best, a very imperfect acquaintance with the languages of India, and were made at once judges. Even the advantage of only acting in that capacity was withheld, the same youth being one day a judge of civil cases, the next a collector of revenue, and the next a police magistrate. Speaking from experience derived from the appeals which had come before him as a member of the judicial committee of the Privy Council, he thought, "as far as regarded the administration of justice in the inferior courts, no language could be too extravagant in describing its enormities."‡

The testimony borne by Mr. Halliday, in Bengal, entirely accords with that given by other witnesses regarding the administration of justice in the North-Western Provinces. Colonel Sleeman, writing in 1853, declared—"There is really nothing in our system which calls so much for remedy." He says, that during his recent tour through Oude, he had had much conversation with the people generally, and with many who had sojourned in our territory in seasons of disturbance. They were all glad to return, rather than remain in our districts and endure the evils occasioned by "the uncertainties of our law, the multiplicity and formality of our courts, the pride and negligence of those who preside over

* Quoted by Mr. Kinnaird, in *Bengal, its Landed Tenure and Police System.* (Ridgway, 1857; p. 14.) The series of measures provided by Lord Cornwallis, to protect the cultivator under the Permanent Settlement from oppression on the part of the proprietors, have been disregarded; and the consequence of this neglect has been to leave too great power in the hands of the zemindars.—(*Ibid.*, p. 6.)

† By the Hon. A. Kinnaird, June 11th, 1856.

‡ *Hansard's Debates*, vol. cxxiv., p. 647.

them, and the corruption and insolence of those who must be employed to prosecute or defend a cause in them, and enforce the fulfilment of a decree when passed." Colonel Sleeman cites the statements made to him by the Brahmin communities of two villages, invited back by the native authorities from the Shahjehanpoor district, and resettled on their lands; "a mild, sensible, and most respectable body, whom a sensible ruler would do all in his power to protect and encourage; but these are the class of landholders and cultivators whom the reckless governors of districts under the Oude government most grievously oppress. They told me:—

"'Your courts of justice are the things we most dread, sir; and we are glad to escape from them as soon as we can, in spite of all the evils we are exposed to on our return to the place of our birth. * * * The truth, sir, is seldom told in these courts. There they think of nothing but the number of witnesses, as if all were alike; here, sir, we look to the quality. When a man suffers wrong, the wrongdoer is summoned before the elders, or most respectable men of his village or clan; and if he denies the charge and refuses redress, he is told to bathe, put his hand upon the peepul-tree, and declare aloud his innocence. If he refuses, he is commanded to restore what he has taken, or make suitable reparation for the injury he has done; and if he refuses to do this, he is punished by the odium of all, and his life becomes miserable. A man dare not put his hand upon that sacred tree and deny the truth—the gods sit in it, and know all things; and the offender dreads their vengeance. In your Adawluts, sir, men do not tell the truth so often as they do among their own tribes or village communities: they perjure themselves in all manner of ways, without shame or dread; and there are so many men about these courts, who understand the 'rules and regulations' (aen and kanoon), and are so much interested in making truth appear to be falsehood, and falsehood truth, that no man feels sure that right will prevail in them in any case. The guilty think they have just as good a chance of escape as the innocent. Our relations and friends told us, that all this confusion of right and wrong, which bewildered them, arose from the multiplicity of the 'rules and regulations,' which threw all the power into the hands of bad men, and left the European gentlemen helpless!'"*

The comment made on the above assertions, tends to establish their accuracy. Colonel Sleeman says—"The quality of testimony, no doubt, like that of every other commodity, deteriorates under a system which renders the good of no more value, in exchange, than the bad. The formality of our courts here, as everywhere else, tends to impair, more or less, the quality of what they receive. The simplicity of courts composed of little village communities and elders, tends, on the contrary, to improve the quality of the testimony they get; and, in India, it is found to be best in the isolated hamlets and forests, where men may be made to do almost anything rather than tell a lie. A Mahratta pundit, in the valley of the Nerbudda, once told me, that it was almost impossible to teach a wild Gond of the hills and jungles the occasional value of a lie. It is the same with the Tharoos and Booksas, who are almost exclusively the cultivators of the Oude Turaee forest, and with the peasantry of the Himalaya chain of mountains, before they have come much in contact with people of the plains, and become subject to the jurisdiction of our courts. These courts are, everywhere, our weak points in the estimation of our subjects; and they should be everywhere simplified, to meet the wants and wishes of so simple a people."†

The Exclusion of the Natives from all Share in the Government, has been acted on as necessary to our retention of India. Yet many leading authorities agree in viewing the degraded state in which they have been held as a great defect in our system. "We exclude them," said Sir Thomas Munro, "from every situation of trust and emolument. We confine them to the lowest offices, with scarcely a bare subsistence. * * * We treat them as an inferior race of beings. Men who, under a native government, might have held the first dignities of the state; who, but for us, might have been governors of provinces, are regarded as little better than menial servants, and are often not better paid, and scarcely permitted to sit in our presence."

Lord Metcalfe, Lord William Bentinck, and others, have taken the same tone; and the opinions of the Duke of Wellington, Sir Robert Peel, and Lord Glenelg, are sufficiently evidenced in the 87th clause of the Charter Act of 1833, which declares the natives eligible to all situations under government, with certain exceptions. This clause,‡ so generously intended, has

* Sleeman's *Journey through Oude*, vol. ii., p. 68.

† *Ibid.*, vol. i., p. 168; vol. ii., p. 415.

‡ The clause runs as follows:—"That no natives of said territories, nor any natural born subject of her majesty resident therein, shall by reason only of his religion, place of birth, descent, colour, or any of them, be disabled from holding any place, office, or employment under the said Company." Mr. Cameron, a gentleman long and intimately acquainted with India, writing in 1853, says—"During the

proved a cruel mockery, by exciting expectations which have been frustrated by the conditions attached to it, and the determined opposition of the Court of Directors, even when those conditions, including the voyage to England, have been fulfilled.

The monopoly of commerce was the worst feature of the E. I. Company, as regarded the British nation; the monopoly of patronage is its worst feature as regards the Indian population, and not its best as regards that of England. Lord William Bentinck stated the case very ably in his evidence before the select committee on steam communication with India in 1837. "The bane of our system is not solely that the civil administration is entirely in the hands of foreigners, but that the holders of this monopoly, the patrons of these foreign agents, are those who exercise the directing power at home; that this directing power is exclusively paid by the patronage; that the value of this patronage depends exactly upon the degree in which all the honours and emoluments of the state are engrossed by their clients, to the exclusion of the natives. There exists, in consequence, on the part of the home authorities, an interest in respect to the administration precisely similar to what formerly prevailed as to commerce, directly opposed to the welfare of India; and, consequently, it will be remarked without surprise, that in the two renewals of the charter that have taken place within the last twenty-five years, in the first, nothing was done to break down this administrative monopoly; and in the second, though a very important principle was declared, that no disability from holding office in respect to any subjects of the Crown, by reason of birth, religion, descent, or colour, should any longer continue, still no provision was made for working it out; and, as far as is known, the enactment has remained till this day a dead letter."*

The number of natives employed in the administration, notwithstanding the large accessions of territory between the years 1851 and 1857 (inclusive), has actually decreased from 2,910 to 2,846. Of the latter number, 856 receive less than £120 *per annum;* 1,377 from £120 to £240 per annum; and only eleven receive above £840.† These figures, when compared with the increased numbers and high salaries of the European covenanted and uncovenanted servants, can hardly fail to suggest a reason why the Hindoos—who frequently filled the chief positions in Indo-Mohammedan states, and almost invariably that of Dewan (or chancellor of the exchequer)—may think the rule of power-loving, money-getting Englishmen, worse for them than that of the indolent Moslem, who, though he sometimes forcibly destroyed the caste of thousands, yet never withheld from their race the honours and emoluments of high office. Rajpoots led the forces of Delhi; Rajpootnies (though that they affected to consider a degradation) sat within its palaces in imperial state—the wives and mothers of emperors: Brahmins filled every revenue office, from that of the treasurer-in-chief to the lowest clerk; all the financial business being transacted by them. The Great Moguls, the minor Mohammedan sovereigns, and their chief retainers, were spendthrifts rather than hoarders: they won kingdoms with their swords; and, like all conquerors, looked to reap where they had not sown; but avarice, or the love of money for its own sake, was very rare among them. They sat on their silver howdahs, on the backs of their elephants, and threw rupees, by bagsful, among the people, who always benefited, at least indirectly, by the lavish expenditure for which they furnished the means.

The modern Brahmins (whatever their ancestors may have done) certainly evince more acquaintance with, and predilection for, the practice of the rules of Cocker, than for the abstract study of the Vedas, and the geographical and astronomical absurdities of the Shastras. They are born diplomatists, as well as financialists. Our greatest statesmen have acknowledged their remarkable ability. The despatches, especially the supplementary ones, of the late Duke of Wellington, abound with evidence of this: and when describing the character of Talleyrand, the duke could find no better comparison than that he was "like Eitel Punt (the

twenty years that have [since] elapsed, not one of the natives has been appointed to any office except such as they were eligible to before the statute." Mr. Henry Richard, commenting on this policy, remarks—"In adopting this course, and treating the natives as a conquered and inferior race, on no account to be admitted to political and social equality with ourselves, we are not only violating the dictates of justice and of Christian morality, but we are disregarding all that the experience of the past has taught us to be wise policy with a view to permanent success."—(*Present and Future of India under British Rule*, p. 37.)

* Parl. Papers, 26th April, 1858; p. 201.

† Parl. Paper (House of Commons), 16th April, 1858.

Brahmin minister of Sindia); only not so clever."* Such men as these can hardly be expected to endure, without resentment, treatment which keeps the promise to the ear, yet breaks it to the sense.

In England we have grown used to the assertion, that there is no such thing as public opinion or discussion among the natives: but this is a mistake, and only proves that we have overlooked its rise and progress. The public meetings held in every presidency, the numerous journals, and, still more, the political pamphlets published by natives, attest the contrary. Of the latter class one now lies before me, written in English—fluent, grammatical English—with just a sufficient tinge of Orientalism to give internal evidence of the veritable authorship. The writer, after admitting the protection afforded by British rule from external violence and internal commotion, adds —"But it has failed to foster the growth of an upper class, which would have served as a connecting link between the government and the mass of the people. The higher order of the natives have, ever since its commencement, been shut out of all avenues to official distinction. They may acquire colossal fortunes in commercial and other pursuits, or obtain diplomas and honours in colleges and universities, but they cannot be admitted into the civil service, or the higher grades in the military service, without undertaking a voyage to England, and complying with other equally impracticable conditions. The highest situations to which they can aspire, are deputy-magistrateships and Sudder ameenships."†

Ignorance of the Languages, and the Aversion evinced towards the Natives, are the causes alleged by Baboo Shew Purshad (inspector of schools in the Benares division), for the "unpopularity of the government, and, consequently, of all the miseries under which the country labours." The reluctance of the English functionaries to mix with the natives, has prevented their acquiring that thorough knowledge of their sentiments and capabilities, social and moral condition, internal economy, wants, and prejudices, which are essential to successful government. "In England," says the writer just quoted, "you have only to pass good acts, and draw good rules, and people will take upon themselves to see that they are worked in the right way, and for their benefit, by the local authorities; but here the case is otherwise: the best regulations can be turned into a source of the worst oppression by an unscrupulous and exacting magistrate; and if you give us a good magistrate, he can keep us happy without any regulation at all. The Punjab owes its happiness more to Sir John Lawrence and Messrs. Montgomery and Macleod, than to any system or regulation. * * * It is owing to these few officers, who come now and then to the lot of some districts, that people have not yet despaired and risen in a body. * * * The government will feel, no doubt, stronger after the suppression of the mutiny than they ever were. If the hatred of their countrymen towards the natives increases in ratio to the increase of power, as hitherto, the disaffection of the people, and the unpopularity of the government, will increase also proportionally. The consequences are obvious: and, be assured, the country will be desolated and ruined."‡

Englishmen, generally, have no gift for languages; and this has been always one of their weak points as rulers of India, where it is of the first importance that all functionaries, whether civil or military, should be—not first-rate Grecians, or versed in black-letter lore—but able to converse, in the vernacular dialect, with the men over whom they bear rule. Had such knowledge been at all general, warnings would, in all human probability, have been received of the combinations (such as they were) which preceded the massacres of Meerut, Cawnpoor, and Jhansi. It is a serious defect in the system (springing, no doubt, from the monopoly of patronage), that so little trouble has been taken to promote the efficiency of the servants of the Company, as administrators of a delegated despotism. Lord Wellesley strove earnestly for this end; but his efforts were coldly received, and are even now insufficiently appreciated.

So far as the natives are concerned, sending out "incapables" to bear rule over them, manifests a shameful indifference to

* Kaye's *Life of Malcolm*, vol. i., p. 241.

† *The Mutinies, the Government, and the People*; by A Hindoo; p. 36. (Printed at Calcutta, 1858.)

‡ *Thoughts of a Native of Northern India on the Rebellion, its Causes and Remedies* (Dalton, Cockspur-street, 1858): with a Preface, written at Calcutta, and signed "M. W."—initials which suggest the name of a well-known member of the Bengal (uncovenanted) service. The Dedication to H. C. T., Esq., is similarly suggestive.

their interests, and is inflicting a wrong, of which we cannot hope to escape the penalty. "It is suicidal to allow India to be a refuge, as it is at present to a great extent, for those of our youth who are least qualified to make their way in their own country; and it is such an insult to the natives, who are full of intelligence, and are making great progress in European knowledge of all kinds, that if anything could excuse them for rebelling, it would be this."

This is plain speaking from an authority like Indophilus; and what he adds with regard to young officers is equally applicable to civilians:—"It should not be left, as it is at present, to the decision of a young man whether he will pass in the native languages or not. The power of understanding his men, and of rendering himself intelligible to them, should be considered an indispensable qualification; and those who cannot, or will not, acquire this necessary accomplishment, should be removed from the service. Every officer should be presumed to understand the language of his soldiers."*

The change which has taken place in Anglo-Indian society, has, without doubt, been a painful one for the natives. The very large increase in the proportion of Englishwomen who now accompany their husbands, fathers, and brothers to India, has tended to decrease the association with the native gentry; and these are becoming yearly less able to vie with the Europeans. One branch of the intercourse of former days has greatly diminished; the conventionalities have become more stringent; the temptations have decreased; the shameless profligacy described by Clive† no longer exists; and a dark-coloured "beebee" (lady), the mother of a large family of Eurasians, would not now be considered a fit head for the household of a distinguished military or civil servant. How far any radical reform has taken place, or whether the great "social evil" has only changed its hue, it is hard to say; but several trustworthy witnesses assert as an evident fact, that the Europeans and natives of all classes associate far less than they used to do, and that many of the former have adopted a supercilious tone towards the latter, which is equally impolitic, unjust, and inconsistent with the usual refining and softening effect of legitimate domestic intercourse.

The repeated use of the word "niggers" in recent books of Indian memoirs, and in the correspondence published in the public journals,‡ is itself a painful and significant symptom. An American traveller asks, how we can reconcile our denunciation of the social inequality of the negro and white races in America with our own conduct to the East Indians? "I allude," he says, "to the contemptuous manner in which the natives, even those of the best and most intelligent classes, are almost invariably spoken of and treated. The tone adopted towards the lower classes is one of lordly arrogance; towards the rich and enlightened, one of condescension and patronage. I have heard the term 'niggers' applied to the whole race by those high in office; with the lower order of the English it is the designation in general use."§

Sir Charles Napier considered, that nothing could be worse than the manners of Englishmen in India towards natives of all ranks. Therefore, when endeavouring to bring into operation the resources of Sinde, he refused British officers a passage on board his merchant steamers, knowing that "if granted, they would go on board, occupy all the room, treat my rich merchants and supercargoes with insolence, and very probably drink and thrash the people."||

Religion and Education.—Missionary operations are alleged to have had their share in jeopardising the permanence of our power; while, on the contrary, the advocates of religious enterprise assert, that had the messengers of the glad tidings of universal peace and good-will been suffered to have free way in India, as in every other dependency or colony of the British empire, such an exposition of the tenets of Protestant Christianity would long since have been afforded to the intelligent and argumentative Hindoos, as would have rendered it impossible for the most artfully-concocted rumours, founded on the most unfortunate combination of circumstances, to persuade them (in the teeth of a hundred years' experience to the contrary), that force and fraud would ever be used to compel the

* Letter to the *Times*, September 25th, 1857.

† *Indian Empire*, vol. i., p. 307.

‡ A writer in the *Times*, "who has passed his life in India," asserts, that "the white and the dark man are no more equal, and no more to be governed by the same rules, than the man and the ape."—("H." Nov. 23rd, 1857.) It is much to be regretted, that such mischievous and exceptional opinions as these should find unqualified expression in a journal which circulates largely throughout India.

§ Taylor's *Visit to India, &c., in* 1853; p. 273.

|| *Life*, by Sir William Napier; vol. iii., p. 473.

adoption of a creed which appeals to the reason, and requires the habitual exercise of the free-will of every disciple.

With some few and partial exceptions, the policy of the home and local government has been steadily and even sternly repressive of all attempts for the extension of Christianity; and every concession made has been wrung from them by the zeal of influential individuals, supported by public opinion. It needs not to establish this fact on evidence, or to remind the reader that English missionaries were not even tolerated in India until the year 1813; that Marshman and Carey were compelled to take up their residence without the British frontier, in the Danish settlement of Serampoor; that Judson and his companions were actually deported; and that Robert Haldane's munificent and self-sacrificing intention of expending £40,000 on the formation of an effective mission for Benares, was frustrated by the positive prohibition of government, despite the efforts of Wilberforce and others.

An Indian director is said to have declared, that "he would rather a band of devils landed in India than a band of missionaries;"* and his colleagues acted very much as if they shared his conviction.

Secular education was long viewed by the East India Company as a question in which they had no concern; and the efforts made by the Marquis Wellesley and others, were treated with an indifference amounting to aversion. At length public opinion became decided on the subject; and, in 1813, the sum of £10,000 was, by the determination of parliament, decreed to be annually appropriated, out of the revenues of India, for the cultivation of exclusively Hindoo and Mohammedan lore.

In 1824, Mr. Mill (the historian, who entered the service of the Company after writing his famous exposition of the worst features of their rule) was ordered to prepare a despatch on the subject of education. He did so, and in it boldly laid down the principle of inculcating sound truth, in opposition to the absurd fictions of the Shastras. The directors accepted his *dictum*, and founded English schools and colleges for exclusively secular instruction. Lord W. Bentinck, in 1834, pursued a similar course; and a few thousand youths (including Nana Sahib) learned to talk English fluently, to quote Shakespeare, Pope, Addison, and Byron, instead of the Ramayana and the Mahabharata, Hafiz or Sadi; and to jeer with the flippancy of superficial scepticism at the ignorance of their parents and countrymen, in asserting that the earth rests on eight elephants, a serpent, a turtle, and such like;† and at the Mussulmans, for believing in Mohammed's journey to the moon. After all, such instruction was a direct and tangible interference with the religious views of the people. No greater would have been committed, had we placed before them a frank and full exposition of our own creed, choosing Moses rather than Milton to narrate the origin and fall of the whole human race, and trusting to the equally inspired record of the evangelists, to impart, with resistless power, the divinely revealed mystery of man's redemption.

We have taught the whole truth as regards material things—that the earth is round, for instance, and that the ocean is everywhere the same; in opposition to the Brahminical doctrine, that the earth consists of seven continents, divided by seas composed respectively of salt-water, wine, sugar-cane juice, clarified butter, curds, milk, and fresh-water. Spiritual truth we have not ventured to set forth; and the conquerors who represent a nation which applauds itself for the maintenance in strict union of church and state, have become the voluntary exponents of a neutral system which closely resembles practical infidelity. And practical infidelity is the cause to which alone our conduct is attributed by the more intelligent class of the natives. They know that the government is firm even to obstinacy in the maintenance of its convictions, and they utterly discredit the reality of a belief which can co-exist with the temporising and cowardly half measures employed by those who are in all other things habitually positive and outspoken.

The Anglo-Indian authorities were not, however, all blind or indifferent to the workings of the "Godless colleges." In Madras, a strong feeling grew up in favour of the teaching of the Bible in government schools. The Marquis of Tweeddale, then governor, shared and ably expressed this opinion, declaring, that "it required a more solid foundation than is to be found in the Hindoo or Mohammedan faith, to bear the change which learning operates on the mind of those who emerge out of a state of ignorance, and attain those mental

* Quoted by the Hon. A. Kinnaird—Exeter Hall, Jan. 5th, 1858.

† Arthur's *Mysoor*, p. 91.

acquirements which enlarged education gives. * * * Nor do I see how native society itself can safely and permanently advance except upon this basis. I would therefore adopt the rule proposed by the council, which recognises the Bible as a class-book in the government schools, but at the same time leaves it free to the native student to read it or not, as his conscience may dictate, or his parent may desire."*

The Court of Directors refused to comply with Lord Tweeddale's recommendation, and persevered in their previous resolve, despite the remonstrances of the Madras council, and their clear exposition of the mistaken view on which that determination was founded. An able pen wrote a denunciation of the system, which now reads like a prophecy:—"The government does not know what it is doing. No doubt it is breaking down those superstitions, and dispersing those mists, which, by creating weakness and disunion, facilitated the conquest of the country; but, instead of substituting any useful truth, or salutary principles, for the ignorance and false principles which they remove, they are only facilitating the dissemination of the most pernicious errors, and the most demoralising and revolutionary principles. I have been appalled by discovering the extent to which atheistical and deistical writings, together with disaffection to the British government and hatred to the British name, have spread, and are spreading, among those who have been educated in government schools, or are now in the service of government. The direction of the government system of education is rapidly falling into the hands of astute Brahmins, who know how to take advantage of such a state of things, and at the same time to strengthem themselves by an alliance with Parsee and Mussulman prejudices; while the European gentlemen who still remain nominally at the head of the system, know nothing of the under-currents which pervade the whole, or consider themselves as bound, either by principle or policy, not to make any exertions in favour of Christian truth; while the professed object of the government is to give secular instruction only."†

* See Lord Tweeddale's Minute, August 24th, 1846, and reply thereto.—Sixth Report of House of Lords, 1853; pp. 189; 152.

† Testimony of Professor Henderson, of the Bombay Government Schools, dated 31st October, 1803; published in a Discourse upon his death, by Dr. Wilson president of the Bombay Literary Society.

In April, 1847, an order was issued by the Court of Directors to the governor-general, requiring, that the principle which had been "uniformly maintained, of abstaining from all interference with the religion of the natives of India," should be rigidly enforced. A paragraph in a previous despatch (to Madras, 21st May, 1845), declared it to be "the duty of government, and not less of its officers, to stand aloof from all missionary labours, either as promoting or as opposing them." At this time, it was well-known that many of the most esteemed officials, civil and military, were, and had been for years past, members of committees of Bible and Missionary societies. A public demand for "specific instructions" regarding the meaning of the directors, was made by their servants; and this, together with the privately expressed opinions which reached the governor-general (Lord Hardinge), induced him to withhold the despatch and recommend its suppression; in which the directors concurred, because its publication "might give rise to discussion on a subject on which it is particularly desired that the public mind should not be excited."‡

In the year 1849, a native of high-caste, occupying a responsible position in the Calcutta college, publicly embraced Christianity, and was immediately dismissed by the English authorities.§

The government pursued the system of excluding the Bible from its schools, while the missionaries persisted in making it the foundation of theirs; and the opinion of the natives was evidenced in the large voluntary contributions made by them to the latter. The statistics of 1853 gave the following result:—Government schools, 404; scholars, 25,362: Christian Mission schools, 1,668; scholars, 96,177. The returns showed some singular facts: among others, that the only school at Bangalore in which Brahmin youths were found, was a missionary one.

In 1854, the duty of adopting measures for the extension of education, was avowed in a despatch by Sir Charles Wood; and the doctrine of grants in aid for the support of all schools, without reference to the religious doctrine taught therein, was plainly set forth.

‡ Parl. Papers (House of Commons), 12th February, 1858; pp. 3, 5, 11.—*Letter from a Layman in India;* pamphlet, published by Dalton, Cockspur-street, 1858; pp. 11, 12.—Speech of Rev. W. Chalmers, Exeter Hall, January 5th, 1858.

§ *Christian Education for India in the Mother-Tongue*, p. 15.

A minister of public instruction for India was appointed, with a salary of £3,000 a-year; four inspectors, with salaries varying from £1,500 down to £750; and a large number of sub-inspectors: but no single vernacular school* was established, neither was any attempt made to frame and circulate tracts on agriculture and mechanics, or to convey, in the native languages, the more elementary and practical portions of the knowledge generally availed of in Europe for the furtherance of various branches of trade and manufacture.†

The extensive scale on which preparations were made surprised the natives, and the unauthorised and improper statement of some of the officials, that "it was the order of government that people should now educate their children,"‡ created much anxiety. Yet proselytising was neither contemplated nor desired. The Calcutta Bible Society requested permission of the Council of Education to place a copy of the Bible, in English and the vernacular, in the library of each government school and college. It was notorious that the Koran and the Shastras were there; yet the council declined to give the Bible a place beside them, because it would be a breach of "neutrality."§

In England, and even in India, the authorities generally seem to have had no misgivings as to the result of purely secular teaching. Some few, however, deprecated education of any kind to any extent; and this party included a late governor-general, Lord Ellenborough, who declared his belief of its incompatibility with the maintenance of British dominion in India—a conviction, the ground of which is explained by a subsequent statement made by his lordship in his place in parliament (in 1852), that "no intelligent people would submit to our government."‖

With such views, it is not surprising that Lord Ellenborough, when addressing the House of Lords on the 9th of June, 1857, on the recent tidings of the mutiny of the Bengal army, should have adverted with extreme astonishment to a statement which he could "scarcely believe to be true," though he had seen it "distinctly stated in the papers, that the governor-general himself, Lord Canning, subscribed largely to a missionary society, which has for its object the conversion of the natives." The reply of Lord Lansdowne was, that if "Lord Canning had so acted as to give countenance to such belief as the noble earl inferred, he would no longer deserve to be continued in his office." These, and similar expressions of opinion, have done good by affording unmistakable evidence of the feelings entertained by men of high talent and position. A cry arose for "Christian emancipation," and several public meetings took place. On one of these, held at Exeter Hall on the 5th of January, 1858, the *Times* commented in the following terms:—"We have made a great mistake in India. The religious policy pursued by the government of that country, has made us, as one of its own servants declared, 'cowards in the eyes of men, and traitors in the eyes of God.' * * * A stranger to the question, after reading the noble chairman's speech on that occasion, might well imagine that the Hindoos were the conquerors, and we the subjects; that we had been tyrannically debarred, for more than a century, from the free exercise of our religion; and that we were at length seizing a favourable moment to demand relief from these unjust disabilities. All that his lordship, and those who followed him, asked for, was Christian emancipation; * * * and that, under a government acknowledging faith in Christ Jesus, the profession of the Gospel should no longer be visited with penalties of civil disqualification. These are literally the conditions to which our policy has driven us. * * * We were never really neutral; we made ourselves partisans; but, unfortunately, in our anxiety to escape the charge of favouring Christianity, we actually favoured heathenism. * * * All this must now end, if not for truth's sake, for the sake of government itself. Our policy has broken down utterly, and proved destructive to its own objects. There is no mistaking the results of the experiment. Where, asked Lord Shaftesbury, did the insurrection break out? Was it in Madras, where Christians are most numerous, and where Christianity has been best treated? Was it in Bombay, where caste was scouted,

* A Vernacular Society is now being organised in London. It is much needed; for, as its chief promoter, Mr. Tucker, truly says, no people have ever been Christianised through a foreign language.

† Report of Public Meeting for the Formation of a Christian Vernacular Education Society, 20th May, 1858; p. 8.

‡ Parl. Papers, 13th April, 1858; p. 2.

§ *Letter from a Layman*, p. 13.

‖ Dickinson's *India under a Bureaucracy*, p. 117.

and Hindoos taught that government could pay no heed to such pretensions? No; it was in Bengal, where idolatry and caste received the greatest reverence; and in the Bengal army, which represented the most pampered class of the whole population."

One last incident, illustrative of the anti-Christian policy of the Indian government, remains to be quoted. The Sonthals—a wild tribe, resembling our gipsies—were driven into rebellion in 1856, by the misconduct of some railway contractors, the exactions of native bankers, and the outrages committed by the native police. The missionaries materially aided in restoring tranquillity, and succeeded in obtaining the confidence of these poor savages, who were without the pale of Hindoo caste; and the Calcutta authorities entered into arrangements with the Church Missionary Society for the establishment of schools of religious and industrial instruction among them, and specially among the females.* When the measure became known in England, the home government refused its sanction, and ordered the establishment of schools on its own plan, the teachers of which were to be "most strictly enjoined to abstain from any attempt to introduce religious subjects in any form."†

It is interesting to learn, from one of the Hindoos themselves, the view taken by them of our so-called neutrality. Shew Purshad says—"It is absurd to think that the English are hated by the Hindoos on account of their religion. * * * It is not religion, but the want of religion, which has brought so much evil to this country. The people know that the government is a Christian one. Let it act openly as a true Christian: the people will never feel themselves disappointed; they will only admire it. * * * Education must be carried on upon a sounder principle, and religion must be fostered. Don't turn India from idolatry to atheism. * * * Who can detest 'religion?' It is the order of their own Shastras‡ that every man is to revere his own religion. You may have a thousand missionaries to preach, and another thousand as masters of the schools, at the expense of the government, or distribute a thousand Bibles at the hands of the governor-general. The people will not murmur out a single syllable, though they may laugh and jeer; but take care that you do not interfere with their caste—you do not force them to eat the food cooked by another in the gaols,§ or thrust grease down their throats with the cartridges made by Europeans. * * * Difference of caste must vanish, with many other offsprings of folly and ignorance, when its proper time comes. To try to exterminate it now must end in bloodshed."||

Mr. Henry Carre Tucker, the son of the late chairman of the East India Company (and himself no mean authority¶), confirms the statement, from long personal experience—that so long as we scrupulously abstain from any direct interference with the ceremonial observances of caste, we may teach Christianity as much as we please, adding—"This view is strengthened by the fact, that during the late mutiny, those large military stations have escaped the best where the governors were most zealous for Christianity." He proceeds to instance Peshawur, under Herbert Edwardes; and Lahore, under "those brave Christian men, John Lawrence and Robert Montgomery:" but here we cannot follow him without anticipating the subsequent narrative. His conclusions, however, are too important to be omitted: they are—"That we ought to assume a bolder position as a Christian gov-

* See Mr. J. M. Strachan's *Letter to Captain Eastwick*. (Seeley, 1858.)

† Parl. Papers (Commons), 24th Aug., 1857; p. 2.

‡ See *Indian Empire*, vol. i., p. 46.

§ "Active resistance to the recently introduced messing system in the gaols of Bengal and the N.W. Provinces, has produced bloodshed."—Col. Sykes' Letter to the *Times*, October 8th, 1857.

|| *Thoughts of a Native, &c.*, pp. 18—34.

¶ Mr. Tucker was connected with the Benares district for twenty-five years: during this period he avowed and acted up to his own high standard of Christian duty, at the risk of being deemed a dangerous fanatic; the more so because the "Holy City" of Benares is the stronghold of the Brahmins, and holds a somewhat similar position, in the estimation of the Hindoos, to what Mecca does in that of the Moslems. Yet, on his departure for Europe in March, 1858, a valedictory address was presented to him, signed by all the principal inhabitants—expressing sorrow at the termination of their official connection, a "deep sense of admiration of his enlarged spirit of philanthropy and almost boundless benevolence," and "gratitude for his zealous exertions in extending the benefits of education." In token of their sense of the manner in which he had employed his few leisure hours in furthering "the welfare, here and hereafter, of those committed to his charge," the subscribers to the address collected among themselves 6,000 rupees, for the obtainment of a full-length portrait of their friend, to be placed in the Benares college; and with the balance, after defraying the cost of the picture, they propose to found a scholarship to commemorate his name. Certainly the Hindoos know how to appreciate Christian disinterestedness when they meet with it.

ernment; that it is quite feasible to Christianise our education; and that, instead of causing alarm and disaffection, those dangerous points have, through God's blessing, been the most quiet where Christian exertion has been the greatest. Oude, destitute of all missionary effort, and the sepoys, to whom Christian instruction was closed, were the worst of all."*

The ignorance displayed by the sepoys, and that large part of the Indian population connected with the army, regarding Christianity, is remarkable, even after making every possible allowance for the rigid exclusion of missionary teaching, and the absolute prohibition of proselytism among their ranks.† The cause is obvious—not simply to the minds of earnest Christians, but to the class who have least sympathy with anything approaching religious enthusiasm.

The *Times*,‡ in one of its leading articles, is constrained to admit, that it is because the superior beneficence and purity of our religion have not been vividly and transparently exhibited in practice, that we "have not converted the people who have witnessed the every-day life of British gentlemen and ladies—we will not say to an acceptance of our religion, but even to any high regard for it. * * * We ought to have stood high in that land of many religions, as a consistent, believing, just, kind, and holy people. That we have not even done this, and that we are regarded simply as unbelievers, with little religion except a few negative tenets, which we find convenient for political purposes, must be deemed a shortcoming in our practice. It must be our fault that we Christians stand so much lower in the religious scale of India than we did in the scale of ancient paganism."

While (according to the above impartial testimony) we have not taught Christianity either by precept or example, and while among the sepoys the Bible has remained a sealed book, no such embargo has ever been laid on the Koran. The Mohammedans, themselves essentially propagandists, have remained masters of the situation. Wrapped in a complacent belief of their own superiority, as believers in a revelation more recent and complete than that of their conquerors, the followers of the False Prophet adopt their own classification of "Jews, English, infidels, and heretics;" and really viewing us (in a certain sense) as we do the Jews, have taken pains to communicate this impression to the Hindoos.

Indeed, who will venture to defend from the charge of practical atheism, a government that causes such sentences as "God is a Spirit," to be expunged from its school-books;§ being apparently ignorant that this fundamental truth is the very essence of all that is sound in Mohammedanism, and is acknowledged, at least in theory, by every Brahmin and Buddhist in India.

Caste, and the panic-terror which the idea of its violation may have occasioned, constitute a social and political, even more than a religious question.‖ Sir Charles Napier well defined the difference when he said, that what the natives dreaded, was "not conversion, but contamination." Caste is no universal, immutable law: it is a pure convention; but one which, by the nature of our position, we are bound to respect to a certain reasonable extent.

The traditional four castes¶ have merged into innumerable others. Human passions have proved too strong for the strongest fetters ever forged by a wily priesthood. Intermarriages have taken place between every variety of caste; and the result is, the general division of the Hindoo population into high-caste (consisting of Brahmins who compose the priest and scholar class, and the Rajpoots, who are hereditary soldiers), low-caste (in which all the Mahrattas, and

* It would seem as if the government had feared the influence of Christianity among the English soldiery; for it is only very recently that chaplains have been appointed to accompany expeditions. No provision of the kind was made in the Cabool war; and Sir Charles Napier loudly complained of a similar deficiency among his force in Sinde.

† Witness the case of Purrub-deen Pandeh, a high-caste Brahmin (a naik in the 25th regiment), who, though "previously much esteemed in the corps," was summarily removed for having received Christian baptism. This occurred at Meerut in 1819.—(Parl. Papers, 8th February, 1858.)

‡ October 6th, 1857.

§ See *London Quarterly Review*, October, 1857: article on the "Sepoy Rebellion;" by the Rev. W. Arthur; p. 259.

‖ No European can form, though they ought to form, a correct idea of the difference between the prejudices of caste and those of religion. Give a couple of gold mohurs to a pundit, and he will cheerfully compose a book in refutation of his own religion; but give him a glass of water openly touched by you, even through the medium of a stick a hundred feet long, and he will not drink it, though you offer him a thousand gold mohurs. Secretly, perhaps, he may not have objection to do anything either to please you or satiate his own passions.—(*Thoughts of a Native, &c.;* p. 18.)

¶ See *Indian Empire*, vol. i., p. 14.

most of the remaining native princes, are included), and, thirdly, out-caste—a section diffused all over India, and forming a large proportion of the entire population. The Abbé Dubois maintained, that they were, in his time, one in five; but an able writer of our own day suggests one in ten as nearer the truth: adding—"Even in this proportion the Indian out-castes would be twenty millions of human beings, or more than the population of all England."*

This class includes the aborigines, or at least the predecessors of the Hindoos, the Gonds, Bheels, Sonthals, &c., who have never accepted caste; and, indeed, could not by Brahminical law find place in it. The barrier is equally impassable for the Mussulmans, whose observance of certain caste rules is worthless in the sight of the Hindoos. No man can venture to foretel how much longer the system may endure, or how soon it may be thrown to the winds. The Jains have caste; the Buddhists (who still linger in India) have none. Then there are the Seiks, originally a peaceable, religious sect, founded by a Hindoo, whose creed was derived from the Vedas and the Koran. Caste was suddenly abolished among them by Govind, their tenth "Guru," or spiritual chief; converts were gladly welcomed from all quarters, and admitted to a perfect equality.†

A similar change may come over the mass of the Hindoos; and as the teaching of St. Paul produced the simultaneous conversion of two thousand persons, so here, whole communities may be led at once to renounce the error which has so long enthralled them. Or, the work may be more gradual—individual enlightenment may be the thin edge of the wedge: but in either case, Christian civilisation is the instrument which alone can prosper in our hands—the only one that affords any rational prospect of leading to the voluntary renunciation of caste. This renunciation does not necessarily accompany conversion to Christianity; though it would seem to be an inevitable consequence.

Some of the Hindoo pamphleteers, however, declare that caste can hardly be deemed incompatible with Christianity, when it exists so evidently, although under peculiar forms, among the English. They ask, whether we do not treat all men whose skins are darker than our own, as if of quite another caste or *breed?* Whether half-caste is not our contemptuous term for an Eurasian? They point to the whole framework of Anglo-Indian society, to its "covenanted" service, to the rigid exclusiveness produced by patronage alike in the military and civil service, in confirmation of their assertion. High-caste, low-caste, and out-caste, with their various subdivisions, are, they say, pretty clearly defined in our practice, however forcibly we may repudiate such distinctions in theory.

To return: the Indo-Mohammedans have, to a certain extent, imitated Brahminical practices as conventional distinctions, and are interested in inciting the Hindoo sepoys to maintain a system which enables them to dictate to their officers the what, when, how, and where, in a service in which unhesitating and unquestioning obedience is otherwise exacted. The natives are perfectly aware that caste is a great inconvenience to the Europeans, and that it materially impedes their efficiency as soldiers and servants. It is this which made them so watchful of every measure of government that might infringe on the caste monopoly of privileges and immunities, which we had unwisely made their "Magna Charta," and which we, strangely enough, took no pains to investigate or define. The consequence of our ignorance of its theory and regulations has been, that we have been perpetually falling into opposite errors—vacillating between absurd deference to pretended scruples, and real infraction of the first and most invariable observances. Persecution on the one hand, undue concessions on the other, have been our Scylla and Charybdis; but it is our ignorance that has made them so.

In considering the operation of caste in India, we must bear in mind that it is a thing hard to preserve intact, and easily destroyed, either by force or fraud. Many comparatively recent instances of both are on record; and Tippoo Sultan especially delighted in compelling Brahmins to forfeit their privileges by destroying kine. The natives know us too well to fear any such ebullitions of insane barbarity or fierce zeal; but it is quite possible they may anticipate our desiring the annihilation of caste on the score of policy, and dread our attempting it by a *coup d'état*. It is alleged that articles in the public journals, regarding the need of soldiers experienced by England in carrying out the Russian, Persian, and Chi-

* *Sepoy Rebellion in India;* by the Rev. W. Arthur.—*London Quarterly Review*, October, 1857.
† See *Indian Empire*, vol. i., p. 154.

nese wars, gave rise to rumours which were circulated among the sepoys, of the anxiety of government to get rid, at once and for ever, of the shackles which prevented the Indian troops from being sent across the Cala-pani, or Black water, to fight our battles in foreign climes.* A Hindoo would naturally cling to the system which was at once his reason and excuse for avoiding expatriation, which he fears worse than death; and his suspicions would easily be roused on the subject.

The readiest way of destroying caste, is by forcing or tempting the party concerned to taste anything prepared by unclean hands—that is, by persons of an inferior, or of no caste; or which contains the smallest particle of the flesh of kine. The Mohammedans abstain as rigidly from tasting the flesh of the impure hog, as the Hindoos from that of the sacred cow. The motive differs, but the result is the same. In both cases, the abstinence respectively practised is one of the first and most generally recognised of their rules. The Indian government could scarcely have been ignorant, when issuing a new description of fire-arms to the sepoys, that to bite a cartridge greased with cows' or pigs' fat, was more to Hindoos and Indo-Mohammedans, than "eating pork to a Jew, spitting on the Host to a Roman Catholic, or trampling on the Cross to a Protestant."† To the Hindoos it was indeed much more, so far as temporal welfare was concerned; for it involved practical outlawry, with some of the pains and penalties specially attached to conversion to Christianity. It is clear, that if it had been necessary to distribute greased cartridges, to be bitten by the troops, not only the greatest care ought to have been taken that no contaminating material should be used in the manufacture, but also that an explicit assurance should have been given to this effect. Yet, the inspector-general of ordnance has stated, that "no extraordinary care appears to have been taken to ensure the absence of any objectionable fat."‡ So that, so far from endeavouring to remove all suspicion from the minds of the sepoys, of any intention to inflict on them the calamity they most dreaded, we did not even guard against its perpetration.

The issue of the greased cartridges, under such circumstances, was unquestionably a gross blunder, and is viewed by many as the exciting cause of the mutiny.

The *Free Press*, and the so-called *Gagging Act* of Lord Canning, have given rise to discussions which bring to mind Dr. Johnson's remark, that opinions formed on the efficacy of a certain branch of scholastic discipline, are apt to be materially influenced by the fact, "of which end of the rod falls to one's share." The evils alleged to have been produced by unrestricted publication, are too circumstantially stated by official authorities to be omitted in the present category; and it becomes necessary to show, if possible, the two sides of the question—that is, the case of those who wield, and those who wince under, the rod of censorship. It is now little more than twenty years since complete freedom of the press was bestowed by Sir Charles Metcalfe.§ The measure was sudden and startling: it was scarcely in accordance with his own previous views; and it was in decided opposition to the opinions which the Court of Directors had from time to time enunciated.

A recapitulation of the restrictive measures adopted in the three presidencies, from 1799 to 1819, is given in an important communication made by "the Chairs"‖ to the president of the India Board, on the 17th of January, 1823. Among other evidence in support of the necessity for a rigid censorship, they quoted the following Minute, written in 1807, by Lord William Bentinck (then governor of Madras), regarding a charge delivered by one of the judges of the Supreme Court (Sir Henry Gwillim) to the grand jury:—

"It is necessary, in my opinion, for the public safety, that the press in India should be kept under the most rigid control. It matters not from what pen the dangerous matter may issue; the higher the authority the greater the mischief. We cannot prevent the judges of the Supreme Court from uttering, in open court, opinions, however mischievous; but it is in our power, and it is our duty, to prohibit them from being circulated through the country by means of the press. Entertaining strongly this sentiment, I would recommend that the order of government may be given to all proprietors of printing-presses, forbidding them, upon pain of the utmost displeasure of the governor in council, to print any paper whatever without the previous sanction of the governor in council, communicated by the chief secretary."¶

* Mead's *Sepoy Revolt*, p. 37. (Routledge and Co.: London, 1858.)

† *Letters of Indophilus*, p. 33.

‡ Parl. Papers (by command), 1857; p. 7.

§ *Indian Empire*, vol. i., p. 431.

‖ The chairman and deputy-chairman of the E. I. Company (J. Pattison and W. Wigram.)

¶ Parl. Papers (Commons), 4th May, 1858.

The opinion pronounced by Sir Thomas Munro, regarding the revolution which a free press would produce throughout the native army, is next quoted; and the writers proceed to express similar and very decided views on the subject:—

"A free press is a fit associate and necessary appendage of a representative constitution; but in no sense of the terms can the government of India be called a free, a representative, or a popular government; the people had no voice in its establishment, nor have they any control over its acts. * * * Can it be doubted that the respect of the natives for our authority would be greatly diminished, and the energy of the government impaired, by a free press? * * * It is impossible to suppose that a foreign government, however strong and beneficent its character, should not be obnoxious in some degree to those who live under it. It is humbling to the pride of the people; and where they differ, as in India, in religion, in language, in manners, in colour, and in customs from those who administer the government, there cannot be much sympathy or attachment between them. Though the situation of the large body of the people may now be greatly better, on the whole, than it was under their native governments, there are not a few, particularly among the Mohammedans, who have suffered from the change. These, we may be sure, will always be ready to avail themselves of any opportunity of retrieving their fortunes, and we know not that they could desire a more efficient auxiliary than a licentious press, labouring daily to extinguish all respect for our character and government in the minds of their countrymen. The tendency and effect of our system, too, has been to beget in the minds of the people at large a respect for themselves, and notions of their own importance, which makes the task of governing them a more difficult one than it was when they first came under our rule. But the delicacy of our situation in India cannot be well understood without special advertence to the circumstance of the government being dependent in a great degree for its security on a native army, which, though better paid, with reference to the wages of labour, than any other army in the world, contains in its organisation some elements of discontent. The exclusion of the natives from its higher ranks must necessarily be a source of heartburning to men of family and ambition; and when a sense of mortification is united with a spirit of enterprise, their joint workings are not easily daunted or repressed. It may be difficult to retain the fidelity of men of this description, with all the care and caution that can be exercised; but it would appear to be either a lamentable infatuation, or unpardonable rashness, to allow them to be goaded on to revolt, by means over which we possess or may obtain control. Whatever English newspapers are published at the presidencies will naturally find their way to the principal military stations. Many of the native officers can read and understand English; and by means of the native servants of the European officers, it will not be difficult for them to obtain the perusal of those papers, containing a perhaps exaggerated representation of their grievances or an inflammatory incentive to rebellion, which, from their assemblage in garrisons and cantonments, they have better means of concerting than any other portion of the population."*

* Parl. Papers, 4th May, 1858; pp. 20—23.

The degree of severity with which the restrictions enacted to control the press were enforced, depended of course materially on the character of those by whom the supreme authority was wielded. Lord Amherst used his power as governor-general in such wise as entirely to stifle all public discussion; and Lord William Bentinck, his successor (in 1828), was so impressed by the mischievous effect of this policy, that though, as has been shown, very ready to repress, in the most summary fashion, any real or imagined excess on the part of journalists, he, nevertheless, deemed it necessary to issue a notice inviting suggestions from any quarter for the improvement of public measures, and the development of the resources of the country; and the result was the publication of letters from various quarters, written with much ability and freedom; among which, the first and most important were those afterwards embodied by the Hon. Frederick Shore, in his *Notes on Indian Affairs*.

Lord William Bentinck quitted India in 1835; Lord Auckland came out as his successor in the same year; and it was during the brief provisional sway of Sir Charles (afterwards Lord) Metcalfe, that the important measure was adopted of giving complete freedom to the press. In explaining the difference between his own opinions and those of his predecessor, Sir Charles says—

"His lordship, however, sees further danger in the spread of knowledge and the operations of the press. I do not, for my own part, anticipate danger as a certain consequence from these causes. I see so much danger in the ignorance, fanaticism, and barbarism of our subjects, that I rest on the spread of knowledge some hope of greater strength and security. * * * The time is past when the operations of the press could be effectually restrained. Even if that course would be any source of safety (which must be very doubtful), nothing so precarious could in prudence be trusted to. If, therefore, increase of danger is really to be apprehended from increase of knowledge, it is what we must cheerfully submit to. We must not try to avert it; and, if we did, we should fail."†

Lord Elphinstone (the present governor of Bombay), in commenting on this passage, truly says, that Lord Metcalfe "considers the freedom of the press, and the diffusion of knowledge, as convertible terms;" and expresses his surprise that a statesman who entertained such alarming notions of the insecurity and unpopularity of our rule, should have been the man to abolish the

† *Selections from the Metcalfe Papers*, p. 197.

few remaining restrictions deemed indispensable by his predecessor.*

In 1841, Lord Auckland revoked an order passed in 1826, prohibiting public servants from being connected with newspapers as editors or proprietors. Next came Lord Ellenborough; who found his tranquillity so disturbed by the "abuse" of the press, that after three months' residence in India, he ceased "to read a word that appeared in the newspapers."† The commander-in-chief, Lord Gough, is alleged to have avowed with yet more stoical philosophy, that "for his part, he never read any paper but the *Tipperary Journal*." The governor-general deemed it the most judicious course to treat all attacks on his administration with silent contempt; and, in 1843, he issued an order of opposite tenor to that of Lord Auckland; which, by enforcing strict secrecy regarding all information officially obtained, neutralised the power which had been freely exercised under the express sanction of the three previous rulers.

"Lord Ellenborough's general order," says Indophilus, "and the disposition which was shown to place a strict interpretation upon it, effectually restrained the pens of the Company's servants; and no government could stand such pounding and kicking, and bedaubing and besmearing, as ensued." Statements, however false, put forth in ignorance or from malice prepense, were left to be copied into the native papers; and no denial, no antidote in any shape, was offered. For instance, a paragraph went the round of the newspapers, that it was intended to annex the Rajpoot states; and although great disquiet was thereby occasioned throughout Rajpootana, no contradiction was ever published.‡

The Afghan war, and the annexation of Sinde, were subjects on which the authorities were perhaps wise in preferring to submit to comments which they might treat as calumnious, rather than engage in controversy; but sometimes leading officials, more sensitive or less discreet than their superiors, broke all bounds, and declaimed against the press in terms of unmeasured invective. The brave, testy, inconsistent general, Sir Charles Napier, who came to India at sixty years of age with five pounds in his pocket, for the sake of providing for his family,§ and who did provide for them magnificently, by what he termed that "very advantageous, useful, humane piece of rascality," the seizure of Sinde;‖—this man (who was as ready with his pen as with his sword, and, in either case, fought ever without a shield) fairly flung himself into a hornet's-nest by his reckless and indiscriminate abuse of those "ruffians,"¶ whom he boasted of taking every public opportunity of calling "the infamous press of India."** One of them excited his special displeasure by taking part against him in the Outram controversy—Dr. Buist, of the *Bombay Times*, whom Sir Charles alternately threatened with a law-suit and a horse-whipping, and of whom he spoke at a public dinner as that "blatant beast;"†† a *mot* which he duly records, and which Sir William has not thought it derogatory to his brother's fame to publish.

With such personal feelings as these, it is not to be wondered that Sir Charles should regard the public statements of the journalists with jealous aversion, and should accuse them of desiring to excite mutiny among the troops; of inciting the hostile tribes to rise against them; of glorying in the sufferings of their countrymen; and many similar accusations in which the fiery old warrior gave vent to his irrepressible belligerence. His is not fair testimony concerning the operation of a free press; and it is necessary to turn to more impartial witnesses. Sir Charles Trevelyan

* Minute of 24th June, 1858. Parl. Papers (House of Commons), 4th May, 1858; pp. 52, 53.

† Debate, 27th Dec., 1857.—*Times* report.

‡ *Letters of Indophilus*, p. 48.

§ *Life*, vol. iii., p. 194. ‖ *Ibid.*, vol. ii., p. 218.

¶ *Ibid.*, vol. ii. p. 305. Dr. Buist (editor of the *Bombay Times*, and sheriff of Bombay), in a pamphlet entitled, "Corrections of a Few of the Errors contained in Sir William Napier's Life of his Brother, in so far as they affect the Press of India," gives some valuable statements regarding the Indian newspapers; of which he says there were, in 1843, about thirty; costing close on £100,000 a-year for their maintenance—deriving their chief support, and nearly all their intelligence from officers of the British army. The *Englishman* (Calcutta) was conducted by Captain McNaughton (Bengal Army) and Mr. (now Sir Ronald McDonald) Stevenson, projector and engineer of the great Bengal railway: *Hurkaru*—Mr. John Kaye, Bengal artillery, now of the India House (author of the *History of the Afghan War*): *Calcutta Star and Morning Star*—Mr. James Hume, barrister, now police magistrate of Calcutta: *Friend of India*—the well-known Mr. John Marshman: *Bombay Courier*, by Mr. W. Crawford, barrister, now senior magistrate of police: and *Bombay Gentleman's Gazette*, by Mr. P. J. McKenna.—(p. 15.)

** *Life*, by Sir William Napier, vol. iii., p. 124.

†† *Ibid.*, vol. iii., p. 294.

asserts, that it has been, "on the whole, highly beneficial:" and that—

"There cannot be a greater evil than that public officers should be exempted from the control of public opinion. In Lord William Bentinck's, Lord Metcalfe's, and Lord Auckland's time, the press was held in wholesome respect by the public functionaries at the most remote stations, and it acted as a sort of moral preventive police. * * * We used to call it the Parliament of the Press. It may safely be said, that there was not a single good public measure which was not powerfully aided by it. As regards the native press, some newspapers were conducted in a creditable manner in the English language, by and for the natives, who had received an English education; others were published in the native language by the missionaries: and it must not be supposed that the remainder, which were written by natives in the native languages, did nothing but preach sedition. Their standard, both of intelligence and morality, was, no doubt, below that of the English newspapers; but they opened the minds of the natives to an interest in general topics, *and taught them to think, from which every thing else might be expected.*"*

Sanscrit literature proves that the Hindoos were a thoughtful people before the English set foot in India; but the spread of European and "non-religious" theories, has been certainly likely to teach them to reason in an entirely different fashion. We know that Voltaire, Rousseau, Diderot, and Condorcet gave currency to ideas which took a very practical form in the French Revolution. These writers, with the English infidel, Tom Paine, have found imitators and admirers in India, and their doctrines are flung abroad like firebrands by the native press. A blind, unreasoning distrust of all governments—a fierce disaffection towards all constituted authorities—thirst for license under the name of freedom; such are the fruits of the tree of knowledge, apart and contra-distinguished from the tree of life. A saying, attributed to the Duke of Wellington, is often cited against the danger attendant on promoting education without religion—that of making men "clever devils." No better illustration of this need be adduced than the terrible scenes enacted by the Bengal sepoys, among whom native newspapers of the worst class have freely circulated. The utter indifference so long evinced by government, regarding the number, tone, and character of the native journals, is almost incredible;† indeed, that complete freedom should have been accorded even to the European press, is strangely at variance with the general policy of the Company.

In 1857, the adult male European population scattered throughout India, not in the service, was estimated at only 4,000.‡ The journals must, therefore, to a great extent, have been maintained by officials. Some of them, especially the *Madras Athenæum*, uniformly deprecated annexation; and thus its supporters contributed with their purses, and sometimes with their pens, to oppose the very acts which, in their official capacity, they were bound to enforce.§ It was impossible that the natives should not take a lively interest in discussions which immediately affected them. Even a child, hearing its own name often repeated, would listen; and the natives have done so to some purpose.

Five years ago, one of the ablest and most disinterested advocates for the necessity of Indian reform, as the sole means of averting the blow which has since fallen, wrote:—

"The free press is doing its work in India: the Parsee merchants, the zemindars, the native heads of castes, are beginning to feel their power, to combine, and to ask for redress of grievances; some of them are violent, and these do not alarm me; but some are remarkably temperate; and I confess, that knowing the strength of their case, I fear the men who begin so temperately, and have reason on their side."‖

Sir Charles Metcalfe, in establishing, and Lord Auckland in confirming, the freedom of the press, especially insisted that the boon thus granted might be withdrawn, in the event of its proving injurious in operation. "Should the safety of the state ever demand such a course, in a single hour a law may be passed to stop or to control every press in India: nothing has been lost of useful power."¶

In the middle of June, 1857, when the mutiny was at its height, the supreme government deemed it necessary to pass an act, which, for the space of the succeeding twelvemonth, was intended to replace the press in the position it occupied

* *Letters of Indophilus*, p. 45.

† On application to the East India House for some additional details to those given in the *Indian Empire* (vol. i., p. 523), the writer was informed that the directors had no information on the subject.

‡ Dr. Buist's *Corrections of Sir W. Napier*, p. 40.

§ The *Edinburgh Review* speaks of the Anglo-Indian press as exclusively representing "the opinions of European settlers in the country, or half-castes not in the Company's service," whom it describes as a class bitterly hostile to government. (October, 1847.) Mr. Mead, on the contrary, affirms, that "six out of seven of the whole body of subscribers are in the Company's service."—*Sepoy Revolt*, p. 183.

‖ Dickinson's *India under a Bureaucracy*, p. 20.

¶ Minute, by Lord Auckland, 8th August, 1836.

in 1835, before the removal of all restrictions by Sir Charles Metcalfe. The authorities were unanimous regarding the necessity of the measure, which involved the re-institution of the licensing system, together with a rigid censorship. The act was passed by the governor-general in council in a sitting; and Lords Harris and Elphinstone, the governors of Madras and Bombay, expressed their entire acquiescence. No distinction was made between the English and the native press, the government being desirous to avoid drawing invidious distinctions between European and native subjects. They add, moreover—

"We do not clearly see how any distinction of the sort could be really carried into effect, for there are now more than one newspaper in the English language written, owned and published by natives, almost exclusively for circulation amongst native readers; and although we have no reason to fear that treasonable matter would be designedly published in any English newspaper, we have to guard in these times against errors, indiscretion, and temper, as well as against international sedition. * * * To show that the necessity of controlling the English as well as the native press, is not merely imaginary, it will be enough to state, that the treasonable proclamation of the king and mutineers of Delhi—cunningly framed so as to influence the Mohammedan population as much as possible against the British government, and ending with the assurance, that the multiplication and circulation of that document would be an act equal in religious merit to drawing the sword against us, was published by a respectable English newspaper of this town without comment. For doing the very same thing, with comments having the outward form of loyalty, the publishers of three native Mohammedan papers in Calcutta, have been committed to the Supreme Court, to take their trial for a seditious libel."*

Lord Harris went further than this, and declared "the larger portion of the British press throughout the country," and particularly in the Madras presidency, to be "disloyal in tone, un-English in spirit, wanting in principle, and utterly regardless of correctness in statement."† He complained especially of the seditious matter circulated among the sepoys by a newspaper entitled the *Examiner*, "the mouth-piece of the Roman Catholic priests."‡ Lord Elphinstone considered the unrestricted liberty of the press incompatible with the continuance of British rule. "Systematic abuse of the government," he writes, "misrepresentation of its acts, and all attempts to create ill-feeling between the different classes of the community, especially between the European officers and the native soldiery, must be prevented."§ The home authorities confirmed the act, declaring that they felt no doubt of its necessity.||

The first English paper threatened with the revoke of its licence, was the well-known *Friend of India*, which, in an article entitled "The Centenary of Plassy," censured the mammon-worship of the East India Company, and declared that "only the intense greediness of traders could have won for us the sovereignty of the country." Mohammedan princes and Hindoo rajahs were spoken of as a class that would speedily die out; and in conclusion, the writer held forth a hope that the second centenary of Plassy might be "celebrated in Bengal by a respected government and a Christian people."

The secretary to government (Mr. Beadon) officially informed the publisher, that the circulation of such remarks, in the existing state of affairs, was dangerous "not only to the government, but to the lives of all Europeans in the provinces not living under the close protection of British bayonets." This communication was published in the *Friend of India*, with satirical comments, which the authorities considered so offensive, that the licence would have been withdrawn but for the resignation of Mr. Mead, who was acting as provisional editor during the absence of the proprietor, Mr. Marshman.¶

The *Bengal Hurkaru* (Messenger) was warned for its exaggerated echo of the vengeance-cry of the London *Times;* a writer, styling himself "Militaire," denouncing the just and wise recommendation of government not needlessly to "embitter the feelings of the natives," and urging that, "for every Christian church destroyed, fifty mosques should be destroyed, beginning with the Jumma Musjid at Delhi; and for every Christian man, woman, and child murdered, a thousand rebels should bleed."**

Ten days later, another article appeared, which contained the following passage:—

* Despatch to the Court of Directors, dated 4th July, 1857. Signed—Canning, Dorin, Low, Grant, and Peacock. Parl. Papers (Commons), 28th August, 1857; pp. 4, 5.

† Minute, by Lord Harris, dated "Fort St. George, 2nd May, 1857"—*Ibid.*, p. 11.

‡ Minute, 22nd June, 1857—*Ibid.*, p. 13.

§ Minute, 24th June, 1857. Parl. Papers (Commons), 4th May, 1858; p. 53.

|| Letter of Court of Directors, 26th August, 1857—*Ibid.*, p. 30.

¶ Parl. Papers—*Ibid.*, pp. 42—46. Mead's *Sepoy Revolt*, pp. 359—376.

** *Bengal Hurkaru*, 5th September, 1857.

"There are many good, honest, simple people in Calcutta, who are both surprised and disappointed that popular indignation has not boiled up to a higher pitch. They are astounded at finding that Lord Canning has not been already ordered home in irons, and that Mr. Beadon has not been sentenced to be tarred and feathered, and ridden upon a rail, previously to being placed in some extremely uncovenanted situation under a native superior. We are very far from saying that these proceedings would not be appropriate in the cases in question; but we would say to our enthusiastic friends, 'My dear sirs, you are too impatient. All in good time.'"*

The licence of the *Hurkaru* was revoked; but the editor (Mr. Blanchard) having resigned, a new licence was issued to the proprietor. Other English papers have been warned for transgressing the conditions of their licences; but the native editors generally do not appear to have incurred censure.

The existing difficulty seems to be, the course to be adopted with regard to the republication of articles from English papers. The following, for instance, is styled by Mr. Frere (commissioner of Sinde), "a very mischievous perversion of an Indian debate, which, in quieter times, might be amusing." A summary of grievances could hardly be deemed amusing at any moment. At the present crisis, it is not only humiliating, but alarming, to find such statements circulating in Hindoostan on the authority of British parliamentary debates; for the so-called perversion is really a summary of the leading arguments advanced by members of both houses against the East India Company, more especially by the Marquis of Clauricarde, whose speech, it was predicted at the time, would occasion great excitement among the natives of India.

"The *Jam-i-Jamsibid* of Meerut relates, that in durbar of ——, the Marquis of Clanricarde complained much of the Indian government; that a vast amount of rupees was expended among the home authorities in the way of pay, they knowing little of the circumstances of the country; that the nobles and great men of Hindoostan were becoming extinct; and the middle classes gradually suffering damage, and poor people being ruined. It would be proper that the country should be so governed, that the people do not suffer. Some zillahs require a decrease of taxation, and the salt-tax is very wrong. In whatever countries there was fitting management, the latter impost had been abolished. Beside this, in Hindoostan, the system of justice was defective. Moreover, on this account, the English name suffered; and, in Hindoostan, amid ten judges, nine are Hindoostanees, but their pay and position was unimportant and inconsistent with their duties. And the heads of the E. I. Company say, that amid fourteen crore (million) of Hindoostanees, not one is worthy of rank or trust; a very sad and distressing statement, enough to break the hearts of the people of Hindoostan, and cow their spirits. Besides which, he said many more things; in answer to which, the Duke of Argyle was unable to advance any clear argument."†

It would be difficult to know on what ground an editor could be warned for the republication of the above statements, unless it were on the strength of the now repudiated axiom, "The greater the truth, the greater the libel!"

In another case—that of a Persian newspaper, edited in Calcutta by one Hafiz Abdul Kadir—the insurrectionary views of the writer were undisguised. The licence was, of course, revoked; and the press and printing materials seized. It would have been madness to suffer such effusions as the following to go forth:—

"Now, when the drum of the power of the English is sounding so loudly, it is in every one's mouth that the state of Travancore also is to be annexed to the British dominions upon the ground of maladministration. It is also said that the principality of Ulwar will be *confiscated*‡ by government. But at present the progress of *confiscation* is *arrested* by the government of the Almighty Ruler.

"The government should first *arrest* the progress of the disturbances and disorders which are raging in all parts of the country, and then address itself to these confiscations again. I formed a design of going to Worms. But the "worms"§ unexpectedly eat off my head. He (God) is Almighty. He does what he will. He makes a world desert in a breath.

"Everybody knows, and now perhaps it has become quite clear to the *lords of annexation*, what kind of mischief the confiscation of Lucknow has done, causing ruin to thousands of their own friends. * * * Come what may, in these degenerate days, the men of Delhi must be celebrated as sons of Rustum, and very Alexanders in strength. Oh! God destroy our enemies utterly, and assist and aid our sovereign (Sultan)."

With the above characteristic extract this section may fitly conclude, without any attempt to hazard conclusions on so difficult a subject as the degree of control necessary to be exercised for the maintenance of a despotic government, in a crisis so arduous and unprecedented as the present.

* *Bengal Hurkaru*, 14th September, 1857.

† Parl. Papers (Commons), 4th May, 1858. p. 48.

‡ All the *italicised* words are exactly rendered from the Persian by their English synonymes.

§ Kirman, the name of a town and province in Persia, also signifies "worms." The conceit can thus be rendered into English. The whole tone of the article, in the original, is highly sarcastic.—*Goolshun Nowbahar*, 27th June, 1857. Parl. Papers (Commons), 4th May, 1858; pp. 46, 47.

*Currency.**—An ill-regulated and insufficient currency has long pressed heavily on the people, and has exercised a singular influence in the present crisis. Until recently there was only one public bank (that of Bengal) in all India: with much difficulty two others, also under the control of government, were established at Bombay and Madras; but the amount of notes issued by them is insufficient for the requirements of even these cities. Three or four joint-stock banks have been lately formed; but the government has continued, up to the present time, to rely on a bulky and indivisible coin, the silver rupee (worth about two shillings), for its standard circulating medium. The exclusive use, by the state, of metallic money, has occasioned the accumulation of treasure, amounting, sometimes, to fourteen millions sterling, in thirty or forty treasuries, scattered all over the country. Forty to fifty thousand sepoys have been annually employed in escorting money from one district to another, an employment properly belonging to a police force; which has occasioned much discontent, and tended to the relaxation of discipline, and general demoralisation of the soldiery. A paper currency would have answered every purpose of local taxation and payments to the troops: it would have been far more easily transmissible, and it would not have offered so tempting a bribe to native cupidity. In several instances, it is evident that the sepoys were stimulated to the commission of crime by the hope of plundering the local treasuries of much larger sums than were ever allowed to remain in them.

The *Times*† has recently published the following forcible remarks on the subject:—

"Regiments that held Company's paper were faithful until they had exchanged it for gold; regiments that had pay in arrear were faithful until the arrears were paid up. The Company's gold has never received credit for the part it played in the mutiny. Yet it had often been pressed upon the authorities at Calcutta, that a paper currency would be a boon to India. Those who wished for this, probably thought little of the danger of carrying bullion in bullock-trunks or palkies through the jungle, or storing it in exposed places; their object was, in all probability, the extension of commerce and the development of the resources of the country. The policy of the Company was, is, and ever must be, to discourage all independent enterprise within their territories, and they were consistent in refusing to listen to any such suggestions. Now, however, when we are commencing a new era—if, indeed, we are commencing, or are about to commence a new era—this subject must be reconsidered. There can be no good reason why India should not in monetary facilities be placed upon a level with England. There is excellent reason why the troops should be paid in paper money. The absence of the gold is the absence of a powerful temptation, and the bank-note is a guardian of the fidelity of the man in whose pocket it lies."

The *Opium Monopoly*, with its concomitant grievances—the forced cultivation of the poppy, and the domiciliary right of search—ranks among the causes of popular disaffection. The Company obtain opium from the ryots at a very low price, by a system of advances, and sell it for the contraband China trade, at a very high one.‡ An official authority declares, that the peasants in the opium districts of Patna and Benares, are compelled to give up fixed portions of their lands for the production of the poppy. The forced cultivation of this poisonous drug brings on the wretched cultivators the persecuting surveillance of the police; the probability that they may be retaining some portion for private sale, exposing them to every sort of ingenuity which spies, authorised and unauthorised, can imagine, as the means of inflicting fines and extorting bribes.§ The deteriorating influence on the consumer cannot be doubted. In China we have notoriously returned evil for good; exporting ship-loads of their refreshing herb to combat our own spirit-craving propensities; and importing, in defiance of the laws of God and man, millions of pounds' worth of a stimulant which we know to be, when once resorted to, almost invariably persevered in, to the destruction of the body, and, it would seem, of the soul even, of its miserable victim. In India we found the debasing indulgence general among certain classes. Baber and his successors, with the exception of Aurungzebe, were all its habitual consumers; and the able historian of Rajast'han, Colonel Tod, attributes the loss of independence by the Rajpoots, their general deterioration, and the diminished productiveness of the country, chiefly to the same suicidal practice.

* The cash balances in the different Indian treasuries, varied from twelve to fourteen millions sterling. In 1856, the amount was £12,043,334: of this sum, there was in Bengal, £5,117,553; in the N. W. Provinces, £2,251,904 = £7,369,457. The Madras presidency had £2,311,365; and the Bombay, £2,362,510.—(Parliamentary Papers, April 20th, 1858.)

† June, 1858.

‡ J. Passmore Edwards' *Evils of the Opium Trade*, p. 18.

§ See *Iniquities of the Opium Trade;* by Rev. A. A. Thelwell.

But though the East India Company did not originate the use or cultivation of opium in all their vast dominions, they have done so in some. It is argued, that the very taxation is itself a discouragement to the cultivation; and this would be the case in a free country; but is not true in India, where there are so many means of compelling the peasant to toil like a serf at any labour for a bare subsistence. That the Company have been voluntarily instrumental in increasing the production, stands on the face of their own records.

On the cession of Malwa by the Mahrattas, measures were taken to raise from that province a revenue similar to that obtained in the Bengal presidency. A powerful impulse was given to the growth of the poppy; but the cost of cultivation was found so far to exceed that of Bahar or Benares, and the transport was likewise so much more difficult, that the excessive production obtained in Central India, scarcely afforded sufficient nett profit to atone for the injury done to the Bengal monopoly. The utmost efforts were made to remedy this, and to prevent diminished cultivation in the old provinces. "Premiums and rewards," says a late chairman of the East India Company, "have been held out; new offices and establishments have been created; the revenue officers have been enlisted in the service; and the influence of that department has been brought into action to promote the production. * * * The supreme government of India, too, have condescended to supply the retail shops with opium, and have thus added a new feature to our fiscal policy. I believe that no one act of our government has appeared, in the eyes of respectable natives, both Mohammedan and Hindoo, more questionable than the establishment of the Abkarry, or tax on the sale of spirituous liquors and drugs. Nothing, I suspect, has tended so much to lower us in their regard. They see us derive a revenue from what they deem an impure source; and when they find the pollution of public-houses spreading around them, they cannot understand that our real object is to check the use of the noxious article which is sold, or to regulate those haunts of the vicious with a view to objects of police. And have we succeeded in promoting these objects? Will any man be so hardy as to maintain, that the use of spirituous liquors and drugs has been diminished by the operation of the tax, or that it has not been everywhere extended? * * * But even if we admit that these objects have been kept in view, or that it is becoming, in the present state of the country, to regulate the vend of spirits and drugs, was it becoming in a great government to exhibit itself as the purveyor of opium to publicans, or—in the words of the Regulation—'to establish shops, on the part of government, for the retail sale of the drug?' Is it desirable that we should bring it to the very door of the lower orders, who might never otherwise have found the article within their reach, and who are now tempted to adopt a habit alike injurious to health and to good morals?"*

Not content with stimulating to the utmost the production of opium in our own territories, we voluntarily extended the curse in the Mahratta districts of Central India, in the Afghan state of Bhopal, in Oodipoor, Kotah, Boondi, and other Rajpoot principalities, by negotiations and treaties, "such as are not, I believe (says Mr. Tucker), to be paralleled in the whole history of diplomacy;" whereby we have bound ourselves to the payment of large annual sums on account of opium. "We make it the interest of the chiefs to increase the growth of the poppy, to the exclusion, in some instances, of sugar-cane, cotton, and other products which constitute the riches of a country, and which ought to minister to the comforts of the people."

These statements are very important, coming from one whose official position, Indian experience, and personal character, give his opinions threefold weight. He adds a brief warning, which, read by the blaze of the incendiary fires of 1857, is pregnant with meaning. "The Rajpoot, with all his heroic bravery and other good qualities, requires very skilful management. The same may be said of the Afghan of Rohilcund, who is still more restless and impatient of control; and if there were not other and better reasons, I should say that it is not safe, with either race—Rajpoot or Afghan—to supply the means of habitual excitement, which must render them more turbulent and ungovernable."†

Sir Stamford Raffles, another acknowledged authority, indignantly denounced the conduct of the European government in

* *Memorials of Indian Government;* a selection from the papers of H. St. George Tucker; edited by Mr. Kaye: pp. 152—134.

† *Ibid.*, p. 156.

overlooking every consideration of policy and humanity, and allowing a paltry addition to their finances to outweigh all regard to the ultimate prosperity of the country. Unfortunately, the financial addition* is paltry only when viewed in connection with the amount of evil which it represents, and which has increased in proportion to the extended cultivation. An experienced authority† states, that wherever opium is grown it is eaten; and considers that "one-half of the crimes in the opium districts, murders, rapes, and affrays, have their origin in opium-eating." Major-general Alexander uses the most forcible language regarding the progressive and destructive course of intoxication by opium and ardent spirits throughout India, appealing to the returns of courts-martial and defaulters' books for testimony of the consequent deterioration of the sepoys; and to the returns of the courts and offices of judges, magistrates, and collectors, for that of the mass of the natives. Under this view of the case, and remembering also the example set by the notorious tendency to drunkenness which disgraces the British troops, there is something terribly significant in the fact, that the fiercest onslaughts and worst brutalities which our countrymen and countrywomen have endured, were committed under the influence of the hateful drugs by which we have gained so much gold, and inflicted so much misery.

The *Neglect of Public Works* must take its place among the indirect causes of revolt; for it has materially impeded the development of the resources of the country, and furnished the people with only too palpable reason for discontent. It was a subject which ought always to have had the special attention of the Anglo-Indian authorities. They should have remembered, that the people over whom they ruled were literally as children in their hands; and should have taken care to exercise a far-seeing, providential, and paternal despotism. Under Mohammedan and Hindoo governments, the princes and nobles have ever delighted in associating their names with some stately edifice, some great road or canal, some public work of more or less utility. It was a fashion which those who made for themselves a fortune and a name, especially delighted in following; and the fact is so well known that it needs no illustration. Every book of travel affords fresh instances. Foreign adventurers have adopted the same beneficent custom: witness the Martinière college at Lucknow. Very few Englishmen, however, have thought of spending on, or in India, any considerable portion of the wealth they made there; the noble Sir Henry Lawrence and others, whose names are easily reckoned, forming the exceptions.

It would occupy too much space to offer anything like an enumeration of our shortcomings in this respect: able pens have already performed the ungracious task; and it needs but a few hours' attentive study of the admirably condensed exposition given by Lieutenant-colonel Cotton (chief engineer of Madras), and of the pamphlets published by Mr. Dickinson and other members of the Indian Reform Society, to be convinced how unjust and impolitic have been our omissions in this important branch of government.

Sir Charles Napier says, that "in India, economy means, laying out as little for the country and for noble and useful purposes as you can; and giving as large salaries as you can possibly squeeze out of the public to individuals, adding large 'establishments.'"‡ The force of this remark is painfully apparent, when the immense number of "collectors," and the extent and enormous expense of the revenue establishment, are compared with the number of engineers, and the cost of the department for public works. The contrast between what is taken from, and what is spent upon India, becomes still more glaring when the items of expenditure are examined, and a division made between the works undertaken on behalf of the government—such as court-houses, gaols, &c.—and those immediately intended for the benefit of the people, such as roads, canals, and tanks.

The injustice of this procedure is surpassed by its impolicy. Colonel Cotton says—

> "Certainly, without any exaggeration, the most astonishing thing in the history of our rule in India is, that such innumerable volumes should have been written by thousands of the ablest men in the service on the mode of collecting the land revenue, while the question, of a thousand times more importance, how to enable the people to pay it, was literally never touched upon; and yet, even the

* See *Indian Empire*, vol. i., p. 582.

† Mr. Andrew Sym, who had charge of the Company's opium agency at Goruckpoor. See pamphlets on the *Opium Trade;* by Major-general Alexander and Mr. W. S. Fry.

‡ *Life*, vol. ii., p. 428.

question of the amount of taxation was utterly insignificant in comparison with that. While we have been labouring for a hundred years to discover how to get twenty lacs out of a district which is not able to pay it, not the least thought has been bestowed on the hundreds of lacs it was losing from the enormous cost of transit, which swallowed up all the value of the ryot produce, if they raised it.* * * * If we take the whole loss to India, from want of communication, at only twenty-five million sterling, it is twelve times as great a burthen as the interest of the [Indian] debt. * * * Public works have been almost entirely neglected in India. The motto hitherto has been—'do nothing, have nothing done, let nobody do anything.' Bear any loss, let the people die of famine, let hundreds of lacs be lost in revenue for want of water, rather than *do* anything. * * * Who would believe, that without half-a-dozen miles of real turnpike-road, with communications generally in the state that they were in England two centuries ago—with periodical famines and a stagnant revenue—the stereotyped answer to any one who urges improvement is, 'He is too much in a hurry—he is too sanguine—we must go on by degrees;' and this, too, in the face of the fact that, almost without exception, money laid out upon public works in India, has yielded money returns of one hundred, two hundred, and three hundred per cent., besides innumerable other advantages to the community. * * * We have already all but lost one century, to the great damage of our finances and the greater injury of the people."†

It is terrible to think of the amount of suffering occasioned by the ignorant apathy of the nation to whom it has pleased Providence to entrust the government of India. "The neglect of public works" is a vague, unmeaning sound in British ears: no nation blessed with free institutions can appreciate its full intent; and no people under the despotism of a single tyrant, but would rise, and cut off the Pharaoh who demanded the tale of bricks, yet withheld the straw. Nothing but the complicated system of our absentee sovereigntyship, can account for such strange persistence in errors which have repeatedly brought the Company to the verge of bankruptcy, and inflicted on the mass of the people chronic poverty and periodical famine.

In England, we are occasionally horror-struck by some case of death from actual destitution; and we know, alas! that large portions of our working population, with difficulty obtain the necessaries of life; but we are also aware that public and individual benevolence is incessantly at work to diminish the sufferings inseparable, at least to some extent, from an over-populated and money-worshipping country. When Ireland was scourged with famine, the whole British empire, even to its farthest colony, poured forth, unsolicited, its contributions in money or in food with eager haste. Is, then, human sympathy dependent on race or colour? No; or the West Indies would still be peopled with slaves and slave-drivers. The same springs of action which, once set in motion, worked incessantly for the accomplishment of negro emancipation, would, if now touched on behalf of the Hindoos, act as a lever to raise them from the deep wretchedness in which they are sunk. The manufacturers of Manchester and of Glasgow are surely blind to their own interests, or long ere this they would have taken up the subject of roads, canals, and tanks for India, if only to encourage the growth of cotton in the country in which it is an indigenous product, and to diminish their dangerous dependence on America. Had they done so, they would have had their reward. But the active and enterprising philanthropical class, which includes many "successful merchants" in its ranks, perhaps requires to be told, that the subject of public works for India is at once a great call for national justice and individual charity; that there is no conceivable means of fulfilling on so large a scale the unquestionable duty of giving bread to the hungry, as by initiating measures to rescue hundreds of thousands of British subjects from probable starvation.

The frightful massacres of Meerut and Cawnpoor have not banished from our minds the recollection of that terrible "Black Hole," where 123 persons perished, some from suffocation, and others in the maddening agonies of thirst; and this not from any purpose of fiend-like cruelty, but simply because the young Nawab, Surajah Dowlah, did not know the size of the prison-chamber of the English garrison in which he had directed his prisoners to be secured; and none of his officers cared to disturb his sleep, to procure a change of orders. When he awoke the door was opened, and the few weak, worn survivors, on whose frames some hours of agony had done the work of years, tottered forth, or were dragged out from amid the already putrefying corpses of their companions.‡

Surajah Dowlah paid, with his throne and life, the forfeit of his apathetic ignorance; and his people were happily delivered from that crowning curse—despotic inca-

* *Public Works in India;* by Lieutenant-colonel Cotton, 1854; p. 8. † *Ibid.*, pp. 294, 295.

‡ *Indian Empire*, vol. i., p. 273.

pacity. His fate ought to have served as a warning of the effects of mere neglect. Has it done so; or has the evil been multiplied a thousand-fold under a Christian government? Can it, or can it not, be proved by public records, that, for every single Englishman who perished while the Indian nawab lay sleeping, many thousand natives have fallen victims to an apathy no less criminal, manifested by the representatives of the E. I. Company? This is the meaning, or at least a part of the meaning, of the "neglect of public works in India;" and the only excuse offered for it is the poverty of the government. It is asserted, that the drain consequent on perpetual wars, which directly enriched and often indirectly ennobled the individuals concerned, occasioned so wide a destruction of native property, created such an unceasing drain on the state revenues, and so increased and complicated the labours of the collectors, that the one-engrossing anxiety of the authorities, how to meet current expenses, unavoidably superseded every other consideration.

The peculiar system of the Company has likewise contributed to induce a selfish and short-sighted policy. The brief period of administration allotted to each governor-general, whatever its advantages, has had the great drawback of rarely sufficing for the initiation, organisation, and carrying through of any large measure of general benefit; and it is, of course, seldom that a new-comer, fresh from England, has the ability or the generosity to appreciate and cordially work out the plan of his predecessor. The consequence has been a lamentable want of any consistent policy for the development of the resources of India. Lord Dalhousie, it is true, exerted himself zealously and successfully in the furtherance of certain great undertakings, in connection with which his name may well be gratefully remembered. The Ganges canal, the Bengal railway, the electric telegraph, are works of undoubted utility; and the good service they have rendered to the supreme government in its hour of need, must be calculated in lives rather than in money. But a few great and costly achievements cannot excuse the general neglect manifested by the non-appropriation of a certain portion of the revenue of every district to meet its own peculiar and urgent requirements. From the absence of any adequate provision, the vast reservoirs, sometimes many miles square, constructed by native princes centuries ago, have been allowed, to a considerable extent, to go to decay, and are now sources of disease instead of fertility, being covered with rank weeds.*

The East India Company have added the tax levied by their Mohammedan or Hindoo predecessors for annual repairs, to their general assessments, but have suffered many of the tanks to go to ruin; while, according to a recent writer (1858), "in many cases they still exact the same money-revenue from the cultivators, amounting, at the present day, to fifty, sixty, and seventy per cent. of the gross produce of the soil, as if the tanks were kept in perfect repair, and the cultivators received the quantity of water required to grow a full crop of produce."†

Water, water! is the primary want of the Indian farmer; yet, according to Colonel Cotton, it is undoubted that, in the worst year that ever occurred, enough has been allowed to flow into the sea to have irrigated ten times as much grain as would have supplied the whole population.‡ The case is put in the clearest light in an extract from a private letter, hastily written, and not meant for publication, addressed by "one of the most distinguished men in India," to Mr. Dickinson, and published by him, under the idea that it was better calculated than any laboured statement, to carry conviction to an unprejudiced mind. The writer, after declaring that the perpetual involvements of the Company had originated in their having omitted not only to initiate improvements, but even to keep in repair the old works upon which the revenue depended; adds—"But this is not the strongest point of the case. *They did not take the least pains to prevent famine.* To say nothing of the death of a quarter of a million of people in Guntoor, the public works' committee, in their report, calculate that the loss in money by the Guntoor famine, was more than two millions sterling. If they could find money to supply these losses, they could have found a hundredth part of the sum to prevent them.

"Lord —— thinks it would be better not to blame the government; how can we possibly point out how improvement can be made without proving that there has been neglect before? * * * Lord —— won-

* Macleod Wylie's *Bengal a Field of Missions*, p. 241.

† *Lectures on British India;* by John Malcolm Ludlow; vol. ii., p. 317.

‡ Quoted in the Madras Petition of 1852.

ders at my vehemence about public works: is he really so humble a man as to think no better of himself, than to suppose he could stand unmoved in a district where 250,000 people had perished miserably of famine through the neglect of our government, and see it exposed every year to a similar occurrence? If his lordship had been living in the midst of the district at the time, like one of our civilians, and had had every morning to clear the neighbourhood of his house of hundreds of dead bodies of poor creatures who had struggled to get near the European, in hopes that there perhaps they might find food, he would have realised things beyond what he has seen in his ——shire park."*

What excuse, even of ignorance, can be offered for a government that turns a deaf ear to statements so appalling as these, made by their own servants? Such impenetrable apathy affords a confirmation of the often-repeated assertion, that nothing but the continual pressure of public opinion in England, will ensure anything being effected in India. Would that this power might be at once exerted! Even now, in the midst of battles, we ought to be doing something to avert the consequences of past neglect, or the scourge of war will be followed by the yet more fatal visitations of famine, and its twin-sister, pestilence.

We may not be able to do much, or anything, in some of the most disturbed districts; but in the great majority, where comparative quiet prevails, a vigorous effort ought at once to be made for the introduction of a better system; that is, one designed to benefit the mass of the people, instead of being exclusively framed to suit the convenience of the European officials. Had this been earlier attempted, we might have had fewer great works to talk about in parliament or at the India House (though that is hardly possible, considering that we are Anglo-Saxons of the nineteenth century): but certainly India would not now be so generally destitute of the means of cheap carriage; neither would it be necessary to urge "the clearing-out of this poisonous old tank; the repairing of that embankment; the metalling of this mud-track through the jungle; the piercing, by a cheap canal of irrigation, of that tongue of land, of a few miles, between two rivers;"† the preservation of bridges; and such-like cheap, homely, obscure labours, as are now urgently needed throughout the length and breadth of the peninsula.

Cheap transit by land and water is a point only secondary in importance to irrigation, as a means of preventing famine, by enabling one part of the country to help another in the event of the failure of local rains. Major-general Tremenheere, in his recent evidence before parliament (May, 1858), when adverting to the brief intervals which have elapsed between the years of scarcity in the present century, forcibly states the necessity for affording the greatest facilities for the transport of produce, as the true remedy for these oft-recurring famines.‡ The evidence of subsequent witnesses before the same committee, shows that, in a country where easy transit is essential to the preservation of life during periodical visitations of dearth, there exists the most remarkable deficiency of means of intercommunication ever heard of under a civilised government.

"There are no roads to connect even Calcutta with any of the great cities of the interior. No road to Moorshedabad; no road to Dacca; none to Patna; no such roads as parish roads in England, to connect villages and market-towns in the interior. Consequently, in the rainy season, every town is isolated from its neighbours, and from all the rest of the country. Besides roads, bridges are wanted: there are hardly any bridges at all in the country; their place is partially supplied by ferries. The grand trunk-road, within the Lower Provinces, is only partially bridged; and half the bridges, I believe, have been washed away from defects of construction."§

In Bengal, Bahar, and Orissa, the maintenance of good roads is a duty to which the government are alleged to be specially pledged; for, in making the decennial settlement (on which the permanent one was subsequently grounded), a separate tax for the purpose was inserted in the rent-roll, but was afterwards merged in the general assessment, and not applied to the roads. The native land-owners have remembered this breach of faith; and when urged, some years ago, to make fresh provision for the maintenance of highways, they objected, on the ground of the misappropriation of their actual yearly payments. Happily for them, their interests are closely allied with those of the British settlers. Both classes are equally without the pale of privilege and patronage, dignities and immunities,

* Dickinson's *India under a Bureaucracy*, pp. 87—90.

† Ludlow's *Lectures*, vol. ii., p. 320.

‡ First Report of the Select Committee on the Colonization and Settlement of India, p. 6.

§ *Ibid.* Evidence of W. Theobald, Esq., p. 74.

with which the East India Company has fenced round its covenanted service; but the storm which has disturbed the immigrant planters in their peaceable avocations, has contributed to procure for them the opportunity of laying before a parliamentary committee, and consequently before the nation at large, the obstructions which impede all attempts to earn an honourable livelihood by developing the resources of India.

Several witnesses declare the want of internal communication to be peculiar to the administration of the East India Company, who have attempted nothing except for military or governmental purposes, and even then very imperfectly; while, under Hindoo and Mohammedan dynasties, the peninsula was intersected with roads, the remains of which are still traceable.* The planters, to some extent, make roads in their immediate vicinity, suitable to their own necessities; but these do not answer for purposes of general traffic, which requires continuous lines. The native land-owners understand road-making, but want the means, not the will, to carry it on extensively. Mr. Dalrymple, an indigo and sugar planter, and silk manufacturer, resident in India upwards of thirty years, adduces, as an instance of the feeling of the natives on this subject, that he has known one of them make a road for a hundred miles from a religious motive.†

For the neglect of many duties, and especially of this one, we are paying a severe penalty; and the hardships so long suffered by the natives, in having to carry their articles of produce or merchandise on their heads, along paths impassable for beasts of burden, now fall with tenfold weight on our heavily-laden soldiery. Individual suffering, great as that has been (including the long list of victims to "solar apoplexy," on marches which, by even good common roads or by canals, would have been short and comparatively innocuous), forms but the inevitable counterpart of the public distress, occasioned by the present insurmountable impediments to the rapid concentration of military force on a given point. Facilities for the movement of troops are important in every seat of war; but particularly so in India, where the extent of country to be maintained exceeds beyond all proportion the number of European troops which can at any sacrifice be spared to garrison it.

The upholders of "a purely military despotism" have not been wise even in their generation, or they would have promoted, instead of opposing, the construction of railways between the chief cities, as a measure of absolute necessity. If only the few already projected had been completed, Delhi could hardly have fallen as it did—a rich, defenceless prize—into the hands of the mutineers, nor afforded them the means of establishing a rallying-point for the disaffected, and doing incalculable damage to European *prestige*, by setting an example of temporarily successful defiance. As it was, the contrast was most painful between the lightning-flash that brought the cry for help from stations surrounded by a seething mass of revolt, and the slow, tedious process by which alone the means of rescue could be afforded. Thus, the appeal of Sir Henry Lawrence for reinforcements for Cawnpoor, received the gloomy response, that it was "impossible to place a wing of Europeans there in less time than twenty-five days." The bullock-train could take a hundred men a-day, at the rate of thirty miles a-day:‡ this was all that could be done; and, with every effort, at an enormous cost of life and treasure, the troops arrived only to be maddened by the horrible evidences of the massacre they were too late to avert.

"Indophilus" views the railroad system as the basis of our military power in India; and considers it "so certain that railways are better than regiments, that it would be for the interest of England, even in a strictly economical point of view, to diminish the drain upon her working population, by lending her credit to raise money for the completion of Indian railways."§ The urgency of the requirement has become so evident as a measure of expediency, for the maintenance of our sovereignty, that it scarcely needs advocating: on the contrary, it seems necessary to deprecate the too exclusive appropriation of Indian revenue to railroads (especially costly ones, in which speed is apt to be made a primary requisite),‖ to the neglect of the far cheaper means of transit which might be opened by single

* Second Report—Evidence of Mr. J. T. Mackenzie, p. 88.

† Second Report, p. 67.

‡ Telegram of the governor-general to Sir Henry Lawrence, May 24th, 1857.—Parl. Papers on the Mutiny; Appendix, p. 315.

§ *Letters of Indophilus*, p. 12.

‖ See Colonel Cotton's *Public Works*, p. 184.

rail, by tram-roads, by the formation of canals for steam navigation, and by the opening and improving of rivers. Measures of this kind must be taken, if we would enable the people to bear the expenses attendant on our system of government.* Labour thus wisely employed and directed, would produce capital; the now insuperable difficulty of raising a sufficient revenue without oppressing the masses, would be removed; and their rulers, relieved from pecuniary pressure, might dare to be just by renouncing opium smuggling, and to be humane by abandoning the less criminal but still obnoxious salt† monopoly, which, as at present conducted, acts as an irregular poll-tax—falling heaviest on those who have farthest to fetch it from the government depôts.

The *Repression of British Enterprise* is closely connected with the neglect of public works; for had European planters been allowed to settle in any considerable numbers, and to give free expression to their opinions, they would certainly have agitated the subject in a manner which no government could have wholly withstood.

The Company, from their earliest days, strove with unremitting care to guard their chartered privileges against the encroachments of their countrymen, and adopted a tone of lofty superiority which was scarcely consistent with their own position as "merchant adventurers." Had there not been in America, the West Indies, and other colonies and dependencies of the British crown, abundant outlet for capital and enterprise, the Indian monopoly would probably have been soon broken through: as it was, the "interlopers" were comparatively few, and easily put down, if they proved in the least refractory, by the strong measure of deportation. Gradually the exclusive system was greatly modified by the effects of the parliamentary discussions which accompanied each renewal of the Company's charter, together with the disclosures of mismanagement involved in the perpetually recurring pecuniary embarrassments, from which they sought relief in the creation and augmentation of an Indian national debt. In 1813 their trade with India ceased entirely: it had long been carried on at an actual loss; the traffic with China, and the Indian territorial revenues, supplying the *deficit*. Yet, notwithstanding the opening up of the Indian trade to all British subjects (followed by a similar procedure with that of China in 1833), the Company were slow in abating their jealous hostility towards "adventurers," and did their utmost to prevent European enterprise from gaining a footing in India. They do not seem to have recognised the change of policy incumbent on them when, ceasing to be traders, they became sovereigns of a vast empire, and were thereby bound to renounce class interests and prejudices, and merge all meaner considerations in the paramount obligation of promoting the general good.

Of course, colonization, in the ordinary sense of the term, is neither practicable nor desirable in a country already well and generally densely peopled, and where land is the most dearly prized of all possessions. Even in certain favoured localities, where outdoor employment can be best undertaken by Europeans, there is no product which they could cultivate on the spot, in which they would not be undersold by the natives. Indeed, it would be manifestly absurd to attempt to compete, as labourers, with men who can support themselves on wages ranging from 1½*d.* to 4½*d.* a-day.‡ It is as the pio-

* The salaries of Englishmen in India are all on a very high scale. The average annual salary received by civilians is estimated at £1,750.—(See article on "British India"—*Quarterly Review*, August, 1858; p. 237.) A Queen's officer, directly he embarks for India, has double pay. The fees of the lawyers and solicitors at Calcutta, are more than double what they are in English courts. No tradesman in Calcutta would be satisfied with the English rate of profit; and, in fact, all European labour is much more highly remunerated in India than elsewhere.—(First Report of Colonization Committee. Evidence of Major-general Tremenheere; p. 36.) It was found necessary to raise the scale of salaries of English functionaries, as a means of preserving them from corruption; and, to a great extent, the measure has succeeded. Even-handed justice requires, that the same experiment should be tried with the natives of the country from which the funds are levied, and it will then be seen whether improved efficiency and integrity may not equally be the result. "A native judge, who has any prospect of promotion, hardly ever is known to be corrupt."—Raikes.

† The difference in the price of salt, between Calcutta and Benares, amounts to 100 per cent. Rice, which sells at a seaport at 2*s.* a bushel, is quoted at an average of 5*s.* 1*d.* per bushel in the Punjab, the Trans-Indus, and the Cis-Sutlej territories; the distance of these states from a seaport being from 800 to 1,200 miles.—Third Report of Colonization Committee, dated July 12th, 1858. Evidence of W. Balston, Esq.; p. 65.

‡ Evidence of R. Baikie, Esq.—First Report of Colonization Committee, 6th May, 1858; p. 52.

neers of skill and capital that Europeans must look to find remuneration and useful employment in India. In that sense the field is wide enough, and the need great indeed; for the native products and manufactures have, in many instances, actually diminished in extent and in value under the sway of the East India Company. Every child knows that calico takes its name from Calicut, whence it was first brought to England; yet domestic manufacture has been overwhelmed by the cheap, coarse fabrics of the Manchester steam-power looms; nor has the encouragement been given which might have opened for them a lucrative market in luxurious England for their own more delicate and durable productions. The Dacca muslin—the famous "woven wind," which, when wet, lay on the grass like the night-dew—this, also, has become almost a thing of the past. Yet, if only a market were assured, the cotton could be grown as before, and the same exquisite manipulation would be as cheaply obtainable.

Much important information regarding the present state of affairs, has been laid before the select committee lately appointed to inquire into questions affecting the settlement of India. Well-informed persons declare, that labour is cheap and abundant almost everywhere throughout India;* that the natives are very tractable; and yet, despite their readiness to learn, and long intercourse with Europeans, the knowledge of agriculture is in about the same position as at the time of Alexander's invasion.† This is in itself a discreditable fact, considering the effects produced by the application of science to agriculture in Europe: and the apathy manifested in India is especially blamable and impolitic, on the part of a government which has virtually usurped the position of landlord over a large portion of the country, more than one-half of the revenues of which, that is to say, £15,500,000 out of £28,000,000, is derived by rents from the land; while four-fifths of the annual exports, namely, £17,500,000 out of £21,500,000, are the direct produce of the soil.‡

While the system pursued has not improved under the rule of the Company, the cultivators themselves have absolutely deteriorated; the better class of farmers are alleged to have become generally impoverished, and to live in less comfort than they used to do under the Hindoo and Mohammedan dynasties; while very many of the ryots are hopelessly in debt.§ Impaired fertility is the natural consequence of over-cropping, and the native tenant has no means of counteracting this; his poverty being so great, that he cannot afford to keep up a farming establishment of sufficient strength, especially as regards cattle, to admit of the due production of manure, or of those requirements which are considered indispensable, in England, to the cultivation of the commonest arable land.‖ The native agriculturist, if he borrow from a native banker and capitalist, pays, it is alleged, from fifty to seventy-five per cent. interest.¶ Usury thrives by sucking the life-blood, already scanty, of tillage and manufacture, and rivets the fetters of that system of advances which is truly described as the curse of India.**

The existence of the prevailing wretchedness above indicated, goes far to prove that the Company, in opposing the settlement of their fellow-countrymen, have not been actuated by a disinterested solicitude for the welfare of the natives. In fact, the fear of an influx of Europeans was almost a monomania with the Court of Directors; and every measure which could in any manner, however indirectly, facilitate the anticipated irruption, met with opposition avowedly on that account. Thus, the chairman and deputy-chairman of the Company, when advocating the enforcement of rigid restrictions on the press in 1823, adverted especially to the possibility of its "affording amusement or occupation to a class of adventurers proceeding clandestinely to India, to encourage whom would be a departure from the policy hitherto observed."††

Lord William Bentinck granted to Englishmen the privilege of holding lands in the interior of India, contrary to the in-

* Second Report of Select Committee on Colonization and Settlement of India, 10th June, 1858.—Evidence of Mr. J. P. Wise; p. 40.

† First Report, 6th May, 1858.—Evidence of Major-general Tremenheere; p. 29.

‡ Second Report.—Evidence of Major-general Tremenheere; pp. 28, 29.

§ *Ibid.*—Evidence of Mr. J. T. Mackenzie; p. 83.

‖ Evidence of Captain J. Ouchterlony.—Third Report, 12th July, 1858; p. 4. Another witness says, the charge for money advances is from fifty to a hundred per cent.; "but when the lenders advance in grain, they generally charge from one to two hundred per cent., because they have to be repaid in kind."—Mr. Mackenzie. Second Report, p. 83.

¶ Evidence of Mr. J. P. Wise.—*Ibid.*, p. 41.

** Evidence of Mr. Fowler.—Third Report, p. 54.

†† Parl. Papers, 4th May, 1858; p. 19.

structions of the Company; and his reasons for so doing are recorded in the minutes in council, of the years 1829 and 1830. At this period the question of settlement in India excited a good deal of interest in England; and a clause was inserted in the East India Charter Act of 1833, giving permission to all British subjects by birth, to purchase land and reside in India; and an enactment, in conformity with this clause, was passed by the local legislature in 1837.

Sir Charles Metcalfe was one of the leading advocates for a change of policy, as indispensable to the continuance of the Anglo-Indian empire; but he held that this change could never be effected until the government of the Crown should be formally substituted for that of the Company. The opinion is remarkable as coming from one of the most distinguished servants of the latter body—one who, trained in the close preserve of the covenanted civil service, rose, under the fostering care of Lord Wellesley, from occupying a clerk's desk, through intermediate grades of office, to the highest place in the council-chamber, and exercised, in a most independent fashion, the supreme authority provisionally entrusted to his care in 1835. His views would lose much of their force if conveyed in terms less full and unequivocal than his own; but, in reading the following extracts, it is necessary to remember that the word colonization has here a very limited application, and that the immigration required is not general; but must, to be beneficial to either of the parties concerned—the natives or the immigrants—consist of the capitalist class; in fact, of precisely those who find in overstocked Europe no field for the development of their resources, and who are deterred from the colonies by the high rate of wages, which constitute their chief attraction to the labouring masses.

"It is impracticable, perhaps [he writes as early as 1814], to suggest a remedy for the general disaffection of our Indian subjects. Colonization seems to be the only system which could give us a chance of having any part of the population attached to our government from a sense of common interests. Colonization may have its attendant evils; but with reference to the consideration above-stated, it would promise to give us a hold in the country which we do not at present possess. We might now be swept away in a single whirlwind. We are without root. The best-affected natives could think of a change of government with indifference; and in the N.W. Provinces there is hardly a man who would not hope for benefit from a change. This disaffection, however, will most probably not break out in any general manner as long as we possess a predominant power." In 1820, he declares—"As to a general reform of our rule, that question has always appeared to me as hopeless. Our rulers at home, and councillors abroad, are so bigoted as to precedent, that I never dream of any change unless it be a gradual declension from worse to worse. Colonization, without being forced or injudiciously encouraged, should be admitted without restraint. * * * I would never agree to the present laws of exclusion with respect to Europeans, which are unnatural and horrible." In 1836, he says—"The Europeans settled in India, and not in the Company's service, and to these might be added, generally, the East Indians of mixed breed, will never be satisfied with the Company's government: well or ill-founded, they will always attach to it the notion of monopoly and exclusion; they will consider themselves comparatively discountenanced and unfavoured, and will always look with a desire to the substitution of a King's government. For the contentment of this class, which for the benefit of India and the security of our Indian empire ought greatly to increase in numbers and importance, the introduction of a King's government is undoubtedly desirable.* * * It must be doubted whether even the civil service will be able to retain its exclusive privileges after the extensive establishment of European settlers. * * * The necessity of employing unfit men in highly important offices, is peculiar to this service, and demands correction."*

The evidence laid before parliament, after an interval of twenty-five years, forms a singular counterpart to the above statements. The persons examined speak from long and intimate experience; and their testimony, though varying in detail, coincides for the most part in its general bearing. They denounce the obstructive policy pursued towards them; and the majority distinctly declare, that permission to settle has not been availed of, because the protection of life and property, common to every other part of the British empire, is not afforded in India to any but the actual servants of government; the interests of all other subjects, European and native, being habitually disregarded. One witness alleges, that, "at this present time" (May, 1858), there are fewer Englishmen settled in the interior of India than there were twenty years ago, government servants excepted.†

* *Metcalfe Papers*, pp. 144; 150; 164; 171. It is, however, only fair to remind the reader, that Lord Metcalfe is declared by his biographer, Mr. Kaye, to have subsequently greatly modified his opinions. Seeing that government by the Crown would be, in fact, government by a parliamentary majority; he said, if that were applied to India, our tenure would not be worth ten years' purchase.—*Papers*, p. 165.

† Mr. G. Macnair.—Second Report, p. 2.

Another gentleman gives a clear exposition of similar convictions; stating, that—

"The real serious impediment to the settlement of Englishmen in India, is to be found in the policy of the system under which our Indian possessions have been hitherto, and, unfortunately, up to the present day, are still governed;—that policy which, giving certain extensive and exclusive privileges to a corporation established for trading purposes, and gradually formed into a governing power, originally shut out the spirit of enterprise, by excluding from the country Englishmen not servants of the Company. Although the extreme severity of this original policy has been somewhat modified and gradually relaxed, its spirit has remained but little changed; and its effects have been to keep the people of this country very ignorant of the resources and great value of India, and of the character, condition, and wants of the natives. Moreover, it is a matter of notoriety, that there has been, and is at the present time, a constant antagonism between the official and non-official Anglo-Indian communities; and that exactly as the adventuresome Englishman, who is called an interloper, with difficulty obtained his admission in the country, so even now he maintains his position in a continuous but unequal struggle with the local government, which he, in turn, regards as an obstacle between himself and the Crown and constitution to which he owns allegiance, and looks for protection in his own country. Then again, the departments of administration, police, the judicial system, both civil and criminal, are notoriously so wretchedly inefficient, oppressive, and corrupt, that they deter the peaceful and industrious from living within their influence, or risking their lives and property under their operations. I believe that even the comparatively few gentlemen settled in the interior of the country, would willingly withdraw, if they could do so without a ruinous sacrifice of property; for little or no heed has been given to their complaints, nor indeed of the natives; while the evils which have been pointed out for many years past are greatly on the increase. The present constitution of the legislative council has made matters worse than they were before; and that body has certainly not the confidence either of Europeans or natives. With the exception of two judges taken from the Supreme Court of Calcutta, it is composed of salaried and government officials, who have been such from the age of twenty, who have really nothing at stake in the country, and who are not likely to live under the operation and influence of the laws which they pass; while those who are directly interested in the well-being of the country, both Europeans and natives, are entirely excluded from any voice in the laws by which they are to be ruled and governed. * * * At present, you have in India a series of antagonisms which works most injuriously for all classes, and completely prevents that union amongst the governing people which appears to me to be essential to the well-being, not only of ourselves, but of the millions of people our subjects, taken under our care and protection avowedly for their own good, and enlightenment, and advancement in civilisation. At present there is an antagonism in the army, by he distinction of two services; and a worse antagonism between the Queen's courts and the Company's courts; between the laws administered in the presidency towns and in the interior; between the covenanted service, who have a monopoly of the well-paid appointments, and the upper, or educated portion of the uncovenanted service, who think themselves most unjustly excluded from advancement: and, finally, between almost every Englishman (I speak of these as facts, not as matters of opinion) not in the service of the Company, and the local government and covenanted service, who not only represent but carry out the policy of the East India Company, so as to shut out the direct authority of the Crown, the intervention of parliament, and the salutary and most necessary influence of public opinion in England. You cannot disconnect the European and the native. If you legislate simply with the idea of what is suitable to the English, without referring to the native and redressing the grievances of the native, there will be that unhappy antagonism between them that will effectually bar Europeans from going out to India."*

The exorbitant rate of interest (from fifteen to eighteen per cent.) charged on advances of money made to an indigo-planter, silk producer, or any settler occupied in developing the resources of the country (though not to be compared with that exacted from the native borrower), is urged by "an English zemindar"† resident some twenty-five years in Bengal, as another proof of the insecurity of property in the mofussil, or country districts, compared with that situated within the Calcutta jurisdiction, where large sums can be readily raised at from six to seven per cent. interest.‡ He enumerates the grievances already set forth in preceding sections, and points to the successful cultivation extensively carried on by European settlers in Ceylon, as a consequence of the perfect security and encouragment to capitalists, afforded by the administration and regulations of that island.§

Another witness declares that, in some parts of India, the land-revenue system actually excludes European capitalists. He instances the Madras presidency, and some portions of that of Bombay, where the Ryotwarree settlement is in force, where the government is the immediate landlord, and is represented in its transactions with its wretched tenants by the revenue police, an ill-paid and rapacious army of some 60,000 men, whose character was pretty well exposed in the Madras Torture Report. The settlement makes no provision for the

* Evidence of Mr. J. G. Waller.—Second Report, pp. 169, 170.

† Evidence of Mr. John Freeman.—First Report, pp. 112; 119; 139.

‡ The fixed legal maximum of interest in Bengal is twelve per cent.; other commissions bring it up to eighteen per cent.—Evidence of Mr. J. P. Wise. Second Report, p. 54.

§ *Ibid.*, p. 113.

introduction of an intermediate class of landlords; and the pauperised labourers emigrate in tens of thousands, to the Mauritius and elsewhere, leaving their own waste lands, to obtain subsistence in better governed countries.

In Bengal, both European and native capital and skill find employment under the permanent settlement, the value of which the natives generally perfectly understand, and call the "Great Charter of Bengal." The same witness adds—"It is invaluable to them and to us too; for it has saved Bengal from insurrection."*

This one great advantage possessed by Bengal, cannot, however, compensate for its other drawbacks; among which, the British settlers especially dwell on the lamentable deficiency of commercial roads, and the contrast thereby offered to the beautiful pleasure-drives for civilians and their ladies, which surround the chief stations. A settler engaged in growing rice, sugar, tobacco, and vegetables, for the Calcutta market, on an estate situated only forty miles from the great English metropolis, describes the difficulty of transit as so great, that the men who come to take the sugar away are obliged to do so upon bullocks' backs, each animal carrying about two maunds (about 1½ cwt. English), and treading warily along the lines separating one rice-field from another, which are generally about a foot in breadth, somewhat elevated above the field, acting also as ledges to keep the water in the fields: but, adds this witness, "some distance from there, where there is a little bit of road, they will take twenty or twenty-five maunds of produce with a cart and a couple of bullocks."†

Despite all discouragements, the British settlers claim to have done good service to their country and to India; and they affirm, "that wherever Europeans have been settled during the late convulsion, those parts have been less disturbed."‡ Their enterprise has been imitated by the native merchants; and many in Calcutta have, during the last twenty years, become large shippers of produce, and send orders for manufactured goods direct to England.§

Articles of great importance have been principally discovered and worked by the "interlopers." The coal-beds found by them after years of research, now give beneficial employment to several associations, including the Bengal Company, which alone pays about £2,000 per month to the railway, for the transit of coal from Raneegunge to Calcutta. The supply furnished by them has proved invaluable to the government during the mutiny; and the fleets of inland steamers belonging to the General Steam Navigation and Ganges Companies, have rendered vital service in the conveyance of the British troops, the naval brigade, and military ammunition and stores. Their efficiency would have been much greater had the authorities heeded the arguments previously addressed to them regarding the want of a canal to Rajmahal, or kept open one of the Nuddea rivers from Nuddea to the Ganges.||

The British settlers were the first to establish direct steam communication between Calcutta and Suez: through their instrumentality the transit through Egypt was carried out, and the first steamer placed on the Nile: they introduced the river steam-tugs, used to facilitate the intricate and dangerous navigation between Calcutta and the pilot station; and they established the horse-carriages, by which Sir Colin Campbell and hundreds of officers and soldiers hastened to the seat of war. Silk, and other valuable and easily-transportable products, such as indigo, the hateful drug opium, together with jute, hemp, tobacco and linseed, have considerably increased in quantity, and improved in quality, under the influence of British capital and energy. The settlers succeeded in growing good tea before it was discovered to be indigenous in so many places

* Evidence of Mr. Theobald.—First Report, pp. 61, 62; 85.

† Evidence of Mr. J. Freeman.—First Report, p. 119. (See further testimony to the same effect—First Report, pp. 114; 157. Second Report, pp. 31; 40; 52; 108. Third Report, pp. 64, 65.)

‡ Evidence of Mr. J. P. Wise.—Second Report, p. 36.

§ Evidence of Mr. Freeman.—First Report, p. 114.

|| The "Nuddea Rivers" is the name given to the network of channels which traverse the country between the Ganges and the Hooghly. These channels are supplied partly from the Ganges and partly from the drainage of the country, and are sometimes all but dry. The general opinion is, that one of them might be kept open for the country-boats and for steamers all the year round, instead of five months, if proper engineering skill were applied to the task; by which means a circuitous and even dangerous route of five hundred miles would be avoided.—First Report. Evidence of Mr. W. Theobald, p. 75.

in the Himalayas; and were beginning the cultivation so successfully in Assam and Kumaon, that, in 1856, 700,000lbs. were exported to England. The Neilgherry coffee is alleged to have obtained an excellent name in the London market, as that of Tellicherry has done long ago. Beer has been brewed on the Neilgherries, and sold at 9*d.* per gallon, which the soldiers preferred to the ordinary description, retailed there at 1*s.* and 1*s.* 2*d.* per quart bottle.*

During the Russian war, there was an export of grains and oil seeds (forming, in 1856, a large item) from the interior of India to England; but it ended on the conclusion of peace, because war prices, or canal irrigation and carriage, were essential conditions of remuneration. The same thing occurred with wheat. At the commencement of the war there was a first export of twenty quarters, which rose to 90,963 quarters in 1856, and fell with declining prices to 30,429 quarters in 1857. Rice is exported largely under any circumstances, because it is produced in great abundance on the coast, and is not subject to the cost of inland carriage.† This, and much similar testimony, tends to corroborate the unqualified declaration previously made by Colonel Cotton, that "India can supply England fully, abundantly, cheaply with its two essentials, flour and cotton; and nothing whatever prevents its doing so but the want of public works."‡

The evidence of British settlers is very satisfactory regarding the possibility of cultivating cotton of good quality to an almost unlimited extent. One witness predicts, that the first three or four large canals (for irrigation as well as transit) made in India, would drive the American cotton entirely out of the market, from the much lower cost of production in India. American cotton costs 6*d.* per pound at the English ports: Indian, of equal quality, might, it is alleged, be delivered there from any part of India at a cost of 1½*d.* per pound.§

Even supposing this representation to be somewhat sanguine and highly-coloured, it is most desirable that a vigorous effort should be made to restore the ancient staple product of India, by making one grand experiment—whether slave labour may not be beaten out of the market by the cheapest and most abundant supply of free labour which could possibly be desired. In the cultivation and manufacture of cotton, all the requirements of England and of India (national and individual) are combined: capital, skill, and careful superintendence, would find remunerative exercise on the one side; and, on the other, large masses of people, now half-starved, would be employed; and men, women, and even children could work together in families—an arrangement always much desired in India.

Neither is there any reason why the manufacture of the finer fabrics—of gold-wrought and embroidered muslins—should not be resumed as an article of export. They are quite peculiar to India, and must remain so. The temperature of the country; the delicate touch of the small supple native fingers; the exquisite, artistic tact in managing the gorgeous colouring: all these points combine in producing effects which have been strangely undervalued in England. The barbaric pearl and gold, the diamonds of Golconda, the emeralds and pearls, have led us to overlook the incomparable delicacy of Indian manufactures.

Shawls are almost the only exceptional article amid general neglect. The French, always discriminating in such matters, have shown more appreciation of the value of native manipulation. Several factories, called "filatures," have been for many years established in their settlement at Pondicherry, and where, properly organised and superintended by practical men, the profit yielded is stated at no less than thirty per cent. per annum on the capital invested. A parliamentary witness says, if three times the amount could have been spun, it would have found ready purchasers.‖ It is, however, asserted, that the assessments are not half as high in Pondicherry as in the neighbouring British territory.

The point long doubtful, whether the English constitution could ever bear permanent residence and active occupation in India, appears to be solved by the concurrent testimony of the planters, whose evidence before a committee of the House of Commons, has been so largely quoted. Their stalwart frames and healthy appearance, after twenty, and even thirty years' experience, went far to confirm their statements, that

* Evidence of Captain Ouchterlony.—Third Report, p. 4.

† Third Report.—Evidence of Mr. W. Balston, pp. 64; 98.

‡ *Public Works*, p. 29.

§ Evidence of Mr. W. Balston.—Third Report, p. 98.

‖ Evidence of Captain Ouchterlony.—Third Report, pp. 13; 37.

out-door employment in the more temperate localities, was, even in India, favourable rather than detrimental to health. It is still an open question, how far their children or grandchildren may thrive there; and to what extent early transplantation to schools in the sanitaria afforded by the Neilgherries and other hilly tracts, may operate in preventing physical deterioration.

The chief attractions to "merchant adventurers" in India, are as prominent now as in the days when good Queen Bess granted the first charter to her subjects; the field for capital and enterprise is quite as wide, and even more promising. Merchants, money-lenders, and government stipendiaries, are the only wealthy natives at present in India; and many of these—some by fair and highly creditable means, others by intrigue and usury—have become possessed of fortunes which would enable them to take rank with a London millionaire.

India is, in truth, a mine of wealth; and if we are permitted to see the sword of war permanently sheathed, it may be hoped that we shall take a new view of things; especially, that the leaders of our large manufacturing towns—Birmingham and Manchester, Glasgow and Belfast—will take up the question of good government for India, and convince themselves, by diligently comparing and sifting the evidence poured forth from many different sources, of the necessity for developing the resources and elevating the condition of their fellow-subjects in Hindoostan. Poverty, sheer poverty, is the reason why the consumption of our manufactures is so small; and its concomitants—the fear of extortion, and personal insecurity, induce that tendency to hoarding, which is alleged to operate in causing the annual disappearance of a considerable portion of the already insufficient silver currency.

This, and other minor evils, are effects, not causes; they are like the ailments which inherent weakness produces: strengthen the general frame, and they will disappear. The temptation of profitable and secure investments, such as urgently-required public works may be always made to offer by a wise government, would speedily bring forth the hoarded wealth (if there be such) of India, and would assuredly attract both European and native capital, which, thus employed, might be as seed sown. The British settlers, and some public-spirited native merchants (such as the well-known Sir Jamsetjee Jeejeeboy, of Bombay, with others in each presidency), have shown what individual effort can accomplish. It is now for the government to follow their example, and prepare for a rich harvest of material and moral progress.

Annexation, and Infraction of the Indian Laws of Inheritance.—The system of subsidiary alliances, established by Lord Wellesley, in the teeth of many and varied difficulties, has, without doubt, been the means of quietly and effectively establishing the supremacy of England over the chief part of the Indian peninsula. It has likewise greatly conduced to the general tranquillity, by compelling the native governments to keep peace with one another. It might have done much more than this, had subsequent governors-general entered into the large and generous policy of its promoter, and viewed it as a protective measure calculated to prolong the existence of native states, and regulate the balance of power. Lord Wellesley had no passion for annexation; he did not even say with Clive, "to stop is dangerous, to recede is ruin:"* on the contrary, he believed that the time had arrived for building up a barrier against further extension; and for this very purpose he bent every energy of his mind to frame the system which has been perverted by his successors, and warped by circumstances, into a preliminary to absorption and extinction.

He desired to preserve the independence of the Rajpoot principalities; and thus, rather than by exterminating wars, to keep in check the then alarmingly turbulent and aggressive Mahratta powers. His plans were perfected, and fairly in operation when he quitted India. Unhappily, his whole policy was, for a little while, misrepresented and misunderstood. Its reversal was decreed, and unswerving "non-intervention" was to be substituted for protective and defensive alliances. In theory, this principle seemed just and practicable; in action, it involved positive breach of contract with the weaker states, with whom, in our hour of peril, we had formed treaties, and whom we were pledged to protect against their hereditary foes.

Mistaken notions of economy actuated the authorities in England; and, unfortunately, Sir George Barlow, on whom the

* *Metcalfe Papers*, p. 5.

charge of the supreme government devolved by the sudden death of Lord Cornwallis, was incapable of realising, much less of forcibly deprecating, the evil of the measures he was called upon to take. Lord Lake, the commander-in-chief, felt his honour so compromised by the public breach of faith involved in the repudiation of treaties which he had been mainly instrumental in obtaining, that he resigned, in disgust, the diplomatic powers entrusted to him.*

No less indignation was evinced by the band of rising statesmen, whose minds had been enlarged and strengthened by participation in the views of the "great little man," who, "from the fire of patriotism which blazed in his own breast, emitted sparks which animated the breasts of all who came within the reach of his notice."† One of these (Charles Metcalfe) drew up a paper on the policy of Sir George Barlow, of remarkable interest and ability. He says—

"The native powers of India understand the law of nations on a broad scale, though they may not adhere to it; but they are not acquainted with the nice quirks upon which our finished casuists would draw up a paper to establish political rights. Our name is high, but these acts must lower it; and a natural consequence is, that we shall not again be trusted with confidence.

"Sir George Barlow, in some of his despatches, distinctly states, that he contemplates, in the discord of the native powers, an additional source of strength; and, if I am not mistaken, some of his plans go directly, and are designed, to foment discord among those states. * * * Lord Wellesley's desire was to unite the tranquillity of all the powers of India with our own. How fair, how beautiful, how virtuous does this system seem; how tenfold fair, beautiful, and virtuous, when compared with the other ugly, nasty, abominable one."‡

All the members of the Wellesley school imbibed the same tone; and though they differed widely on many points, and subsequently became themselves distinctive leaders, yet Elphinstone and Malcolm, Adams and Jenkins, Tucker and Edmonstone, consistently maintained the rights of native states, and regarded any disposition to take advantage of their weakness or promote strife, as "ugly, nasty, and abominable."

When the non-intervention system proved absolutely impracticable, the authorities fell back on that of subsidiary alliances; but instead of proceeding on the broad basis laid down by Lord Wellesley, and organising such relations of mutual protection and subordination between the greater and the minor states, as might be necessary for the preservation of general tranquillity, a system of minute and harassing interference was introduced into the affairs of every petty state. "We established," writes Sir Charles Metcalfe in 1830, when a member of the supreme council, "a military police throughout Central India, with a view to maintain order in countries belonging to foreign potentates."§ The arrangements made were costly, clumsy, and inefficient; and, in the end, have worked badly for all parties.

The British contingents, which have now joined the rebel Bengal army, were, for the most part, forced on the native princes, and their general tendency has been to foster the inherent weakness, corruption, and extortion of the states in which they have been established. The benefit of exemption from external strife, has been dearly purchased by increased internal oppression; the arm of the despot being strengthened against his subjects by the same cause which paralysed it for foreign aggression. Then has arisen the difficult question—how far we, as the undoubted supreme power, were justified in upholding notoriously incapable and profligate dynasties, even while the cruel wrongs of the people were unceasingly reported by the British residents at the native courts? As is too frequently the case, the same question has been viewed from different points of view at different times, and, at each period, the decision arrived at has run the risk of being partial and prejudiced.

In the time of Warren Hastings, Sir John Shore, and Lord Wellesley, the increase of territory was deprecated by the East India Company and the British nation in general, as equally unjust in principle and mistaken in policy. The fact that many of the Hindoo, and nearly all the Mohammedan, rulers were usurpers of recent date, ruling over newly-founded states, was utterly ignored; and their treacherous and hostile proceedings against us, and each other, were treated as fictitious, or at least exaggerated. At length a powerful reaction took place; people grew accustomed to the rapid augmentation of our Anglo-Indian empire, and ceased to scrutinise the means by which it was accomplished. The rights of native princes, from being over-estimated, became as unduly disregarded.

* See *Indian Empire*, vol. i., p. 406.
† *Metcalfe Papers*, p. 10.
‡ *Ibid.*, pp. 6, 7.
§ *Ibid.*, p. 178.

The system of annexation recently pursued, which has set at nought the ancient Hindoo law regarding the succession of adopted sons and female representatives, is alleged to have been a special cause of the revolt.* From time immemorial, the adoption of heirs in default of natural and legitimate issue, has been the common custom of the Hindoos. If a man have no son, it is an imperative article in his religious belief that he should adopt one; because it is only through the ceremonies and offerings of a son, that the soul of the father can be released from *Put*—which seems to be the Brahminical term for purgatory. The adopted child succeeds to every hereditary right, and is treated in every respect as if lawfully begotten. Lord Metcalfe has expressed a very decided opinion on the subject. After pointing out the difference between sovereign princes and jagheerdars—between those in possession of hereditary sovereignties in their own right, and those who hold grants of land, or public revenue, by gift from a sovereign or paramount power—he adds, that Hindoo sovereign princes have a right to adopt a successor, to the exclusion of collateral heirs; and that the British government is bound to acknowledge the adoption, provided that it be regular, and not in violation of Hindoo law. "The supposed reversionary right of the paramount power," Lord Metcalfe describes "as having no real existence, except in the case of the absolute want of heirs; and even then the right is only assumed in virtue of power; for it would probably be more consistent with right, that the people of the state so situated should elect a sovereign for themselves."†

Many of our leading statesmen have concurred not only in deprecating the use of any measures of annexation which could possibly be construed as harsh or unjust, but also in viewing the end itself, namely, the absorption of native states, as a positive evil. Mountstuart Elphinstone, who has probably had more political intercourse with the highest class of natives than any other individual now living, has always continued to entertain the same views which he set forth as interpreter to Major-general Wellesley, in the memorable conferences held to negotiate the treaties of Surjee Anjengaum and Deogaum, in 1803, with Sindia and the rajah of Berar;‡ when he described the British government as uniformly anxious to promote the prosperity of its adherents, the interests of such persons being regarded as identified with its own.

Many years later, Mr. Elphinstone wrote—"It appears to me to be our interest as well as our duty, to use every means to preserve the allied governments: it is also our interest to keep up the number of independent powers: their territories afford a refuge to all whose habits of war, intrigue, or depredation, make them incapable of remaining quiet in ours; and the contrast of our government has a favourable effect on our subjects, who, while they feel the evils they are actually exposed to, are apt to forget the greater ones from which they have been delivered."

Colonel Wellesley, in 1800, declared, that the extension of our territory and influence had been greater than our means. "Wherever we spread ourselves," he said, "we increase this evil. We throw out of employment and means of subsistence, all who have hitherto managed the revenue, commanded, or served in the armies, or have plundered the country. These people become additional enemies, at the same time that, by the extension of our territory, our means of supporting our government and of defending ourselves are proportionately decreased."§

Marquis Wellesley, in 1842, wrote—"No further extension of our territory is ever desirable in India, even in the event of war for conquest, if that could be justified or were legal, as the law now wisely stands."‖

Lord Ellenborough (despite the annexation of Sinde) advised, that even "what are called rightful occasions of appropriating the territories of native states," should be avoided; because he considered, that the maintenance of those states, and "the conviction that they were considered permanent parts of the general government of India, would materially strengthen our authority. I feel satisfied, that I never stood so strong with my own army as when I was surrounded by native princes; they like to see respect shown to their native princes. These princes are sovereigns of one-third of the population of Hindoostan;

* *Vide Rebellion in India;* by John Bruce Norton.

† *Metcalfe Papers* (written in 1837); p. 318.

‡ *Supplementary Despatches of F. M. the Duke of Wellington;* edited by the present Duke: vol. iii.

§ *Wellington Despatches.* Letter to Major Munro, dated 20th August, 1800.

‖ Letter from the Marquis Wellesley to Lord Ellenborough, 4th July, 1842.

and with reference to the future condition of the country, it becomes more important to give them confidence that no systematic attempt will be made to take advantage of the failures of heirs to confiscate their property, or to injure, in any respect, those sovereigns in the position they at present occupy."

Sir John Malcolm went further still, and declared, that "the tranquillity, not to say the security, of our vast Oriental dominions, was involved in the preservation of the native principalities, which are dependent upon us for protection. These are also so obviously at our mercy, so entirely within our grasp, that besides the other and great benefits which we derive from these alliances, their co-existence with our rule is, of itself, a source of political strength, the value of which will never be known till it is lost. * * * I am further convinced, that though our revenue may increase, the permanence of our power will be hazarded in proportion as the territories of native princes and chiefs fall under our direct rule."

Henry St. George Tucker likewise lifted up his voice in warning, declaring, that the annexation of a principality to our gigantic empire, might become the source of weakness, by impairing our moral influence over our native subjects.*

These opinions so far prevailed, that down to the viceroyalty of Lord Dalhousie, the Hindoo custom of adoption was not only sanctioned, but urged by the supreme government on native princes in the absence of natural heirs. The majority of Indian dynasties have been maintained in this manner. The famous Mahratta leaders, Dowlut Rao Sindia of Gwalior, and Mulhar Rao Holcar of Indore, both died childless: the latter adopted a son; the former left the choice of a successor to his favourite wife, who exercised the right, and herself filled the position of regent.†

On the death of the adopted prince, in 1843, his nearest relative, a boy of eight years of age, was proclaimed maharajah. The war which took place in the same year, and which terminated in the capture of the fortress of Gwalior by the British troops, on the 4th of January, 1844, did not lead to the extinction of the principality, as it would unquestionably have done under the course of policy which subsequently prevailed. The young maharajah was confirmed in the position, for which, as he advanced in age, he showed himself well qualified; and his name, like that of his contemporary the rajah of Indore, now takes high rank amid the faithful allies of England.

Lord Ellenborough's opinions regarding the maintenance of native states, were not, however, shared by his zealous champion, Sir Charles Napier, who expressed himself on this point, as on most others, in very strong terms. "Were I emperor of India," he said, when his views were most matured, "no Indian prince should exist." He would dethrone the Nizam, he would seize Nepaul: in fact, he considered, that without the abolition of the native sovereignties no great good could be effected, and the Company's revenues must be always in difficulty.‡

Sir Charles was probably singular in his desire to extend the British frontier indefinitely, and "make Moscowa and Pekin shake;" but many persons, including Mr. Thoby Prinsep and other leading India House authorities, looked forward to the extinction of the subsidiary and protected states within our boundary as desirable, both in a political and financial point of view, especially in the latter.§

In India, the majority of the governing "caste," as Colonel Sykes called the civilians,‖ were naturally disposed to favour extensions of territory which directly conduced to the benefit of their body, and for the indirect consequences of which they were in no manner held responsible. To them, the lapse of a native state was the opening of a new source of promotion, as it was to the directors in England of "patronage"—an advantage vague in sound, but very palpable and lucrative in operation. No wonder that the death of the "sick man" should have been often anticipated by his impatient heirs as a happy release, which it was excusable and decidedly expedient to hasten. It was but to place the sufferer or victim within reach of the devouring waves of the Ganges,

* Several of the above opinions, with others of similar tendency, will be found collected in a pamphlet entitled *The Native States of India;* published by Saunders and Stanford, 6, Charing-cross: 1853.

† *Indian Empire*, vol. i., p. 427.

‡ See review in the *Times*, May 25th, 1857, of Sir W. Napier's *Life of Sir C. Napier*.

§ See Mr. Prinsep's pamphlet on the *Indian Question in* 1853.

‖ Third Report of Colonization Committee, 1858; p. 88.

and the result, according to Hindoo notions, is paradise to one party, and pecuniary advantage, or at least relief, to the other. The whirlpool of annexation has been hit upon as offering advantages of a similar kind; namely, complete regeneration to the native state subjected to its engulphing influence, and increased revenue to the paramount power. Bengal civilians began to study "annexation made easy," with the zeal of our American cousins, and it was soon deemed indispensable to hasten the process by refusing to sanction further adoptions. The opinions quoted in preceding pages were treated as out of date, and the policy founded on them was reversed. The experience of the past showed, that from the days of Clive, all calculations founded on increase of territorial revenue, had been vitiated by more than proportionate increase of expenditure. It might have also taught, that the decay of native states needed no stimulating, and that even if their eventual extinction should be deemed desirable, it would at least be well to take care that the inclined plane by which we were hastening their descent, should not be placed at so sharp an angle as to bring them down, like an avalanche, on our own heads. These considerations were lost sight of in the general desire felt "to extinguish the native states which consume so large a portion of the revenue of the country;"* and few paused to consider the peculiar rights of native administrators, as such, or remembered that, in many cases, the profit derived from the subsidy paid for military contingents, was greater than any we were likely to obtain from the entire revenue. In fact, the entire revenue had repeatedly proved insufficient to cover the cost of our enormous governmental establishments, civil and military.

The expenditure consequent on the war with, and annexation of, Sinde,† was the subject of much parliamentary discussion, the immense booty obtained by the army being contrasted with the burden imposed upon the public treasury and highly-taxed people of India. Still the lesson prominently set forth therein was unheeded, or treated as applicable only to projects of foreign aggrandisement, and having no relation to questions of domestic policy.

The Marquis of Dalhousie expressed the general sentiments of the Court of Directors, as well as his own, in the following full and clear exposition of the principles which prompted the series of annexations made under his administration:—"There may be a conflict of opinion as to the advantage, or to the propriety, of extending our already vast possessions beyond their present limits. No man can more sincerely deprecate than I do any extension of the frontiers of our territories, which can be avoided, or which may not become indispensably necessary from considerations of our own safety, and of the maintenance of the tranquillity of our provinces. But I cannot conceive it possible for any one to dispute the policy of taking advantage of every just opportunity which presents itself for consolidating the territories that already belong to us, by taking possession of states which may lapse in the midst of them; for thus getting rid of these petty intervening principalities, which may be made a means of annoyance, but which can never, I venture to think, be a source of strength; for adding to the resources of the public treasury, and for extending the uniform application of our system of government to those whose best interests, we believe, will be promoted thereby."

Lord Dalhousie differed from Lord Metcalfe and others above quoted, not less with regard to the nature of the end in view, than as to the means by which that end might be lawfully obtained; and he has recorded his "strong and deliberate opinion," that "the British government is bound not to put aside or to neglect such rightful opportunities of acquiring territory or revenue, as may from time to time present themselves, whether they arise from the lapse of subordinate states by the failure of all heirs of every description whatsoever, or from the failure of heirs natural, when the succession can be sustained only by the sanction of government being given to the ceremony of adoption, according to Hindoo law."

It is not surprising that the process

* *Modern India;* by Mr. Campbell, a civilian of the Bengal service.

† Mr. St. George Tucker asserted, that the proceedings connected with the annexation of Sinde were reprobated by every member of the Court of Directors of the East India Company, "as characterised by acts of the grossest injustice, highly injurious to the national reputation:" and that the acquisition of that country was "more iniquitous than any which has ever stained the annals of our Indian administration."—*Memorials of Indian Government*, pp. 351, 352.

of absorption should have been rapid, when the viceroy, who held the above opinions, was essentially a practical man, gifted with an "aptitude for business, unflagging powers of labour, and clearness of intellect;" which even the most decided opponents of his policy have applauded. In reviewing the result of his eight years' administration, Lord Dalhousie dwells, apparently without the slightest misgiving, on the large increase of the British territories in the East during that period; four kingdoms, and various chiefships and separate tracts, having been brought under the sway of the Queen of England. Of these, *the Punjab* was the fruit of conquest.* *Pegu and Martaban* were likewise won by the sword in 1852; and a population of 570,180 souls, spread over an area of 32,250 square miles, was thereby brought under the dominion of the British Crown.†

The *Raj or Principality of Sattara*, was the first state annexed by Lord Dalhousie, to the exclusion of the claims of an adopted son. There was only one precedent—and that a partial one—for this measure: it occurred under the administration of Lord Auckland, in 1840, in the case of the little *state of Colaba*, founded by the pirate Angria, whose chief fort, Gheria, was taken by Watson and Clive in 1756.‡ Colaba was dependent on the government of the Peishwa at Poona; and, on the extinction of his power, the British entered into a treaty with Ragojee Angria, the existing chief, guaranteeing the transmission of his territories in their integrity to his "successors." With the sanction of the Bombay government, Ragojee adopted a boy, who died soon after him. Permission was asked for a fresh adoption, but refused; and the territory was treated as having escheated for want of heirs male, although, it is alleged, there were many members of the Angria family still in existence, legally capable of succeeding to the government.

Sattara was altogether a more important case, both on account of the extent and excellent government of the kingdom, and because its extinction involved a distinct repudiation of the practice of adoption previously sanctioned by the British authorities, and held by the Hindoos as invariably conferring on the adopted child every privilege of natural and legitimate issue.§ The fact was so generally recognised, that there seems no reason to doubt that the native princes, in signing subsidiary or other treaties, considered that children by adoption were included, as a matter of course, under the head of legitimate heirs and successors. The exception, if intended, was sufficiently important to demand mention. But the conduct of the government, in repeated instances (such as those of the Gwalior and Indore principalities, of Kotah in 1828, Dutteah in 1840, Oorcha, Banswarra, and Oodipoor, in 1842, and, several years later, in Kerowlee),‖ was calculated to remove all doubt by evidencing its liberal construction of the Hindoo law of succession.

Lord Auckland declared, in the case of Oorcha, that he could not for a moment admit the doctrine, that because the view of policy upon which we might have formed engagements with the native princes might have been by circumstances materially altered, we were therefore not to act scrupulously up to the terms and spirit of those engagements; and again, when discussing the question of the right of the widow of the rajah of Kishenghur to adopt a son without authority from her deceased husband, his lordship rejected any reference to the "supposed rights" which were suggested as devolving on the British government as the paramount power, declaring that such questions must be decided exclusively with reference to the terms and spirit of the treaties or engagements formed with the different states; and that no demand ought to be brought forward than such as, in regard to those engagements, should be scrupulously consistent with good faith.

By this declaration Lord Auckland publicly evinced his resolve to adhere to the principle laid down by high authority forty years before, under very critical circumstances. It was not an obedient dependency, but the fortified border-land of a warlike principality, that was at stake, when Arthur Wellesley urged the governor-general to abide by the strict rules of justice, however inconvenient and seemingly inexpedient. On other points of the question the brothers might take different views; on this they were sure to agree; for they

* Norton's *Rebellion in India*, p. 65.
† *Indian Empire*, vol. i., p. 456.
‡ *Ibid.*, p. 458. Parl. Papers, 16th April, 1858.
§ See *Indian Empire*, vol. i., p. 271.

‖ The social grounds on which the practice of adoption is based, are well set forth by General Briggs. See Ludlow's *Lectures*, vol. ii., p. 226; and *Native States*, pp. 21; 23.

were equally ready to "sacrifice Gwalior or every other frontier in India ten times over, in order to preserve our credit for scrupulous good faith."*

The recent mode of dealing with Sattara has not contributed to raise the British name either for generosity or unflinching integrity. The deposition of that most able ruler, Pertab Sing, on a charge of conspiracy against the supreme government,† was earnestly deprecated in England by many eminent men, and excited great indignation among his subjects. The secret and hurried manner in which his seizure and trial were conducted, increased the apparent hardship of his sentence; and an able writer asserts his conviction that, at the present time, not a native in India, nor five persons in the world, believe in his guilt.‡ He died in 1847, leaving an adopted son, around whom the affections of the people still cling.§ The remembrance of his misfortunes has not passed away; and one of the mutineers, hung at Sattara in 1857, addressed the surrounding natives while he was being pinioned, to the effect that, as the English had hurled the rajah from his throne, so they ought to be driven out of the country.‖ The deposition of Pertab Sing was not, however, accompanied by any attempt at annexation of territory; the government, on the contrary, "having no views of advantage and aggrandisement," resolved, in the words of the new treaty (5th September, 1839), to invest the brother and next in succession to the rajah with the sovereignty. This brother (Appa Sahib) died in 1848. He, also, in default of natural issue, had adopted a son, whose recognition as rajah was strongly urged by Sir George Clerk, the governor of Bombay, on the ground that the terms of the treaty, "seemed to mean a sovereignty which should not lapse for want of heirs, so long as there was any one who could succeed, according to the usages of the people." "In a matter such as this question of resumption of territory, recovered by us, and restored to an ancient dynasty,"¶ he observes, "we are morally bound to give some consideration to the sense in which we induced or permitted the other party to understand the terms of a mutual agreement. Whatever we intend in favour of an ally in perpetuity, when executing a treaty with him on that basis, by that we ought to abide in our relations with his successors, until he proves himself unworthy."

Sir G. Clerk further advocated the continuance of the independence of Sattara, on account of its happy and prosperous state. Mr. Frere, the British resident, said that no claimant would venture to put forward his own claim against the adopted sons of either of the late rajahs; but that there were many who might have asserted their claim but for the adoption, and who would "be able to establish a very good *primâ facie* claim in any court of justice in India." These arguments did not deter Lord Dalhousie from making Sattara the first example of his consolidation policy. "The territories," he said, "lie in the very heart of our own possessions. They are interposed between the two military stations in the presidency of Bombay, and are at least calculated, in the hands of an independent sovereign, to form an obstacle to safe communication and combined military movement. The district is fertile, and the revenues productive. The population, accustomed for some time to regular and peaceful government, are tranquil themselves, and are prepared for the regular government our possession of the territory would give." With regard to the terms of the treaty, he held that the words "heirs and successors" must be read in their ordinary sense, and could not be construed to secure to the rajahs of Sattara any other than the succession of heirs natural: and the prosperity of the state, he did not consider a reason for its continued independence, unless this prosperity could be shown to arise from fixed institutions, by which the disposition of the sovereign would always be guarded, or compelled into an observance of the rules of good government. (This, of course, could not be shown, such security being peculiar to countries blessed with free institutions, and utterly incompatible with any form of despotism.) In conclusion, the governor-general argued, that "we ought to regard the territory of Sattara as lapse, and should incorporate it at once with the British dominions in India."**

The Court of Directors were divided in opinion on the subject: nine of them agreed

* *Wellington Despatches*, 17th March, 1804.
† See *Indian Empire*, vol. i., p. 432.
‡ Ludlow's *Lectures*, vol. ii., p. 171.
§ *Ibid.*, p. 171.
‖ *Bombay Telegraph*, 19th June, 1857.
¶ *Indian Empire*, vol. i., p. 419.
** Minute by Lord Dalhousie, 30th August, 1848.

with, and five differed from, Lord Dalhousie.* The dissentients were Messrs. Tucker, Shepherd, Melville, Major Oliphant, and General Caulfield. Regarding the precedent established in the case of Colaba, Mr. Tucker said—

"I remonstrated against the annexation (I am disposed to call it the confiscation) of Colaba, the ancient seat of the Angria family, to which the allusion has been made in the Bombay minutes; and far from having seen reason to modify or recall the opinion recorded by me on that proceeding, I have availed myself of every suitable occasion to enforce my conviction, that a more mischievous policy could not be pursued than that which would engross the whole territory of India, and annihilate the small remnant of the native aristocracy. There are persons who fancy that landed possessions in India cannot be successfully administered by native agency. In disproof of this notion I would point to the Rampoor jaghire in Rohilcund, which was a perfect garden when I saw it long ago, and which still remains, I believe, in a state of the highest agricultural prosperity. Nay, I would point to the principality of Sattara, which appears to have been most successfully administered both by the ex-rajah, Pertab Sing, and his brother and successor, Appa Sahib, who have done more for the improvement of the country than our government can pretend to have done in any part of its territory."†

This, and other energetic protests, are said to have produced so strong an impression, that a vote seemed likely to pass in the Court of Proprietors, repudiating the annexation of Sattara.. The majority of the directors perceiving this, called for a ballot, and so procured the confirmation of the measure by the votes of some hundreds of ladies and gentlemen, for the most part utterly ignorant of the merits of the case.‡

The provision made by the supreme government for the widows and adopted son,§ was censured by the directors; and Lord Dalhousie writes, that although the Hon. Court had declared "their desire to provide liberally for the family, and their wish that the ladies should retain jewels, furniture, and other personal property suitable to their rank, they still objected that the grant of so much property, which was fairly at the disposal of the government, was greatly in excess of what was required."‖

The Kingdom of Nagpoor "became British territory by simple lapse, in the absence of all legal heirs;" for the government, says Lord Dalhousie, "refused to bestow the territory, in free gift, upon a stranger,¶ and wisely incorporated it with its own dominions."**

Absorption was becoming a very familiar process to the British functionaries, and the addition of a population of about 4,650,000, and an area of 76,432 square miles,†† appeared to excite little attention or interest. Parliamentary returns prove, however, that the kingdom was not extinguished without palpable signs of dissatisfaction, and even some attempt at resistance on the part of the native government. The ranees, or queens, on the death of the rajah in December, 1853, requested leave to take advantage of the Hindoo law, which vested in them, or at least in the chief of them—the right of adopting a son, and of exercising the powers of the regency. They offered to adopt, according to the pleasure of the supreme government, any one of the rightful heirs, who, they alleged, existed, and were entitled to succeed to the sovereignty; "both according to the customs of the family and the Hindoo law, and also agreeably to the practice in such cases pursued under the treaties." The reply was a formal intimation, that the orders issued by the government of India having been confirmed by the Hon. Court of Directors, the prayer of the ranees for the restitution of the raj to the family could not be granted. The maharanee, called the Banka Bye (a

* The question of the right of adoption, says Mr. Sullivan, was treated by all the authorities at home and abroad as if it had been an entirely new one, and was decided in the negative; whereas, it appeared, by records which were dragged forth after judgment was passed in the Sattara case, that the question had been formally raised, and as formally decided in favour of the right, twenty years before; and that this decision had been acted upon in no less than fifteen instances in the interval.—Pamphlet on the *Double Government*, published by India Reform Society; p. 24.

† Lieutenant-general Briggs, in his evidence before the Cotton Committee appointed in 1848, mentioned having superintended the construction of a road made entirely by natives for the rajah of Sattara, thirty-six miles long, and eighteen feet wide, with drains and small bridges for the whole distance.

‡ Sullivan's *Double Government*, p. 26.

§ They were allowed to retain jewels, &c., to the value of sixteen lacs, and landed property worth 20,000 rupees a-year. Pensions were also granted (from the revenue) to the three ranees, of £45,000, £30,000, and £25,000 respectively.—Parl. Papers (Commons), 5th March, 1856; p. 10.

‖ Parl. Papers, &c., p. 10.

¶ Lord Dalhousie, in a minute dated 10th June, 1854, admits that lineal members of the Bhonslay family existed; but adds, "they are all the progeny of daughters."—Parl. Papers (Commons), 16th June, 1856.

** Minute, dated 28th February, 1856; p. 8.

†† Parl. Papers (Commons), 16th April, 1858.

very aged woman, of remarkable ability, who had exercised the authority of regent during the minority of her grandson, the late rajah), and the younger ranees, were not entirely unsupported in their endeavours for the continuance of the state, or at least for the obtainment of some concessions from the paramount power. The commissioner, and former resident, Mr. Mansel, represented the disastrous effect which the annexation of Nagpoor was calculated to produce upon certain influential classes. The dependent chiefs, the agriculturists, and the small shopkeepers would, he considered, "if not harshly agitated by new measures," be easily reconciled to British rule; but—

"The officers of the army, the courtiers, the priesthood, the chief merchants and bankers who had dealings with the rajah's treasury and household—all the aristocracy, in fact, of the country, see in the operation of the system that British rule involves, the gradual diminution of their exclusive consequence, and the final extinction of their order."*

The extinction of the aristocracy was calculated to affect the mass of the population more directly than would at first seem probable. Mr. Mansel truly says—

"The Indian native looks up to a monarchical and aristocratic form of life; all his ideas and feelings are pervaded with respect for it. Its ceremonies and state are an object of amusement and interest to all, old and young; and all that part of the happiness of the world which is produced by the gratification of the senses, is largely maintained by the existence of a court, its pageantry, its expenditure, and communication with the people. Without such a source of patronage of merit, literary and personal, the action of life in native society as it is and must long be, would be tame and depressing. * * * It is the bitter cry on all sides, that our rule exhibits no sympathy, especially for the native of rank, and not even for other classes of natives. It is a just, but an ungenerous, unloveable system that we administer, and this tone is peculiarly felt in a newly-acquired country. It may be that we cannot re-create, but we may pause ere we destroy a form of society already existing, and not necessarily barren of many advantages. * * * The main energies of the public service in India are directed to, or absorbed in, the collection of revenue and the repressing of rural crime; and the measures applied to the education of the native people are of little influence; while many of our own measures—as in the absorption of a native state (if we sweep clean the family of the native prince and the nobility gradually from the land)—are deeply depressing on the national character and social system."†

He therefore recommended, with a view of reconciling the past with the future, in a change of government from Oriental to European hands, that the Nagpoor royal family should be permitted to exercise the right of adoption; to enjoy the privileges of titular chieftainship; and to retain possession of the palace in the city of Nagpoor, with a fixed income and a landed estate.

The reply to these recommendations was, that the governor-general in council could not conceal his surprise and dissatisfaction at the advocacy of a policy diametrically opposed to the declared views of the supreme authority. The grounds on which the British commissioner advocated the creation of a titular principality, were pronounced to be weak and untenable; while all experience was alleged to be opposed to the measure which he had "most inopportunely forced" on the consideration of government. The king of Delhi, the nawab of Bengal, and the nawab-nizam of the Carnatic, were cited as so many examples of its impolicy: but "in all these cases, however, some purpose of great temporary expediency was served, or believed to be served, when the arrangement was originally made; some actual difficulty was got over by the arrangement; and, above all, the chiefs in question were existing things [?] before the arrangement." In the present instance, however, the official despatch declares there was no object of even temporary expediency to serve; no actual difficulty of any sort to be got over; no one purpose, political or other, to be promoted by the proposed measure.‡

The provision suggested by Mr. Mansel as suitable for the ranees in the event of his proposition being rejected, was condemned as extravagantly high; the hereditary treasure of the rajah, the governor-general considered, in accordance with the decision of the Hon. Court in an analogous case (Sattara), was "fairly at the disposal of the government, and ought not to be given up to be appropriated and squandered by the ranees."§

The money hoarded, having been accumulated, it was alleged, out of the public funds, was available to defray the arrears of the palace establishments—a reasonable

* Parl. Papers (Commons)—Annexation of Berar: No. 82; March 5th, 1856; p. 4.

† *Ibid.*, p. 6.

‡ *Ibid.*, pp. 12, 13.

§ The mode of appropriating the personal and hereditary treasure of the late rajah, suggested by the commissioner as likely to be approved by the ranees, was the building a bridge over the Kumaon river; and thus, in accordance with Hindoo custom, linking the family name to a great and useful work.

plea, which could not be urged in defence of the same seizure of personal savings in the case of Sattara.

This unqualified censure of the commissioner was followed by his removal, a proceeding directly calculated to inculcate the suppression not only of opinions, but even of facts, of an unpalatable kind. The half-measure which he had suggested might possibly have worked badly, as most half-measures do; but it was avowedly proposed as a compromise, and as a means of meeting difficulties, which the Calcutta authorities saw fit to ignore. No notice whatever was taken of Mr. Mansel's statement, that in arguing with the people at Nagpoor on the practice of putting the members of the family of a deceased chief on individual life pensions, upon the absorption of a state, they immediately (though not before unsubservient to the execution of orders from Calcutta for the extinction of sovereign powers) fell back upon the law and rights of the case, and contended that the treaty gave what was now being arbitrarily taken away.*

Nothing, indeed, could be more arbitrary than the whole proceeding. A military officer, Captain Elliot, was made officiating commissioner, and a large body of troops was placed at his disposal to overawe opposition, in the event of the royal family or their late subjects evincing any disposition to resist the fulfilment of the orders of the governor-general for the seizure of the treasure, hereditary jewels, and even the personal property and household effects of the deceased rajah, which were advertised to be sold by public auction, to provide a fund for the support of his family.

The ranees sent a vakeel, or ambassador, to Calcutta, to intreat that a stop should be put to the sale of effects held as private property for a century and a-half; "and, further, for the cessation of the unjust, oppressive, and humiliating treatment shown by the commissioner, under the alleged orders of government, towards the maharanees and the other heirs and members of the family of the late rajah, whose lives are embittered and rendered burdensome by the cruel conduct and indignities to which they have been obliged to submit."

Repeated memorials were sent in by the ranees, concerning "the disrespect and contumely" with which they were treated by the acting commissioner, and also regarding the manner in which the sales by auction were conducted, and property sacrificed; particularly cattle and horses: a pair of bullocks, for instance, estimated to be worth 200 rupees, being sold for twenty.

The official return of the proceeds of the rajah's live stock, tends to corroborate the statement of the ranees. A hundred camels only realised 3,138 rupees, and 182 bullocks only 2,018; elephants, horses, and ponies in large numbers, sold at equally low prices. The remonstrances of the ranees were treated with contemptuous indifference. The government refused to recognise their envoys, and would receive no communications except through the official whose refusal to forward their appeals was the express reason of their having endeavoured to reach the ear of the governor-general by some other channel.

The removal of the property from the palace was attended by considerable excitement. The native officer employed by the English government, was "hustled and beaten" in the outer courtyard of the palace. The sepoys on duty inside the square, are described by Captain Elliot in his rather singular account of the matter, "as not affording that protection and assistance they were bound to do; for, setting aside Jumal-oo-deen's [the native officer's] rank, position, and employment, he was married, and somewhat lame." There was great excitement in the city, as well as in and about the palace, and great crowds had assembled and were assembling. It was doubtful to what extent opposition might have been organised, for the aged maharanee was asserted to have sent a message to the British officer in command, that if the removal of property were attempted, she would set the palace on fire. This threat, if made, was never executed: reinforcements of troops were introduced into the city, and the orders of the government were quietly carried through. The governor-general considered that the "scandalous conduct" of the sepoys and rifle guards on duty, ought to have been punished by dismissal from the service; but it had been already passed over in silence, and so no martyrs were made to the cause, and the affair passed over as an ebullition of that "floating feeling of national regret," which Mr. Mansel had previously described as ready to discharge itself in dangerous force upon any objects within its range.

* Parl. Papers on Berar, p. 7.

The maharanee denied having incited or approved the resistance offered by her people; but the Calcutta authorities persisted in considering that a plan of resistance had been organised by her during the night preceding the disturbances which took place in the morning of the 11th of October, 1854, and threatened to hold the ranees generally responsible, in the event of any repetition of such scenes as those which had already brought down upon them the displeasure of government.

The ladies were, no doubt, extremely alarmed by this intimation, which the officiating commissioner conveyed to them, he writes, in "most unmistakable language." The sale of the chief part of the jewels and heirlooms (estimated at from £500,000 to £750,000 in value)* was carried on unopposed in the public bazaars; a proceeding which the then free press did not fail to communicate to the general public, and to comment on severely.† Of the money hidden within the sacred precincts of the zenana, 136 bags of silver rupees had been surrendered; but there was a further store of gold mohurs, with the existence of which the Banka Bye had herself acquainted the British functionaries immediately after the death of her grandson, as a proof of her desire to conceal nothing from them. When urged, she expressed her readiness to surrender the treasure; but pleaded as a reason for delay, the extreme, and as it speedily proved, mortal sickness of Unpoora Bye, the chief widow, in whose apartments the treasure was hidden, and her great unwillingness to permit its removal. The commissioner appears to have treated this plea as a continuation of "the old system of delay and passive resistance to all one's instructions and wishes." Nevertheless, he deemed it objectionable "to use force;" and "was unwilling that Captain Crichton [the officer in command] should go upstairs on this occasion, or take any active part in this matter," it being "better to avoid a scene:" and, as an alternative, he advised "writing off the amount known to be buried, to the debit of the ranees, deducting the same from their annual allowance, and telling them the same was at their disposal and in their own possession."‡

* Parl. Papers (Annexation of Berar), p. 9.

† *Indian News*, 2nd April, 1855.

‡ Letter from officiating commissioner, Capt. Elliot, to government, 13th Dec., 1854.—Parl. Papers, p. 44.

The princesses would have been badly off had this arrangement been carried out, for the amount of hoarded treasure had been exaggerated, as it almost invariably is in such cases; and although no doubt is expressed that the formal surrender of 10,000 gold mohurs (made immediately after the delivery of the governor-general's threatening message) included the entire hoard, yet double that sum was expected; the other half having, it is alleged, been previously expended.

The maharanee excited the angry suspicions of the Calcutta government by a despairing effort for the maintenance of the state, with which she felt the honour of her house indissolubly allied. It appeared, that Major Ramsay, then resident at Nepaul, had, when occupying the same position at the court of Nagpoor, been on very bad terms with the deceased rajah. The Banka Bye attributed the extinction of the raj to his representations, and sent a vakeel to him, in the hope of deprecating his opposition, and obtaining his favourable intervention. The errand of the vakeel was misunderstood, and attributed to a desire to communicate with the Nepaulese sovereign on the subject of the annexation of Nagpoor. Under this impression, the governor-general in council declared, that the ranees had no right whatever to communicate with native courts; that it was impossible to put any other than an unfavourable construction on their attempt to do so: and the acting commissioner was officially desired to acquaint them, that the repetition of such an act would "certainly lead to substantial proof of the displeasure of government being manifested to them."

On the mistake being discovered, the following minute was recorded by the governor-general, and concurred in by the four members of council whose names have become lately familiar to the British public. Its curt tone contrasts forcibly with that adopted by the Marquis Wellesley, and his great brother, in their arrangements for the royal family of Mysoor: yet the dynasty of Hyder Ali had been founded on recent usurpation, and overthrown in open fight; while that of Berar represented a native power of 150 years' duration, and long in peaceful alliance with the Company as a protected state. The age and reputation of the Banka Bye, her former position as regent, the remarkable influence exercised by her during the late reign, and her uniform adhesion to the British government,—these, together with the dying state of Unpoora Bye, the eldest of the rajah's widows, and the bereaved condition of them all, might well have dictated a more respectful consideration of their complaints and misapprehensions, than is apparent in the brief but comprehensive account given by the supreme government, of the groundless charge which had been brought against the princesses:—

"It now appears that the vakeel sent by the ranees of Nagpoor to Nepaul, was intended, not for the durbar, but for Major Ramsay, the resident there. Major Ramsay, when officiating resident at Nagpoor, was compelled to bring the late rajah to order. The rajah complained of him to me, in 1848. The officiating resident was in the right, and, of course, was supported. It seems that these ladies now imagine that Major Ramsay's supposed hostility has influenced me, and that his intercession, if obtained, might personally move me. The folly of these notions need not to be noticed. The vakeel not having been sent to the durbar, nothing more need be said about the matter."*

The means used by Major Ramsay "to bring the rajah to order," had been previously called in question, owing to certain passages in the despatch which had occasioned the supersession of Mr. Mansel. These passages are given at length, in evidence of the entirely opposite manner in which successive British residents at Nagpoor exercised the extraordinary powers entrusted to them; interfering in everything, or being absolutely nonentities (except as a drain upon the finances of the state they were, barnacle-like, attached to), according to their temper of mind and habit of body.

"In my arguments," says Mr. Mansel, "with natives upon the subject of the expediency and propriety of the British government dealing with the Nagpoor case as a question of pure policy, I have put to them the position, that we had all of us at Nagpoor, for the last two years, found it impracticable to carry on the government decently. I remarked that Major Wilkinson, after a long struggle, succeeded in getting the rajah within his own influence, and, by his fine sagacity and perfect experience, had controlled him whenever he chose. Colonel Speirs, from decaying health, was latterly unable to put much check upon the rajah, though his perfect knowledge of affairs of the day here, and of Oriental courts in general, would otherwise have been most valuable. Major Ramsay† pursued a course of uncompromising interference, and, in a state of almost chronic disease, attempted a perfect restoration to health. Mr. Davidson, as his health grew worse, left the rajah to do as he liked; and under the argument, that it was better to work by personal influence than by fear, he left the rajah to do as he pleased, with something like the pretence of an invalid physician—that his patient would die with too much care, and required gentle treatment. During my incumbency, I found the rajah so much spoiled by the absolute indulgence of my predecessor, that I was gradually driven to adopt the radical reform of Major Ramsay, or the extreme conservatism of Mr. Davidson; and in the struggle which latterly ensued between myself and the rajah, his end was undoubtedly hastened by vexation at my insisting on his carrying out the reform in spirit as well as to the letter. * * * The argument of the natives, with whom I have frequently conferred on this subject, is, that the British residents at Nagpoor should participate in the blame charged to the rajah by myself; for if the same system of advice and check which was contemplated by the last treaty, had been carried out from first to last, the rajah would never have been tempted into the habits of indolence and avarice that latterly made him make his own court and the halls of justice a broker's shop, for the disposal of official favours and the sale of justice. The answer to this is, that the British government does its best; that it sends its highest servants to a residency; and if the principles or abilities of the different incumbents vary, it is only natural and incidental to any colonial system in the world. The result, however, is, that the management of the country gets into all kinds of embarrassment, of death, judicial corruption, and irresponsibility of ministers, when the readiest course is to resume those sovereign powers that were delegated on trust."‡

Surely the foregoing statements of the last "incumbent" of the Nagpoor residency, afford a clear exposition of the mischievous effects of establishing, at the courts of native princes, a powerful functionary, whose office combines the duties of a foreign ambassador with those of a domestic counsellor, or rather dictator. If the

* Minute, dated November, 1854. Parl. Papers (Annexation of Berar), p. 41. Signed—Dalhousie, J. Dorin, J. Low, J. P. Grant, B. Peacock.

† Major Ramsay denies this; and, while bearing testimony to the "high character" of Mr. Mansel, says, that the policy adopted by the latter was radically opposed to his own, for that he had pursued the most rigid system of non-interference with any of the details of the local government; whereas Mr. Mansel appointed, or caused the appointment of, several individuals to responsible offices in the Nagpoor government, and set apart particular days in the week on which the heads of departments waited upon him at the residency, and submitted their reports and proceedings.—Letter of Major Ramsay to government, 5th February, 1855—Parl. Papers, pp. 46; 53.

‡ Letter of Commissioner Mansel, 29th April, 1854—Parl. Papers, p. 7. See *Indian Empire*, vol. i., p. 420, for an account of the circumstances under which the so-called delegation of sovereign powers was made in the case alluded to.

resident be an upright man, he can scarcely fail to be distracted by the conflicting interests of the paramount and dependent states—the two masters whom he is bound to serve; and if of a sensitive disposition, he cannot but feel the anomalous character of his situation at the elbow of a dependent sovereign, who must naturally regard him as something between a schoolmaster and a spy. No doubt there have been British residents whose influence has been markedly beneficial to native states; not only formerly, when their position was better defined, and, from circumstances, involved less temptation to, or necessity for, interference in the internal affairs of the state, but even of late years. The general effect, however, has been the deterioration and depression painted with half unconscious satire by Mr. Mansel, in the case of Nagpoor.

The circumstances attending the annexation of this state, have been dwelt on more on account of the incidental revelations which they involve of the practical working of a pernicious system, than from any special interest which attaches to the particular question so summarily decided by Lord Dalhousie. No connected statement of the case has been made public on behalf of the princesses, notwithstanding the spirited attempts made by the Banka Bye to obtain a fair hearing. When the governor-general refused to receive any communication through her envoys, she sent them to England, in the hope of obtaining a reversal of the decision pronounced at Calcutta. The vakeels complained of the treatment which the ranees had met with, especially of the strict surveillance under which they were placed: their statements were published in the newspapers, and the new commissioner for Nagpoor (Mr. Plowden) took up the matter in resentment. Meantime, Unpoora Bye died (14th Nov., 1855), her end being embittered, and probably accelerated, by the same mental distress which is acknowledged to have hastened that of her husband. The aged maharanee abandoned further opposition, and wrote to London to dismiss her vakeels (2nd Dec., 1855), on the ground that, instead of obeying her orders, and laying her case before the authorities in a supplicating way, so that her "honour and humble dignity might be upheld," they had displayed a great deal of imprudence, and used calumnious expressions against the British officers. She informed them, with significant brevity, of the death of Unpoora Bye; adding—"Well, what has happened, has happened." This letter, which is alike indicative of the character of the writer and of the dictation (direct or indirect) under which it was written, closes the series of papers, published by order of parliament, regarding the annexation of Berar.

The territory resumed from Ali Morad, one of the Ameers of Sinde, in 1852, comprised an area of 5,412 square miles. The reason of the resumption has been already stated.*

Odeipore is mentioned, in a Return (called for by the House of Commons in April, 1858) "of the Territories and Tributaries in India acquired since the 1st of May, 1851," as having been annexed in 1853. The area comprises 2,306 square miles, with a population of 133,748 persons. This place must not be confounded with the two Oodipoors (great and small) in Rajast'han, the absorption of which even Lord Dalhousie would scarcely have ventured on attempting.

The territory resumed from Toola Ram Senaputtee, in Cachar, in 1853, comprises 2,160 acres of land; but, unlike Odeipore, has only the disproportionate population of 5,015.†

Hyderabad.—In 1853, the Nizam concluded a new treaty with the Company, by which he transferred to them one-third of his country, to meet the expenses of the contingent maintained by him, but disciplined and commanded by British officers. The resident, Major-general Fraser, when the proposition for the cession of territory first came under consideration in 1851, recommended nothing less than the deposition of the Nizam, and the assumption of sovereign power by the Company for a definite number of years—a measure which he considered justified by the weak character of the Nizam, and the disorganised state of his administration. This proposition was at once rejected by Lord Dalhousie, who ably argued, that the transfer of the administration to the British government would never be consented to by the Nizam; that to impose it upon him without his consent, would be a violation of treaties; that the Nizam was neither cruel, nor ambitious, nor tyrannical; that his maladministration of his own kingdom did not materially affect the security of British territory, or the interests of British subjects; and that the

* See *Indian Empire*, vol. i., p. 452.

† Parl. Paper (Commons), 16th April, 1858.

British authorities were neither called on, nor at liberty, to set aside an independent native government because, in their opinion, that government exercised its authority in a manner injurious to its subjects.* "The debt," Lord Dalhousie says, "which burdens the Nizam has been produced by the contingent. The monthly subsidy for which the resident at Hyderabad maintains a perpetual wrestle with the dewan [native chancellor of the exchequer], and which transforms the representative of the British government, by turns, into an importunate creditor and a bailiff in execution, is the pay of the contingent." The governor-general proceeds to expose the misinterpretation of the article of the treaty of 1800; which provided that the British army should, in time of war, be reinforced by a body of 15,000 of the Nizam's troops; but which had "been made to justify our requiring the Nizam to uphold a force of about 5,000 infantry, 2,000 horse, and four field batteries, officered by British officers, controlled by the British resident, trained on the British system, not in war only, but permanently, at a very costly rate, and so as to be available for the use of the Nizam only when the representative of the British government has given his consent."†

The scale of expenditure on which the contingent was maintained, was inordinate. Lord Dalhousie, in a minute of the 25th of September, 1848, declared—"I agree with Colonel Low in thinking that we cause the contingent to become a much heavier burden on the Nizam's finances than it ought to be. The staff, in my humble judgment, is preposterously large. The pay and allowances, and charges of various kinds, are far higher than they ought to be." Still, nothing was done to reduce this ruinous waste of public funds; for in March, 1853, another minute, by the same ready pen, described the contingent as having no less than five brigadiers, with brigade-majors, attached to it, and a military secretary, who drew the same salary as the adjutant-general of the Bengal army. By the rules of the force, the officers were promoted to superior grades, and to higher pay, earlier than they would have been in their own service; and, altogether, the expenses were "unusually and unnecessarily heavy."‡

The plan devised for compelling the payment, by the Nizam, of expenditure thus recklessly incurred in the maintenance of a contingent which no treaty bound him to support, and which had existed on sufferance from the time of the Mahratta war, without any formal sanction on the part of either government, is vaunted as extremely liberal, apparently because it fell short of total annexation.

The sum claimed was about seventy-five lacs,§ or £750,000 (including interest at six per cent.); to provide for the payment of which, the supreme government demanded the transfer of "districts to the value of not less than thirty-five lacs per annum, so as to provide for the payment of the principal of the debt within three years, and further to afford a margin, which should in each year be applicable to meet any partial deficiencies which might still occur in the supply of monthly pay for the troops of the contingent."‖ The resident pointed out, as the districts of which the British government might most fitly and advantageously demand possession, the Berar Payeen Ghaut, the border districts from thence down to Shorapoor,¶ and the territory of the dooab, between the Kistnah and the Toombuddra; which, together, comprised the whole frontier of the Nizam's kingdom along its northern and western boundaries, and along its southern boundary, as far as the junction of the above-named rivers.

"The Berar Payeen Ghaut (he adds) is, without exception, the richest and most fertile part of the Nizam's country, and the Raichore dooab is the next to it in this respect. These two districts hold out great prospect of improvement in regard to revenue and commerce, from an extended culture of the two articles of cotton and opium. * * * The quantity of opium now cultivated in Berar Payeen Ghaut,

* Parl. Papers, 26th July, 1854; p. 3.

† Minute by the governor-general, June, 1851.—Parl. Papers—*Ibid.*, p. 100.

‡ Parl. Papers—*Ibid.*, pp. 4; 103.

§ Minute by governor-general, 27th May, 1851.—Parl. Papers—*Ibid.*, p. 32.

‖ *Ibid.*, p. 34.

¶ The resident, Major-general Fraser, adds a remark on Shorapoor, which illustrates the systematic encroachment, manifested in so many ways, and excused by such various pretexts. The rajah of Shorapoor, he says, "is near his majority; but, I presume, that when that district is given over to his charge, measures will be taken by the supreme government for keeping it, for some years at least, subject to the control of a British officer. It is at present in a favourable and improving state; but if given up to the young rajah's exclusive and uncontrolled authority, it will quickly revert to the same state of barbarism in which it was before."—Parl. Papers—*Ibid.*, p. 14. Shorapoor is inhabited by the Bedars, a warlike aboriginal tribe, whose chief claims a descent of more than thirty centuries.

as well as of cotton, might be greatly increased, and the duty upon them would form, in itself, a very productive source of revenue."

Captain Meadows Taylor likewise gave an extremely tempting account of the same districts; he referred to the reported existence of very valuable anicuts, and described the Raichore district as well supplied with tanks.

Temporary occupation, for the liquidation of the outstanding debt, was all that was to be immediately demanded; but Lord Dalhousie avowedly anticipated the probability of being compelled to retain these districts permanently, for the regular payment of the contingent. Major-general Fraser entered more fully into the subject; and his statements show, in the clearest manner, the irremediable disorder into which the proposed step was calculated to plunge the finances of Hyderabad. He writes (4th February, 1851):—

"We are about to assume, in pursuance of a just right to do so, which cannot be denied, the temporary management of a tract of country yielding from thirty to forty lacs of rupees; and the Nizam, therefore, will have so much income less to meet those demands, to which his whole and undivided revenue has long been proved to be quite unequal. He has been unable, for the last five years, to pay the contingent, except by partial instalments only, although he considers this the first and most important payment incumbent on his government to make; and it cannot, therefore, be expected that he should be able to meet this essential claim upon him with his financial means diminished to the extent above mentioned. It is all but certain that he will not be able to pay the contingent [*brigadiers, brigade-majors, military secretaries, and all*] for any further period than perhaps the next two months, and this, probably, but in small proportion only. The ultimate consequence, then, must be (and I see no reason why this argument should not be set before him in a plain and distinct light), that we should be under the necessity of retaining, permanently, in our possession the territory of which we are now about to assume the temporary charge."

The Nizam felt the iron pale which surrounded his kingdom closing in, and made an attempt at resistance which astonished the supreme authorities, and disconcerted, or at least delayed, the execution of their arrangements. Open resistance the governor-general was prepared to overwhelm by taking military possession of the specified districts. The Nizam was too prudent, or too powerless, to offer any. Suraj-ool-Moolk, the chief minister, appointed in compliance with Lord Dalhousie's suggestion, and pronounced by him to be the only man who seemed to possess the capacity to grapple with the difficulties of the state, pointed out the certain ruin which the proposed cession would involve. The districts demanded, he said, afforded one-third of the entire revenue; another third would be required for the regular monthly payment of the contingent, &c.: and only one-third being left to carry on the entire administration, both the Nizam and his subjects would be reduced to distress for the means of existence.

Arguments of this nature had been anticipated, and would probably have made little impression, had they not been followed up by a distinct offer for the immediate liquidation of arrears. The resident had received no instructions how to act in so unexpected a case, and he therefore wrote word to Calcutta, that pending further orders, he had judged it his duty to consent to leave the question of the transfer of the districts in temporary abeyance, the Nizam having found means to take upon himself the entire and immediate payment of his debt, and to give "the best security that could be offered for the future regular payment of the contingent, short of the actual transfer, to us, of part of his country for this purpose."*

The first half of the debt was paid at once; the second proved more difficult to be raised in the precise manner required, although the Nizam contributed thirty lacs of rupees (£30,000) from his private funds. Suraj-ool-Moolk requested that a favourable rate of exchange might be allowed for the Nizam's bills, in consideration of the interest paid by him direct to the British government, of that exacted by usurers on sums borrowed on the same account, and especially because of the notorious embarrassments of the state. He asked that the existing average rate of exchange on the Company's bills should be applied to the Nizam's, and that these latter should be credited according to their dates. In support of his first request, he urged that it was the universal practice to pay a debt at the current rate of exchange, and not at the rate which prevailed when the loan was made; adding, that it ought to be borne in mind, that the present debt had accumulated, in the course of seven years, by comparatively small sums; and the whole of it was now required to be paid within four months. With regard to the

* Letter of Resident Fraser, 16th July, 1851.—Parl. Papers (Nizam's Territory), p. 52.

second point, he said—"If instead of hoondees [bills], the Circar [state] paid the amount of the debt to you in cash, and you found it expedient to remit the money to the residencies, you would have to pay ready money to the soucars [bankers] for the hoondees you procured for this purpose; and as I send you hoondees so purchased, instead of the coin, I do not think I am unreasonable in requesting that credit may be given to this Circar [state] on the dates the hoondees are delivered to you."*

But the resident would hear of no allowance; no deductions in any way. The financial difficulties of the Nizam were a subject of regret; but it was not "equitable, that the loss of which Suraj-ool-Moolk complained, should be lessened at the expense of the British government."

The 31st of October—the time specified for the payment of the second and final instalment—arrived. The Nizam, though unable to raise the entire sum required, yet managed to furnish a considerable portion of it, and acted in such a manner as to convince the resident that he was really "exerting himself, in good faith, to liquidate the whole." The governor-general records this, in a minute dated 3rd January, 1852; yet, at the same time, he was occupied in framing a treaty which was to deprive the Nizam of the territory he had made so strenuous an effort to retain. Colonel Low was dispatched to Hyderabad to conduct the negotiations; "his judgment, firmness, and conciliatory demeanour" being relied on to bring about the issue desired by the supreme government. The task was neither an easy nor a pleasant one.

The proposals now made were, that the Nizam should cede the frontier districts in perpetuity, and receive, in return, a receipt in full for the portion of the instalment he had failed to pay in October, and likewise for the future subsistence of the contingent, which the Company proposed to reorganise in their own name, on a reduced scale, transforming it from the Nizam's force into one to be maintained for him by the government. There was, moreover, a subsidiary force, which the Company were bound to maintain in perpetuity by the treaty of 1800, within the state of Hyderabad; the funds being provided by the cession of the Nizam's share of the territory acquired from Mysoor.† The government had need of these troops, and desired to obtain, by a new treaty, the right of employing the chief part of them elsewhere, on the plea of there being no necessity for them in Hyderabad; the danger of external foes which existed when the arrangement was first made, and when the Mahrattas were in the height of their power and turbulence, having long since passed away.

It was true that, by this particular part of the proposed arrangement, the Nizam would be no loser; because the contingent, and the large number of troops in his immediate service, alone exceeded the ordinary requirements of the state. Only, as Lord Dalhousie wanted the services of the subsidiary force elsewhere, and as the contingent force, to a great extent, performed its duties and supplied its place, it is evident that there could be no excuse for appropriating the services of the former body without contributing to the expenses of the latter, which amounted to £30,000 a month.‡

This was never even contemplated; and the state of Hyderabad having been made to furnish funds in perpetuity for a subsidiary force, was now to be compelled to cede territory for the support of another distinct but very similar body of troops, and to place the former at the service of the British government without receiving any compensation whatever.

It is true the Nizam was to be given the option of disbanding the contingent; but then the immediate ruin of the country was anticipated by the resident as so palpable and certain a consequence of such a measure, that the idea was viewed as one of the last the Nizam would entertain. Even in the event of his choosing this hazardous alternative, in a desperate endeavour to relieve his finances from the incubus with which they had been so long burdened, the transfer of territory was still to be insisted on, at least temporarily, for the payment of arrears, "and for covering the future expenses of the force during the time necessary for its absorption, in the gradual manner required by good faith to existing personal interests."§

* Letter from Sooraj-ool-Moolk, 14th August, 1851.—Parl. Papers (Nizam's Territory), p. 70.

† For the origin and establishment of the subsidiary force, see *Indian Empire*, vol. i., pp. 373; 378.

‡ Parl. Papers (Nizam's Territory), 26th July, 1854; p. 94.

§ Despatch from directors, 2nd November, 1853.—Parl. Papers—*Ibid.*, p. 8.

"Beneficial as these proposals are, especially to the Nizam," writes Lord Dalhousie, "it is anticipated that his highness will be reluctant to assent to them:" and, in the event of his reluctance amounting to a positive refusal to sign the new treaty, military possession was ordered to be taken of the coveted districts.

The Nizam was, as had been anticipated, incapable of appreciating the advantages offered him: he saw no occasion for any new treaty at all; earnestly craved for time to pay off the debt; and promised to meet the expenses of the contingent with regularity for the future—a promise which, however, there is reason to fear he lacked the means of performing. At first, he seems to have been inclined to stand at bay; and in the opening conference with Colonel Low, he took up the strong point of his case, and put it very clearly.

"In the time of my father," said the Nizam, "the Peishwa of Poona became hostile both to the Company's government and to this government, and Sir Henry Russell (the resident) organised this contingent, and sent it in different directions, along with the Company's troops, to fight the Mahratta people; and this was all very proper, and according to the treaty; for those Mahrattas were enemies of both states; and the Company's army and my father's army conquered the ruler of Poona, and you sent him off a prisoner to Hindoostan, and took the country of Poona.* After that, there was no longer any war; so why was the contingent kept up any longer than the war?"

Colonel Low was not prepared to meet an argument which went at once to the gist of the question; and he made, as an honest man could not help doing, a very lame reply, excusing himself on the plea, that thirty-six years had elapsed since the occurrence of the events alluded to by the Nizam; that he (the colonel) was not in Hyderabad at the time; but that he supposed the reigning prince had considered the maintenance of the contingent a good arrangement, and therefore consented to it. He proceeded to represent the necessity of retaining this force to overawe the Arabs, Rohillas, Seiks, and other plunderers, and to enable the Nizam to collect his revenues: adding, that the governor-general was so much disposed to act liberally in the matter, that he would probably aid in reducing the expenses of the contingent, if that were desired. The Nizam here abruptly terminated the conference.

A draft treaty was sent in, providing for the required cession; and the Nizam was reminded, that he would thereby gain relief, in future, from the heavy interest he had been compelled to pay on money borrowed for the maintenance of the contingent. His reiterated reply was—"A change in a treaty, be it what it may, can never be an advantage to a sovereign who prefers, as I do, that there should not be any change at all." He reluctantly consented to discuss the subject again with the resident, and received him at the second interview with a flushed face and excited manner, which, at first sight, resembled the effects of wine or opium. This was not the case; for the Nizam had never shown himself more acute in argument, nor more fluent in conversation; but he was very angry, and had been sitting up nearly all night examining the treaty with his chief nobles. "Two acts," he said, "on the part of a sovereign prince are always reckoned disgraceful: one is, to give away, unnecessarily, any portion of his hereditary territories; and the other is, to disband troops who have been brave and faithful in his service. * * * Did I ever make war against the English government, or intrigue against it? or do anything but co-operate with it, and be obedient to its wishes, that I should be so disgraced?"† Again and again he asked to be allowed to pay the forty-six lacs of rupees then owing, and provide security for future regularity; but the resident reminded him that similar pledges had been repeatedly violated, and urged him to accept the governor-general's proposition, and apply the sum he spoke of in lessening the heavy arrears of his own troops and servants. The Nizam, in reply, made what impartial readers may consider a natural and sensible speech; but which the resident reported as illustrative of "his highness's peculiar and strange character."

"Gentlemen like you," he said, "who are sometimes in Europe, and at other times in India; sometimes employed in government business, at other times soldiers; sometimes sailors, and at other times even engaged in commerce (at least I have heard that some great men of your tribe have been merchants), you cannot understand the nature of my feelings in this matter. I am a sovereign prince, born to live and

* See *Indian Empire*, vol. i., p. 419.

† Parl. Papers (Nizam's Territory), p. 119.

die in this kingdom, which has belonged to my family for seven generations. You think that I could be happy if I were to give up a portion of my kingdom to your government in perpetuity: it is totally impossible that I could be happy; I should feel that I was disgraced. I have heard that one gentleman of your tribe considered that I ought to be quite contented and happy if I were put upon the same footing as Mohammed Ghouse Khan [the Nawab of Arcot]; to have a pension paid to me like an old servant, and have nothing to do but to eat and sleep and say my prayers. Wah!"*

Other remarks followed; the Nizam went over all the most disputed portions of former negotiations, and said that the Company ought to give him territory instead of taking any away. He complained bitterly of the discreditable transactions connected with the firm of Palmer & Co., by which his father had sustained both territorial and pecuniary loss;† and adverted sarcastically to the high value the British power placed on money. The second interview terminated as unsatisfactorily as the first. A third followed, at which the Nizam received the resident with "something of sadness in his expression of countenance," yet "with due courtesy and politeness." But he soon grew excited, and said angrily, "Suppose I were to declare that I don't want the contingent at all?" In that case, he was told, some years might elapse before the men could be otherwise provided for, and the specified districts would still be required to provide for them in the interim.

The conversation came to a standstill, and the resident broke silence by asking a decided answer to the question—whether the Nizam would consent to form a new treaty? "I could answer in a moment," was the retort; "but what is the use of answering? If you are determined to take districts, you can take them without my either making a new treaty, or giving any answer at all."

Once more the discussion was adjourned. The government had resolved, in case of necessity, "to take possession of the districts by physical force;"‡ but a difficulty arose as to the troops to be employed. There were, indeed, more than sufficient for the purpose already stationed within the limits of Hyderabad; but the employment of troops ostensibly organised for the Nizam's service, in direct opposition to his will, would, one of the members of government observed, be a measure of doubtful propriety in the case of the subsidiary force, but, beyond all doubt, wrong in the case of the contingent. The same minute shows how completely native contingents were viewed as identified with British interests, and how little anticipation was then entertained that a time was coming when the majority would mutiny, murder their officers, and fight to the death against the united power of their own princes and the British government: it also illustrates the anomalous condition of contingent troops in general, on whom such divided allegiance as is here described, must necessarily have sat lightly; and who were counted upon by the supreme government, as being ready, at any moment, to march against the person and the capital of their ostensible master, to whom they had sworn allegiance, and whose salt they ate.

"I am quite satisfied," writes Sir Frederick Currie, "that the troops of the contingent would, at the command of the resident and their officers, march against the other troops of the state, against Hyderabad, and against the person of the Nizam himself, if so ordered, as readily as against any other parties, so entirely have they been taught to consider themselves our soldiers; but we must not, on that account, lose sight of the fact, that they are *bonâ fide* the Nizam's troops, enlisted (by British officers, it is true, but by British officers in the pay and service of the Nizam) in his name, sworn to allegiance to him, and obedience to his orders. It would be, to my mind, the very height of anarchy to order these troops to coerce their master in any way; but more especially so, to use them for the purpose of taking violent possession of a part of that master's territories in order to provide for their own pay."§

The government had therefore a special reason for desiring to procure the consent of the Nizam to their occupation of the frontier districts; beside which, the use of the subsidiary troops for their own purposes, could only be obtained by an article framed to supersede the rule by which they were "hampered"‖ in the treaty of 1800; and further, it was desirable to secure a legal sanction for the continued maintenance of the contingent.

At length a modification of the draft treaty was agreed upon, chiefly through

* An Arabic exclamation, indicative of anger and surprise, and uttered with uncontrollable passion.—Parl. Papers (Nizam's Territory), p. 120.

† *Indian Empire*, vol. i., p. 421.

‡ Resident's Letter.—Parl. Papers—*Ibid.*, p. 129.

§ Minute by Sir F. Currie, 2nd April, 1853.

‖ Minute by Mr. Dorin, 1st June, 1853.—Parl. Papers, p. 154.

the mediation of Shums-ool-Omrah, the uncle-in-law of the Nizam; who was described by the resident as having been famed, throughout a long life, for truthfulness and general respectability of character, and who evinced, at a very advanced age, remarkable manliness and good sense. The Nizam positively refused to sign away any of his territory in perpetuity; but he reluctantly consented to the temporary transfer of the districts to British management, on condition of regular accounts being rendered to him, and the surplus revenue being paid into his treasury, after the liquidation of the old debt, and the regular payment of the contingent, with some other items, should have been provided for.

The governor-general had previously declared, that "much consideration" was due to the Nizam on account of the unnecessary expense at which the contingent had been maintained; and had dwelt forcibly on the heavy pecuniary sacrifice the government was willing to make by cancelling the old debt. Why this benevolent intention was not carried out, does not clearly appear. The Nizam would have joyfully accepted the boon, if assured that it involved no latent responsibility; but it never seems to have been placed within his reach. Lord Dalhousie, in his long minute on the subject of the advantages procured by the treaty, says, "that in providing, beyond risk, the means of regularly paying the contingent, and of terminating all pecuniary transactions and consequent causes of dispute with the Nizam, the government of India secured an all-important object; to obtain which, it was prepared not merely to accept an assignment of districts only, but further to cancel the fifty lacs of rupees due to it." His lordship adds—"The government may well be content with a treaty which gives it what it sought without requiring the sacrifice it was ready and willing to make in return."

No doubt the new arrangement was an extremely favourable one for the British government, when viewed in the light of temporary financial expediency. The benefit to be derived by the prince, whom Lord Dalhousie truly called our "old and staunch ally," is by no means equally apparent.* Yet it would seem to have been so to the Calcutta council; for, in sending home to the Court of Directors the documents from which the preceding account has been exclusively framed, and the precise words of which have been, as far as possible, adhered to, entire confidence is expressed in the irrefragable proofs contained therein, "that the conduct of the government of India towards the Nizam, in respect of the contingent and of all his other affairs, has been characterised by unvarying good faith, liberality, and forbearance; and by a sincere desire to maintain the stability of the state of Hyderabad, and to uphold the personal independence of his highness the Nizam."

The directors evidently sympathised with Lord Dalhousie's views of the course prompted by such laudable motives, including "a due regard for our own interests."† They rejoiced to find the Indian government relieved "from the unbecoming position of an importunate creditor;" and presented their "cordial thanks to the governor-general, and the officers employed by him, in negotiating so satisfactory a treaty."

The transfer was effected in 1853. Since then, the annexation of Hyderabad has been openly canvassed, and, probably, would have been ere now completed, only the turn of Oude came first, and then—the mutiny. Fortunately for us, the Nizam died in the interim; otherwise, "the mingled exasperation and humiliation," which Lord Dalhousie himself declares the proceedings of the governor-general *must* have produced in his mind, would perhaps have taken a tangible form; and, to our other difficulties, might have been added that of struggling with "one of the most dangerous and fanatical Mussulman districts in India."‡

* Parl. Papers, p. 40.

† Minute and despatch by gov.-general, pp. 8, 9.

‡ See *Quarterly Review*, August, 1858; article on "British India," pp. 265, 266. The writer (believed to be Mr. Layard) refers to the "garbled" Blue Book from which the statement in the foregoing pages has been framed, as affording some insight into the manner in which Lord Dalhousie bullied the Nizam into a surrender of his three richest districts; and speaks of a letter full of unworthy invective and sarcasm, in which the latter is likened, by the former, "to the dust under his feet." This sentence is not printed in the only letter from the governor-general to the Nizam in the Parl. Papers; which contains, however, the strange assertion, that the efficient maintenance of the contingent force was a duty imposed upon the government of Hyderabad, by the stipulations of existing treaties —a statement refuted by his lordship in repeated minutes. The Nizam is also threatened with the resentment of that great government "whose power can crush you at its will;" and an anticipation is expressed, of the pain and anxiety which must be caused to his highness by "the plain and peremptory

The present Nizam was suffered to ascend his hereditary throne in peace, and will, it is to be hoped, reap the reward of his allegiance in the restoration of the assigned districts, which a recent authority has declared, "were filched from his father by a series of manœuvres as unjust and discreditable as any that may be found in the history of our administration of British India."*

The Principality of Jhansi (a name with which we have been of late painfully familiar), annexed in 1854, added to our dominions 2,532 square miles of territory, peopled by 200,000 souls. The attendant circumstances were peculiar. In 1804, a treaty was concluded with Sheo Rao Bhao, subahdar or viceroy of Jhansi, by Lord Lake, under what the government truly described as the "nominal" sanction of the Peishwa. The adhesion of this chief was then deemed of much importance, and his influence had effect in inducing many others to follow his example, and thus facilitated our operations in Bundelcund. In 1817, the Peishwa having ceded to us all his rights, feudal, territorial, and pecuniary, in that province, a new treaty was entered into, by which the governor-general, "in consideration of the very respectable character" borne by the lately deceased ruler, Sheo Rao Bhao, "and his uniform and faithful attachment to the British government, and in deference to his wish expressed before his death," consented to confirm the principality of Jhansi, in perpetuity, to his grandson Ram Chandra Rao, his heirs and successors.†

The administration of Ram Chandra was carried on so satisfactorily, that, in 1832, the title of maharajah was publicly conferred on him, in lieu of that of subahdar, by Lord William Bentinck, who was returning by Jhansi to Calcutta, from a tour of inspection in the Upper Provinces. The little state was then well ordered. Its ruler was a sensible, high-spirited young man; his aristocracy and army were composed of two or three thousand persons, chiefly of his own family and tribe; and his villages and people had as good an appearance as any in India. After the ceremony had been performed in the presence of all orders of his subjects, the maharajah approached the governor-general in the attitude of supplication, and craved yet another boon. His subjects watched with deep interest the bearing of their ruler, which, in their view, implied unqualified devotion and allegiance; but they noticed (according to a native writer) the smile of surprise and derision with which the ladies and officials in the viceregal suite regarded the scene. Lord William himself had a juster appreciation of native character, but he naturally feared some embarrassing request, and heard with relief, that the boon desired was simply permission to adopt the English ensign as the flag of Jhansi. A union-jack was at once placed in his hands, and forthwith hoisted, by his order, from the highest tower of his castle under a salute of one hundred guns. The significance of the act thus gracefully carried through, was beyond misapprehension; for the adoption of the flag of the supreme power by a dependent chieftain, was the expressive and well-known symbol of loyalty and identity of interest.‡

Upon the death of Ram Chandra in 1835, without male heirs, the succession was continued in the line of Sheo Rao. Gungadhur Rao, the son of Sheo, while yet a young man, was suddenly carried off by dysentery, on the 21st of November, 1853. The day before his death, the maharajah sent for the political agent of Bundelcund (Mr. Ellis), and the officer in command (Captain Martin), and delivered to them the following *khareeta*, or testament, which he caused to be read to them in his presence, before all his court.

"[After compliments.] The manner in which my ancestors were faithful to the British government, previous to the establishment of its authority [in Bundelcund], has become known even in Europe; and it is well known to the several agents here, that I also have always acted in obedience to the same authority.

"I am now very ill; and it is a source of great grief to me, that notwithstanding all my fidelity, and the favour conferred by

language" addressed to him. Mr. Bright quoted the sentence already given from the *Quarterly Review*, in his place in parliament (June 24th, 1858); adding—"Passages like these are left out of despatches when laid on the table of the House of Commons. It would not do for the parliament, or the Crown, or the people of England, to know that their officer addressed language like this to a native prince." It is further alleged, that when forced to make the transfer in question, the Nizam had a counter pecuniary claim, exceeding in demand that urged against him; which claim, though of old standing and repeatedly advanced, Lord Dalhousie refused to discuss, until the coveted districts should have been surrendered.

* *Quarterly Review*, p. 266.

† Parl. Papers (Jhansi), 27th July, 1855; pp. 1; 17.

‡ Indophilus' *Letters to the Times*, p. 11.

such a powerful government, the name of my fathers will end with me; and I have therefore, with reference to the second article of the treaty concluded with the British government, adopted Damoodhur Gungadhur Rao, commonly called Anund Rao, a boy of five years old, my grandson through my grandfather.* I still hope that, by the mercy of God, and the favour of your government, I may recover my health; and, as my age is not great, I may still have children; and should this be the case, I will adopt such steps as may appear necessary. Should I not survive, I trust that, in consideration of the fidelity I have evinced towards government, favour may be shown to this child, and that my widow, during her lifetime, may be considered the regent of the state (Malika) and mother of this child, and that she may not be molested in any way."

Lakshmi Bye addressed the governor-general in favour of the adoption. She argued, that the second article of the treaty was so peculiarly worded, as expressly to state the right of succession in perpetuity, either through *warrisan* (heirs of the body, or collateral heirs) or *joh nasheenan* (successors in general); which the widow interpreted as meaning, "that any party whom the rajah adopted as his son, to perform the funeral rites over his body necessary to ensure beatitude in a future world, would be acknowledged by the British government as his lawful heir, through whom the name and interests of the family might be preserved." She likewise pleaded, that the fidelity evinced by the Jhansi chiefs in past years, ought to be taken into consideration in coming to a final decision on the fate of the principality.†

Major Malcolm, the political agent for Gwalior, Bundelcund, and Rewah, in forwarding the above appeal, speaks of the first point as an open question for the decision of government; but with regard to the latter plea, he says—"The Bye (princess or lady) does not, I believe, in the slightest degree overrate the fidelity and loyalty all along evinced by the state of Jhansi, under circumstances of considerable temptation, before our power had arrived at the commanding position which it has since attained."‡ In a previous communication, the British agent wrote—"The widow of the late Gungadhur Rao, in whose hands he has expressed a wish that the government should be placed during her lifetime, is a woman highly respected and esteemed, and, I believe, fully capable of doing justice to such a charge." Major Ellis, the political assistant for Bundelcund, considered the particular question of the right of adoption in Jhansi as settled by the precedent established in the case of Oorcha; treaties of alliance and friendship existing with both states, and no difference being discernible in the terms, which could justify the withholding the privilege of adoption from the one after having allowed it to the other. Moreover, he considered that the general right of native states to make adoptions, had been clearly acknowledged and recorded by the directors.§

The governor-general, after having "carefully considered" the above statements, decided that Jhansi, having "lapsed to the British government, should be retained by it, in accordance equally with right and with sound policy." Measures were immediately taken for the transfer of the principality to the jurisdiction of the lieutenant-governor of the North-Western Provinces. The native institutions were demolished at a blow, all the establishments of the rajah's government were superseded, and the regular troops in the service of the state were immediately paid up and discharged.||

The Gwalior contingent, and the 12th Bengal native infantry, were the troops chiefly employed by the British government in carrying through these unpopular measures; but reinforcements were held in readiness to overawe opposition. Employment such as this, on repeated occasions, was not calculated to increase the attachment of the sepoys to the foreign masters whom they served as mercenaries, in what many of them considered the confiscation of the rights and property of native royalty. If they had any latent patriotism, or any capacity for feeling it, nothing could have been more calculated to arouse or implant it than this ruthless system of absorption. Their sympathies would naturally be enlisted in favour of Lakshmi Bye, who fierce, relentless tigress as she has since appeared,

* This term is used to denominate cousins in the third and fourth degrees, tracing their descent in the male line to a common ancestor.—Jhansi Papers, p. 8.

† Letters from the Ranee.—Parl. Papers, pp. 14; 24.

‡ Jhansi Papers, pp. 14; 24, 25.

§ Major Ellis referred especially to a despatch from the Court of Directors, dated 27th March, 1839 (No. 9), for an explicit statement of their views on the subject of adoption.—Jhansi Papers, p. 16.

|| *Ibid.*, p. 31.

was then venerated as a marvel of youth, ability, and discretion. "This lady," said Major Malcolm, "bears a very high character, and is much respected by every one in Jhansi;" and he urged especially (in the event of the annexation of the state), "that in compliance with her husband's last request, all the state jewels and private funds, and any balance remaining in the public treasury, after closing the accounts of the state, should also be considered as her private property."*

The governor-general replied, in general terms, that the property of the rajah would belong by law to his adopted son; because, the adoption, if legally made, was good for the conveyance of private rights, though not for the transfer of the principality. Thus the ranee was not only deprived of the regency, but was held to be cut off from other claims by the very means her dying husband had taken to ensure her future position. The first part of her history ends here. We have no account of the manner in which she bore her disappointment; but we know that she rose at the first signal of the mutiny, and that her name is now inseparably connected with thoughts of massacre and war. Her subsequent career does not, however, belong to this introductory chapter. The supreme council were by no means unanimous regarding the seizure of Jhansi. Messrs. Low and Halliday, while professing themselves convinced by Lord Dalhousie's reasoning on the legality of the annexation, stated, that they would have preferred the pursuance of a similar course towards Jhansi to that lately taken with regard to Kerowlee.

Now Kerowlee was a Rajpoot principality, the annexation of which was only prevented by the interference of the home government, on a threatened motion of the House of Commons.†

Indophilus (whose opinion on the subject is especially interesting, on account of his tendency towards the annexation policy in particular, and generally in favour of the Company) says, that Kerowlee had neither been so well governed, nor had entered into such an interesting relation with us, as Jhansi: but its rajah was descended from the Moon (Chandrabunsee); and some thousands of half-civilised relations and retainers were dependent for their social position and subsistence upon the continuance of the little state. He also died without children; but the native institutions of the state were suffered to continue, and the ruling chief has remained faithful to us during the insurrection. The larger Rajpoot states of Jeypoor, Joudpoor, Bikaneer, and others, have been also on our side. "The case of their Brother of the Moon was justly regarded by them as a test of our intentions towards them, and they were in some degree reassured by the result. There can be no doubt (adds Indophilus) that these small national states, which must be dependent upon the central government, and cannot, if treated with common fairness, combine against it, are an important element of the Indian system."

The Nawab of the Carnatic died in 1855, leaving no son. The claims of his paternal uncle, Azim Jah (who had been regent), were urged as entitling him, by Mohammedan law, to succeed to the musnud; but the decision was given against him, and the title of nawab placed "in abeyance," on the ground that the treaty by which the musnud of the Carnatic had been conferred on the nawab's predecessor, had been purely a personal one, and that both he and his family had disreputably abused the dignity of their position, and the large share of the public revenue which had been allotted to them.‡

Mr. Norton, an English barrister of the Madras bar, who had been present at the installation of the deceased nawab, and had resided at Madras throughout the whole of his occupation of the musnud, says, he was neither of bad parts nor of bad disposition; and had he been only moderately educated, his presence at Madras might have entailed great benefits upon the people, especially the Mussulman population. The nawab had been under the tutelage of the Company from his earliest infancy; and instead of superintending his moral and intellectual training, they gave him over "to the offices of panders and parasites, and left him to sink, from sheer neglect, into the life of sensuality and extravagance common to Eastern princes." He died suddenly, while still young; and Mr. Norton argues, that

* Letter of political agent (Malcolm), 16th March, 1854.—Parl. Papers on Jhansi, p. 28.

† *Quarterly Review*, July, 1858; article on "British India," p. 269.

‡ *Letters of Indophilus*, p. 11. Minute of Governor-general Dalhousie, 28th February, 1856. Return to order of House of Lords; printed 16th June, 1856; pp. 12, 13.

foolish and improvident as his conduct had been, he had committed no offences sufficiently heinous to justify the penalty inflicted on the family; adding, "we might just as reasonably have refused to allow the heirs of George IV. to succeed him, on account of his irregular habits and extravagance."

The same writer states, that Azim Jah, the rejected claimant of the musnud, had been on several occasions officially recognised, in writing, as the lawful heir.*

The titular Raj of Tanjore was abolished by alleged right of lapse on the death of its last rajah, Sevajee, in 1855. The resident, Mr. Forbes, pleaded strongly in behalf of the daughter of the deceased. He urged that Tanjore was not a conquered country; that its acquisition had not cost the life of a single soldier, nor the value of a single rupee; and that during fifty years' possession, a revenue of no less than twenty crores, or as many millions sterling, had been derived from it by the British government. After entreating favourable consideration for the daughter of a line of princes who, when their aid was needed, had always proved our firm allies—he sets forth another and very pertinent view of the case, declaring, that "it is impossible to doubt that the now prosperous condition of the country would be very greatly affected by the sudden withdrawal of a circulation amounting to about eleven lacs a-year. So great a diminution of the expenditure within the province, must certainly lead to a difficulty in realising the revenue: it is a small tract of land from which to raise fifty lacs a-year; and it cannot be a matter of indifference to the producers, whether more than a fifth of the revenue be spent among them or not."

Mr. Norton gives his personal testimony with regard to the unnecessary and impolitic harshness with which the extinction of the titular principality was accomplished. A company of sepoys was marched suddenly into the palace; the whole of the property, real and personal, was seized, and the Company's seals put upon all the jewels and other valuables. The soldiery were disarmed, and in the most offensive way. The private estate of the rajah's mother, of the estimated value of three lacs a-year, was sequestered, and has remained so. The occupier of every piece of land in the district, which had at any time belonged to a former rajah, was turned out of his possession, and ordered to come before the commissioner to establish a title to his satisfaction. The whole of the people dependent upon the expenditure of the raj revenue among them, were panic-struck at the prospect of being thrown out of employ; and, in a week, Tanjore, from the most contented place in our dominions, was converted into a hotbed of sullen disaffection. The people venerated the raj, and were indignant at its suppression: the very sepoys refused to receive their pensions.

According to Mr. Norton, the terms of the treaty promised the succession to "heirs" in general, and not exclusively to heirs male; but he considers the prior claim to be that of the senior widow, in preference to the daughter; and quotes a precedent in the history of the Tanjore dynasty, and many others in Hindoo history, including that of Malcolm's favourite heroine, Ahalya Bye, the exemplary queen of Indore.†

Kamachi Bye, the senior widow, intends contesting her claims to the raj, in England. She has filed a bill in the Supreme Court, for the recovery of the personal private estate of her late husband, and has obtained an injunction against the Company, to restrain them from parting with the property.‡

Passing over some minor absorptions, we arrive at the last and greatest of Lord Dalhousie's annexations—one which, both from its importance and special character, requires to be entered into at some length.

Oude, or *Ayodha*, was famous in ancient Hindoo lore as the kingdom of Dasaratha, the father of Rama, the hero of the famous epic the *Ramayana*. With the details of its fall as a Hindoo kingdom, and its history as a province of the Mogul empire, we are almost entirely unacquainted; but we know that it has retained its institutions to the present day, and that, in all respects, the Hindoo element largely predominates throughout Oude. The question of immediate interest is its connection by treaties with the East India Company, and the proceedings of its Mussulman rulers.

It has already been shown that their independence was founded on simple usurpation, having been obtained by taking advantage of the weakness of their rightful sovereigns, the Moguls of Delhi.§

Sadut Khan, nick-named the "Persian pedlar," the founder of the dynasty, was a

* Norton's *Rebellion in India*, pp. 98—107.

† *Indian Empire*, vol. i., p. 392.

‡ Norton's *Rebellion in India*, pp. 107—118.

§ *Indian Empire*, vol. i., p. 159.

merchant of Khorasan, who, by dint of ability and intrigue, eventually procured for himself the position of governor (or soubah, or nawab) of the province of Oude, together with that of vizier, which he held when Nadir Shah invaded India in 1738-'9.

The reigning emperor, Mohammed Shah, was powerless in the hands of his ambitious servants; their plots and peculations facilitated the progress of the invader; and their private quarrels incited the pillage and massacre which desolated Delhi. Sadut Khan was perpetually intriguing against his wily rival, the Nizam-ool-Moolk (or regulator of the state), "the old Deccani baboon," as the young courtiers called him; from whom the Nizams of the Deccan (Hyderabad) descended.

The death of Sadut Khan is said to have been indirectly caused by the Nizam.* It occurred before Nadir Shah quitted Delhi.† His son and successor, Sufdur Jung, was likewise able and unprincipled. The third of the dynasty was Shuja Dowlah,‡ who succeeded, in 1756, to the nawabship, which the weakness, not the will, of the Moguls of Delhi had suffered to become hereditary. The unfortunate emperor, Shah Alum, had indeed no worse enemy than his nominal servant, but really pitiless and grasping gaoler, the nawab-vizier of Oude.§ It was Shuja Dowlah who was conquered by the British troops in the battle of Buxar, in 1764; and with whom, in 1773, Warren Hastings concluded the infamous treaty of Benares, whereby the districts of Allahabad and Corah were, in defiance of the rights of Shah Alum, sold to the nawab-vizier; and British forces were hired out to the same rebellious subject, for the express purpose of enabling him to "annex" Rohilcund, and "exterminate"‖ the Rohilla chiefs, with whom we had no shadow of quarrel.

Immediately after the defeat and massacre of the Rohillas on the bloody field of Bareilly in 1774, Shuja Dowlah was seized with mortal sickness, and died after many months of agony. The cause was said to have been a wound inflicted by the daughter of Hafiz Rehmet, the principal Rohilla chief, who perished, sword in hand, at Bareilly. The unhappy girl had been captured; and when the nawab strove to add to the murder of the father the dishonour of his child, she stabbed him, and was immediately seized, and put to death. The wound inflicted by the unhappy girl was slight; but the dagger's point had been dipped in poison, which slowly and surely did its work.¶

The next nawab, Asuf-ad-Dowlah, was a weak and sensual youth, who had no strength of character to enable him to resist the evil counsels of unworthy favourites. The subsidiary troops at first obtained from the English for purposes of the most direct aggression, became a heavy drain on the resources of the misgoverned country. Warren Hastings saw, in his indolent neighbour, an instrument for increasing the dominions of the Company, and refilling their treasury; and then followed new treaties, new loans, new cementing of eternal friendships, and, lastly, the shameless plunder of the begums of Oude, which inflicted indelible disgrace alike on the nawab and the governor-general.**

The Marquis Cornwallis, in this as in other cases, took a very different view to that acted on by his predecessor. He saw the increasing disorganisation of Oude, and remonstrated forcibly with its ruler; who urged, in extenuation, the exactions of the Company, amounting, within a period of little more than nine years, to £2,300,000 sterling.†† The annual subsidy settled by treaty, had been raised, on one pretext or another, until it averaged eighty-four lacs per annum; and Warren Hastings himself acknowledged the "intolerable burden" which was inflicted upon the revenue and authority of the nawab-vizier, by the number, influence, and enormous amount of the salaries, pensions, and emoluments of the Company's service, civil and military; which called forth the envy and resentment of the whole

* *Indian Empire*, vol. i., p. 166. † *Ibid.*, p. 173.

‡ A memorandum on the Oude dynasty, drawn up by Fletcher Hayes, assistant-resident at Lucknow, is inserted in the Oude Blue Book of 1856. Shuja Dowlah is there described "as the infamous son of a still more infamous Persian pedlar," and as enjoying "the extensive province of Oude as a reward for a service of uncommon villanies." This and other statements are quoted on the authority of Ferishta, the famous Mohammedan annalist; but Mr. Hayes overlooks the fact, that Ferishta (or Mahomed Kasim) was born about the year 1570 during the reign of the emperor Akber, and was the cotemporary of the French traveller Bernier. It is therefore not the *Annals of Ferishta* which Mr. Hayes quotes from, but the continuation of them, known as Dow's *History of Hindoostan*, a work which, though honestly and ably written, occasionally records rumours of the day as historical facts.

§ *Indian Empire*, vol. i., p. 299.

‖ The word used in the treaty of Benares.—*Vide Indian Empire*, vol. i., p. 329.

¶ *Indian Empire*, vol. i., p. 330. ** *Ibid.*, p. 363.

†† Despatch of directors, 8th April, 1789.

country, by excluding the native servants and adherents of the vizier from the rewards of their services and attachment.*

Lord Cornwallis reduced the amount of tribute to fifty lacs; checked the interference, and curtailed the salaries and perquisites, of officials; and insisted on the disbandment of the temporary brigade, which had been subsidized by the vizier for so long a time only as he should require its services, but from the costly maintenance of which he had afterwards in vain sought relief.

The measures of the governor-general in favour of the Oude government were, unhappily, not attended by any corresponding internal reforms. Profligacy, incapacity, and corruption at court; tyranny, extortion, and strife among the semi-independent Hindoo chiefs; neglect and abject wretchedness among the mass, continued to prevail up to the death of Asuf-ad-Dowlah in 1797.

The succession was disputed between his brother Sadut Ali, and his son Vizier Ali, a youth of seventeen, of a disposition violent even to madness. The Calcutta government (of which Sir John Shore was then at the head) at first decided in favour of Vizier Ali; but clear proof of his illegitimacy, and consequent unfitness to succeed according to Mussulman law, being adduced, the decision was reversed in favour of Sadut Ali, who entered into a new treaty with the Company; by which he consented to surrender the fortress of Allahabad, to increase the annual subsidy, and to receive into his service the additional troops deemed necessary for the protection of Oude.

The Marquis Wellesley (then Lord Mornington) became governor-general in 1798; and his attention was at once drawn to the notorious misgovernment of Oude. The three brothers—the Marquis, Colonel Wellesley (the future duke), and Henry Wellesley (afterwards Lord Cowley)—discussed the subject publicly and privately; and the colonel drew up a memorandum on the subject, which, in fact, anticipates all that has since been said on the evils of subsidiary troops.

"By the first treaty with the nabobs of Oude, the Company were bound to assist the nabob with their troops, on the condition of receiving payment for their expenses. The adoption of this system of alliance is always to be attributed to the weakness of the state which receives the assistance, and the remedy generally aggravates the evil. It was usually attended by a stipulation that the subsidy should be paid in equal monthly instalments; and as this subsidy was generally the whole, or nearly the whole, disposable resource of the state, it was not easy to produce it at the moments at which it was stipulated. The tributary government was then reduced to borrow at usurious interest, to grant tuncaws upon the land for repayment, to take advances from aumildars, to sell the office of aumildar, and to adopt all the measures which it might be supposed distress on the one hand, and avarice and extortion on the other, could invent to procure the money necessary to provide for the payment of the stipulated subsidies.

"As soon as this alliance has been formed, it has invariably been discovered that the whole strength of the tributary government consisted in the aid afforded by its more powerful ally, or rather protector; and from that moment the respect, duty, and loyalty of its subjects have been weakened, and it has become more difficult to realise the resources of the state. To this evil must be added those of the same kind arising from oppression by aumildars, who have paid largely for their situations, and must remunerate themselves in the course of one year for what they have advanced from those holding tuncaws, and other claimants upon the soil on account of loans to government; and the result is, an increasing deficiency in the regular resources of the state.

"But these financial difficulties, created by weakness and increased by oppression, and which are attended by a long train of disorders throughout the country, must attract the attention of the protecting government, and then these last are obliged to interfere in the internal administration, in order to save the resources of the state, and to preclude the necessity of employing the troops in quelling internal rebellion and disorder, which were intended to resist the foreign enemy."†

Lord Wellesley was ambitious, and certainly desirous of augmenting, by all honourable means, the resources and extent of the dominion committed to his charge. He had, however, no shade of avarice in his composition, for himself or for the Company he served: all his plans were on a large scale—all his tendencies were magnificent and munificent. He saw that the Company, by their ostensible system of non-interference in the internal affairs of the nawab's government, and by the actual and almost inevitable exercise of authority therein for the restraint of intolerable acts of oppression and disorder, had created a double government, which was giving rise to the greatest extortion and confusion.

Successive governors-general had borne testimony to the absence of law, order, and justice throughout Oude, and had endeavoured to introduce remedial measures; which, however, had all produced a directly contrary effect to that for which they were

* Quoted in *Dacoitee in Excelsis; or, the Spoliation of Oude*, p. 28. London: Taylor.

† Memorandum on Oude.—*Wellington Supplementary Despatches:* edited by the present Duke. London: Murray, 1858.

designed, by complicating the involvements of the state, and increasing the extortions practised on the people by the aumildars and licentious native soldiery. These latter had become so perfectly mutinous and ungovernable, that Sadut Ali required the presence of British troops to secure him against the anticipated treachery of his own; and declared that, in the day of battle, he could not tell whether they would fight for or against him.

The consideration of these circumstances induced Lord Wellesley to frame a treaty, concluded in 1801, by which the nawab ceded one-half of his territories to the Company (including the districts now forming part of the North-Western Provinces, under the names of Rohilcund, Allahabad, Furruckabad, Mynpoorie, Etawa, Goruckpoor, Azimghur, Cawnpoor, and Futtehpoor), in return for a release from all arrears of subsidy, and for all expenses to be hereafter incurred in the protection of his country, which the Company bound themselves to defend in future, alike against foreign and domestic foes. They distinctly promised that no demand whatever should be made upon his territory, whether on account of military establishments; in the assembling of forces to repel the attack of a foreign enemy; on account of the detachment attached to the nawab's person; on account of troops which might be occasionally furnished for suppressing rebellions or disorders in his territories; nor on account of failures in the resources of the Ceded Districts, arising from unfavourable seasons, the calamities of war, or any other cause whatever.

The Company guaranteed to Sadut Ali, his heirs and successors, the possession of the reserved territories, together with the exercise of authority therein; and the nawab engaged to establish therein such a system of administration (to be carried into effect by his own officers) as should be conducive to the prosperity of his subjects, and calculated to secure their lives and property. He likewise bound himself to disband the chief part of the native troops; which he immediately did by reducing them from 80,000 to 30,000. The treaty of 1801 gave the nawab a certainty for an uncertainty; and restored to the remaining portion of Oude something of the vigour of an independent state. It would probably have done much more than this, had the Company confirmed the appointment of Henry Wellesley, by the governor-general, to superintend the working of the new arrangements, and assist in initiating and carrying out useful reforms. The ability, tact, and courtesy which he had manifested in the previous negotiations, had won the confidence of Sadut Ali; and, as the brother of the governor-general, Henry Wellesley might have exercised an influence beneficial to both parties, similar to that which contributed so largely to the tranquil settlement of Mysoor, under the auspices of Colonel Wellesley. But the directors would not sanction such a breach of the privileges of the covenanted service, and the appointment was cancelled. The papers of the late Lord Cowley, and the Wellesley MSS. in the British Museum, abound with evidence of judicious reformatory measures projected for Oude, but neutralised or set aside by the home government. While Sadut Ali lived the treaty worked well, although the manner in which he availed himself of the stipulated services of British troops, repeatedly made the Calcutta government sensible of the responsibility they had assumed, and the difficulty of reconciling the fulfilment of their engagements to the ruler, with a due regard to the rights and interests of his subjects.

The nawab conducted his affairs with much discretion and economy; and, on his death in 1814, he left fourteen millions sterling in a treasury which was empty when he entered on the government.

The partition of Oude was not, however, accomplished without bloodshed. The Hindoo landowners in the ceded country—who were, for the most part, feudal chieftains of far older standing than any Mussulman in India—resisted the proposed change, and were with difficulty subdued.* The fact was significant; and it would have been well had the subsequent annexators of Oude remembered, that the danger to be apprehended lay with the feudal and semi-independent chiefs, rather than with their sensual and effete suzerain.

Sadut Ali was succeeded by Ghazi-oo-deen, who is described by one authority as "indolent and debauched;"† and, by another, as bearing some resemblance to our James I.‡ He lent the Company two millions of the treasure accumulated by his predecessor, to assist them in carrying on their wars with

* *Indian Empire*, vol. i., p. 386.
† Sleeman's *Journey through Oude*, vol. ii., p. 192.
‡ Heber's *Journal*.

Burmah and Nepaul; and they gave him, in return, a share of their conquests; namely, the Turaee*—a fertile, richly-wooded, but unhealthy tract, which extends along the foot of the Himalayas; and sanctioned his assumption of regal dignity.

The acceptance of a loan, under the circumstances, was unworthy of a great government; and the confirmation of Ghazi-oo-deen's sovereignty was of doubtful policy. Complaints of misgovernment were rife, and appear to have been supported by forcible evidence. Bishop Heber, who travelled through Oude in 1824-'5, gave a more favourable account than other witnesses of the condition of the country; but his observations were necessarily cursory. He reasoned with Ghazi-oo-deen on the duty of attending to the condition of the people; and "the reply was, that he was powerless, having lent to the British government all the money which would have enabled him to ease his subjects of their burdens." Had the money remained in the Oude treasury, it is highly improbable that it would have benefited the people, except, indeed, indirectly, through the reckless expenditure of an unscrupulous minister, and a most unworthy set of favourites. Still, it is painful to learn that English governors should have exposed themselves to such a reproach, or should have acknowledged a loan from a dependent prince, in such a strain of fulsome and profane flattery as that in which Lord Amherst invokes the blessing of the Almighty on "the Mine of Munificence;" and declares, that "the benefits and fruits of our amity, which have existed from days of yore, are impressed upon the heart of every Englishman, both here and in Europe, as indelibly as if they had been engraven on adamant; nor will lapse of time, or change of circumstance, efface from the British nation so irrefragable a proof, so irresistible an argument, of the fraternal sentiments of your majesty."†

Nevertheless, the internal management of the "Mine of Munificence" was far from satisfactory, and the resident was officially reminded (July 22nd, 1825), that "by the treaty of 1801, the British government is clearly entitled, as well as morally obliged, to satisfy itself by whatever means it may deem necessary; that the aid of its troops is required in support of right and justice, and not to effectuate injustice and oppression." In conformity with these instructions, the resident, and the officers commanding troops employed in the king's service, exercised a scrutiny which became extremely distasteful; and the treaty was violated by the increase of the native force (which was available, unchallenged, for any purpose, and afforded emolument and patronage to the native ministers and favourites), until, within the last few years of the reign of Ghazi-oo-deen, it comprised about sixty thousand men.

Nuseer-oo-deen, the son of Ghazi, succeeded him on the musnud in 1827. This is the "Eastern king" whose private life has been gibbeted to deserved infamy, in a sort of biographical romance‡ written by a European adventurer, for some time member of the royal household (as librarian or portrait-painter.) Recollecting the scandalous scenes revealed by contemporary diaries and memoirs regarding our nominally Christian kings—the Merry Monarch, and Nuseer's contemporary, the Fourth George—we need not be too much surprised by the mad vagaries and drunken cruelties of the Moslem despot, who prided himself on his adoption of certain English habits and customs§—such as wearing broadcloth and a beaver hat under the burning sun of Oude; and usually terminated his daily drinking bouts with his boon companions, under the table, after the most approved English fashion. The favourite, shortly before the death of Nuseer, was a barber from Calcutta, who had come out to India in the capacity of a cabin-boy, and from that became a river trader. Hairdressing, however, continued to be a lucrative resource to him: the natural curls of the governor-general were widely imitated; and when the barber went on his other affairs to Lucknow, he was employed in his old vocation by the resident. The king, delighted with the change produced in the appearance of this powerful English functionary, tried a similar experiment on his own lank locks, and was so gratified by the result, that he appointed the lucky *coiffeur* to a permanent post in his house-

* *Indian Empire*, vol. i., p. 413.

† Letters of Lord Amherst to the King of Oude, October 14th, 1825; and June 23rd, 1826. Quoted in *Dacoitee in Excelsis; or, the Spoliation of Oude*: pp. 68—70.

‡ *Private Life of an Eastern King;* by a member of the household of his late majesty, Nuseer-oo-deen, King of Oude. London, 1855.

§ Nuseer substituted a chair of gold and ivory for the musnud, or cushion, of his ancestors.

hold, with the style of Sofraz Khan (the illustrious chief), and gave him a seat at his table. The barber had a fund of low humour: he amused the king by pandering to his vitiated taste; and soon made himself indispensable. The existence of Nuseer-oo-deen was embittered by a well-grounded suspicion of treachery among his own family and household: the fear of poison was continually present with him; and he would touch no wine but that placed before him by his new favourite, who consequently added the office of wine-merchant to his other lucrative monopolies.

The European papers learned something of what was passing at the palace of Lucknow, despite the care which the European adventurers installed there, naturally took to keep things quiet. The *Calcutta Review*, and *Agra Ukbar*, published squibs and pasquinades upon the "low menial" who had ingratiated himself with the King of Oude; but the object of their jeers set them at nought, and continued to accumulate wealth, and to retain his influence at court by ever-new inventions of buffoonery and indecency, until the European members of the household threw up their appointments in uncontrollable disgust; and such scenes of open debauchery disgraced the streets of Lucknow at mid-day, that the resident, Colonel Low, was compelled to interfere, and at length succeeded in procuring the dismissal of the barber.*

These and other statements of the anonymous memoir-writer, are quite compatible, and, indeed, frequently correspond with the entries in the journal of Sir William Sleeman, of accounts furnished by natives of the character and habits of Nuseer-oo-deen.

Both writers dwell much on the repeated declaration of the king that he should be poisoned; and Sir William states, that for some time before his death, Nuseer wore constantly round his neck a chain, to which was attached the key of a small covered well in the palace, whence he drew water. His death was very sudden. It occurred shortly after a glass of sherbet had been administered to him by one of the women of his harem, in the night of the 7th of July, 1837.

The question of succession was stormily contested. The king had had several wives, whose history forms a not very edifying episode in Sir William Sleeman's journal. The most reputable one was a grand-daughter of the King of Delhi—a very beautiful young woman, of exemplary character; who, unable to endure the profligacy of the court, quitted it soon after her marriage, and retired into private life, on a small stipend granted by her profligate husband. Then there was Mokuddera Ouleea, originally a Miss Walters, the illegitimate daughter of a half-pay officer of one of the regiments of British dragoons, by a Mrs. Whearty, a woman of notoriously bad character, although the daughter of one English merchant, and the widow of another. She was married to the king in 1827, and was seen by Mrs. Park, in her visit to the zenana in 1828, sitting silently on the same couch with her successful rival, the beautiful Taj Mahal.†

Mulika Zamanee (Queen of the Age) entered the palace of Lucknow while Nuseer-oo-deen was only heir-apparent, in the capacity of wet-nurse to his infant son, Moonna Jan (by another wife called Afzul-Mahal); and so fascinated the father, that, to the astonishment of the whole court (in whose eyes the new-comer appeared very plain and very vulgar), he never rested until she became his acknowledged wife. Her former husband (a groom in the service of one of the king's troopers, to whom she had previously been faithless) presumed to approach the palace, and was immediately thrown into prison; but was eventually released, and died soon after the accession of Nuseer. Her two children, a boy and girl, were adopted by Nuseer; who, when he became king, declared the boy, Kywan Jah, to be his own son, and publicly treated him as such.

When Viscount Combermere visited Lucknow in 1827, in the course of his tour of inspection as commander-in-chief, Kywan Jah was sent, as heir-apparent, with a large retinue and a military escort, to meet his lordship and attend him from Cawnpoor. The king was, no doubt, desirous to propitiate his guest. He came outside the city to welcome him, invited him to share the royal howdah on the state elephant, and escorted him to the palace in full procession, flinging, meantime, handfuls of coin among the multitude who accompanied the cavalcade.

The Orientals dearly love pageantry; it would seem as if it reconciled them to des-

* The barber carried off £240,000.—*Private Life of an Eastern King*, p. 330.

† Mrs. Park's *Wanderings*, vol. i., p. 87.

potism: and the present occasion must have been an interesting one; for the externals of royalty sat gracefully on the handsome person of the sensual and extravagant Nuseer-oo-deen; and the British general, besides being in the zenith of his fame as the conqueror of Bhurtpoor (which had successfully resisted the British troops under Lord Lake), had a manly bearing, and a rare gift of skilful horsemanship—befitting the soldier pronounced by the great Duke the best cavalry officer in the service—united to an easy, genial courtesy of manner, calculated to gain popularity everywhere, but especially in India.

Lord Combermere occupied the residency for a week, during which time, a succession of hunts, sports, and *fêtes* took place, which formed an era in the annals of Lucknow. Nuseer-oo-deen was, in turn, sumptuously entertained by the commander-in-chief; to whom, on parting, he gave his own portrait, set in magnificent diamonds. The Company appropriated the diamonds; but the picture remains in the possession of Lord Combermere, and is an interesting relic of the fallen dynasty of Oude.

Nuseer-oo-deen subsequently demanded from the resident the formal recognition of Kywan Jah, as his heir-apparent, by the British government. The resident demurred, on the plea that the universal belief at Lucknow was, that Kywan Jah was three years of age when his mother was first introduced to his majesty. But this had no effect: Nuseer-oo-deen persisted in his demand; and, to remove the anticipated obstacle, he repudiated Moonna Jan publicly and repeatedly.* The consequence of his duplicity was, that he was held to have left no legitimate son. According to Sir William Sleeman (who, during his situation as resident, had abundant means of authentic information), the general impression at Lucknow and all over Oude was, that the British government would take upon itself the management of the country on the death of the king, who himself "seemed rather pleased than otherwise" at the thought of being the last of his dynasty. He had repudiated his own son, and was unwilling that any other member of the family should fill his place. The ministers, and the other public officers and court favourites, who had made large fortunes, were favourable to the anticipated measure; as it was understood by some, that thereby they would be secured from all scrutiny into their accounts, and enabled to retain all their accumulations.†

The reader—recollecting the custom in Mussulman kingdoms, of a complete change of officials at every accession, generally accompanied by the spoliation of the old ones—will understand this was likely to prove no inconsiderable advantage. Lord Auckland, the governor-general, had, however, no desire for the absorption of Oude, but only that measures should be taken for its better government. He decided that the eldest uncle of the late king should ascend the musnud, and that a new treaty should be formed with him.

On the death of Nuseer-oo-deen, a British detachment was sent to escort the chosen successor from his private dwelling to the palace. He was an old man, had led a secluded life, and was weakened by recent illness. On arriving at his destination, he was left to repose for a few hours in a small secluded room, previous to the tedious formalities of enthronement. But the succession was not destined to be carried without opposition. The Padshah Begum (the chief queen of Ghazi-oo-deen, and the adoptive mother of Nuseer, with whom she had been long at variance) asserted the claims of her grandson, the disowned child but rightful heir of the late ruler. She made her way to the palace in the middle of the night, on the plea of desiring to see the dead body of the king—forced the gates with her elephants, and carried in with her the youth Moonna Jan, whom she succeeded in literally seating on the musnud; while she herself took up her position in a covered palanquin at the foot of the throne. Amid the confusion, the sovereign selected by the Company remained unnoticed, and apparently unknown. His sons, grandsons, and attendants were, however, discovered, and very roughly treated; nor did the resident (Colonel Low) escape severe handling. On learning what had occurred, he proceeded to the palace with his assistants, and remonstrated with the begum on the folly of her procedure; but his arguments were stopped by the turbulence of her adherents, who seized him by the neckcloth, dragged him to the throne on which the boy sat, and commanded him to present a complimentary offering on pain of death. This he positively refused; and the begum's vakeel, Mirza Ali, seeing the dangerous excitement of her rabble followers, and dreading the

* Sleeman's *Oude*, vol. ii., p. 40.

† Sleeman's *Oude*, vol. ii., p. 152.

sure vengeance of the Company if the lives of their servants were thus sacrificed, laid hold of the resident and his companions, and shouted out, that by the command of the begum they were to be conducted from her presence. The resident and his party, with difficulty and danger, made their way to the south garden, where Colonel Monteath had just brought in, and drawn up, five companies in line. The temper of the troops, generally, seemed doubtful. At this crisis Colonel Roberts, who commanded a brigade in the Oude service, went in, and presented to Moonna Jan his offering of gold mohurs; and then absconded, being seen no more until the contest was decided. Captain Magness drew up his men and guns on the left of Colonel Monteath's, and was ordered to prepare for action. He told the resident that he did not feel quite sure of his men; and a line of British sepoys was made to cover his rear.*

Meanwhile the begum began to think the game in her own hands. The palace and *baraduree*, or summer-house, were filled with a motley crowd; nautch-girls danced and sang at one end of the long hall, in front of the throne; and the populace within and without enjoyed the tumult, and shouted acclamation: every man who had a sword or spear, a musket or matchlock, flourished it in the air, amid a thousand torches. Everything portended a popular insurrection. The begum saw this, and desired to gain time, in the hope that the British troops in the garden would be surrounded and overwhelmed by the armed masses which had begun to pour forth from the city. Had this catastrophe occurred, the British authorities would have borne the blame for the deficiency of the subsidized British troops, and for having indiscreetly omitted to watch the proceedings of the Padshah Begum, whose character was well known. The fault, in the latter case, is attributed to the negligence of the native minister.

The resident was anxious to avoid a collision; yet convinced of the necessity for prompt action: therefore, on receiving a message from the begum, desiring him to return to her presence, he refused, and bade her and the boy surrender themselves immediately; promising, in the event of compliance, and of the evacuation of the palace and city by her followers, that the past should be forgiven, and that the pension of 15,000 rupees a-month, accorded by the late king, should be secured to her for life. But in vain: the begum had no thought of surrendering herself; the tumult rapidly increased; the rabble began to plunder the palace; several houses in the city had already been pillaged; and the British officer in command urged the resident to action, lest his men should no longer have room to use their arms.

The native commanders of the state troops manifestly leant towards the begum. One of them declared that "he was the servant of the throne; that the young king was actually seated on it; and that he would support him there:" whereupon he also presented his offering of gold mohurs. The armed crowds grew momentarily more menacing: a ringleader attempted to seize a British sepoy by the whiskers; and an affray was with difficulty prevented. The resident, taking out his watch, declared, that unless the begum consented to his offer within one quarter of an hour, the guns should open on the throne-room. She persisted in her purpose, encouraged by the increasing numbers of her followers. The stated time elapsed; the threat of the resident was fulfilled; and, after a few rounds of grape, a party of the 35th regiment, under Major Marshall, stormed the halls.

As soon as the guns opened, the begum was carried by her attendants into an adjoining room; and Moonna Jan concealed himself in a recess under the throne. They were, however, both captured, and carried off to the residency. None of the British troops were killed; but one officer and two or three sepoys were wounded. Many of the insurgents perished; from forty to fifty men being left killed and wounded, when their companions fled from the palace. The loss would probably have been much greater, had not the soldiers of the 35th, on rushing through the narrow covered passage, and up the steep flight of steps by which they entered the throne-room, seen, on emerging from the dim light, a body of sepoys with fixed bayonets and muskets, drawn up (as they imagined) behind the throne. At these they fired; a smash of glass followed, and proved their first volley to have been spent, on their own reflection, in an immense mirror. This happy mistake saved a needless waste of blood. No further resistance was attempted; order was gradually restored; and the sovereign selected

* Sleeman's *Oude*, vol. ii., p. 162.

by the Company was publicly crowned in the course of the morning.

Strangely enough, the innocent and ill-used Delhi princess, after years of seclusion, was involved in the tumult, but escaped injury by the zeal and presence of mind of her female attendants. The begum, on her way from her own residence to the palace, had passed that of the princess, whom she summoned to accompany her. Perhaps awed by her imperious mother-in-law—perhaps desirous of looking once again on the face of the man whose conduct had doomed her to long years of widowhood, the princess obeyed, and appears to have been a silent witness of the whole affair. When the firing began, her two female bearers carried her in her litter to a small side-room. One attendant had her arm shattered by grapeshot; but the other tied some clothes together, and let her mistress and her wounded companion safely down, from a height of about twenty-four feet, into a courtyard, where some of the retinue of the princess found and conveyed them all three safely home.

The claim of Moonna Jan appears to have been a rightful one, despite the formal declaration of the late king, that he had ceased to cohabit with the boy's mother for two years before his birth. The decision arrived at by the British government cannot, however, be regretted; for Moonna Jan was said, even by the members of his own family who asserted his legitimacy, to be of ungovernable temper, and the worst possible dispositions.* Both he and the begum† were sent to the fort of Chunar, where they ended their days as state prisoners.

The new king, Mohammed Ali Shah, succeeded to an empty treasury and a disorganised government: he had the infirmities of age to contend with; nevertheless, he displayed an amount of energy and shrewdness very rare in his family.

A new treaty with Oude was alleged to be necessary, because no penalty had been attached, in that of 1801, to the infraction of the stipulation for reforms to be made in the government. Another article had been violated by the increase of the native army greatly beyond the stated limit. Of this latter infraction the British government were well disposed to take advantage, having, in fact, themselves violated the spirit, if not the letter, of the treaty, by keeping Oude very ill supplied with troops. Thus, at the time of the death of Nuseer-oo-deen (previous to the arrival of the five companies under Colonel Monteath), the whole of the British force in charge of Lucknow and its million inhabitants, consisted of two companies and a-half of sepoys under native officers. One of the companies was stationed at the treasury of the resident; another constituted his honorary guard; and the remaining half company were in charge of the gaol. All the sepoys stood nobly to their posts during the long and trying scene; but no attempt was made to concentrate them for the purpose of arresting the tumultuous advance of the begum's forces: collectively, they would have been too few for the purpose; and it was, moreover, deemed unsafe to remove them from their respective posts at such a time.‡

Something more than tacit consent had probably been given to the increase of the native force of Oude; which, in 1837, numbered about 68,000 men. By the new treaty, Mohammed Ali was authorised to increase his military establishment indefinitely; but bound to organise, as a part of it, an auxiliary British force, and to provide a yearly sum of sixteen lacs (£160,000) for the maintenance of the same. The concluding articles stipulated, that the king, in concert with the resident, should take into immediate and earnest consideration the best means of remedying the existing defects in the police, and in the judicial and revenue administration of his dominions; and set forth, that "if gross and systematic oppression, anarchy, and misrule should hereafter at any time prevail within the Oude dominions, such as seriously to endanger the public tranquillity, the British government reserves to itself the right of appointing its own officers to the management of whatsoever portions of the Oude

* Sleeman's *Oude*, vol. ii., p. 170.

† The previous history of the begum appears to have been very remarkable. Ghazi-oo-deen had conceived a strong dislike to his son Nuseer, and considered him utterly unfit to mount the throne. The begum stanchly and successfully asserted his rights, as her husband's lawful heir. When he, in turn, conceived a violent aversion to his own child Moonna Jan, she took her grandson under her protection, armed her retainers, and, after a contest in which many lives were lost, succeeded in maintaining her ground until the resident interfered, and satisfied her by guaranteeing the personal safety of the boy, for whose sake she eventually sacrificed the independence of her latter years, and died a prisoner of state.—*Private Life of an Eastern King*, p. 205.

‡ Sleeman's *Oude*, vol. ii., p. 168.

territory—either to a small or to a great extent—in which such misrule as that above alluded to may have occurred, for so long a period as it may deem necessary; the surplus receipts in such case, after defraying all charges, to be paid into the king's treasury, and a true and faithful account rendered to his majesty of the receipts and expenditure of the territory so assumed." In the event of the above measure becoming necessary, a pledge was given for the maintenance, as far as possible, of the native institutions and forms of administration within the assumed territories, so as to facilitate the restoration of those territories to the sovereign of Oude when the proper period for such restoration should arrive.*

The above treaty was executed at Lucknow on the 11th of September, 1837, and was ratified on the 18th of the same month by the governor-general. It is necessary that the manner in which the compliance of Mohammed Shah was ensured, should be clearly understood. The death of Nuseer occurred at midnight, and the resident, as has been stated, instantly sent off one of his assistants to the house of Mohammed Shah, with orders to conduct him to the palace, after having secured his signature to a paper promising consent "to any new treaty that the governor-general might dictate." This was obtained.

Lord Auckland was rather shocked by such undisguised dictation; and declared, "he should have been better pleased if the resident had not, in this moment of exigency, *accepted* the unconditional engagement of submissiveness which the new king had signed. This document may be liable to misconstruction; and it was not warranted by anything contained in the instructions issued to Colonel Low."†

If Lord Auckland was startled by the means taken to ensure the consent of the king to any terms which might be required from him, the resident was not less painfully surprised by the draft treaty framed by the governor-general in council. Colonel Low wrote, that the concessions so unexpectedly demanded, were "of a nature that would be very grating to any native sovereign of respectable character;" especially to the present king, "who, to the best of my belief at least, knows by experience how to manage a country properly, and really wishes to govern with moderation and justice." The resident especially deprecated the requisition for the payment of a very large annual sum for the maintenance of an army, which was not to be under the command of the king, or even at his own disposal—"a heavy payment, in fact, which he must clearly perceive is more for our own purposes and interests than for his, or for the direct advantage of his subjects." Colonel Low requested a reconsideration of the unfavourable opinion which had been expressed regarding the preliminary pledge he had exacted from Mohammed Ali, declaring, that so far from its being superfluous, it was indispensable; otherwise, the "desired objects of the Indian government could never have been gained without some forcible and most unpleasant exercise of our power." In a significant postscript, he asked whether, in the event of the present king's death before the ratification of the treaty, he ought to take any, and, if so, what, agreement from the next heir? adding, that the residency surgeon lately in attendance on Mohammed Shah, was decidedly of opinion, that "any unusual excitement, or vexation of mind, would be likely to bring on apoplexy."‡ All this the resident stated in a public letter; but he wrote another in the secret department, in which he earnestly advised a revision of the treaty; urging, that the formation of the proposed auxiliary force would create great discontent in Oude, and inflict a burden which would necessarily be felt by all classes; and that it would be considered "as distinctly breaking our national faith and recorded stipulations in the former treaty."§

Lord Auckland persisted in his policy: the resident was told that he had "misapprehended" the spirit of the treaty, which the king was compelled to sign, literally at the hazard of his life; for, on being made acquainted with its terms, "the idea of such new rights being ordered in his time, so hurt the old man's feelings, that it had an immediate effect on his disease;" producing an attack of spasms, from which he did not entirely recover for twenty-four hours.‖

The authorities in England, to their honour be it spoken, refused to sanction such a shameless breach of faith as this repudiation of the terms on which half Oude had been annexed in 1801. They unanimously de-

* Treaty between E. I. Company and King of Oude: printed in Parl. Papers relating to Oude (Commons), 20th July, 1857; pp. 31—33.

† Parl. Papers, p. 13.

‡ *Ibid.*,—pp. 14, 15.

§ *Ibid.*, p. 17.

‖ Letter of Resident, July 30, 1837.—Parl. Papers.

creed the abrogation of the recent treaty, and desired that the king should be exonerated from the obligations to which his assent had been so reluctantly given. Nothing could be more thoroughly straightforward than the view taken by the directors. They declared, that it would have been better to have given the king a fair trial, without any new treaty; and condemned the preliminary engagement as having been "extorted from a prince from whom we had no right to demand any condition on coming to his lawful throne." The proposed auxiliary force was pronounced inadmissible, on the ground that the payment "would constitute a demand upon the resources of Oude that we are not entitled to make; for we are already bound, by the treaty of 1801, to defend at our own expense, that country against internal and external enemies; and a large cession of territory was made to us for that express purpose."

The sentiments expressed on this occasion are directly opposed to those which animated the annexation policy, subsequently adopted. The directors conclude their despatch with the following explicit opinion:—"The preservation of the existing states in India is a duty imposed upon us by the obligations of public faith, as well as the dictates of interest; for we agree in the opinion expressed by Lieutenant-colonel Low, in his letter of the 26th of September, 1836, that the continued existence of such states will afford the means of employment to respectable natives, which they cannot at present obtain in our service; and, until such means could be provided in our own provinces, the downfall of any of the native states under our protection might, by depriving numerous influential natives of their accustomed employment, be attended with consequences most injurious to our interests. Our policy should be to preserve, as long as may be practicable, the existing native dynasties; and should the fall of them, or of any one of them, from circumstances beyond our control, become inevitable, then to introduce such a system of government as may interfere in the least possible way with the institutions of the people, and with the employment of natives of rank under proper superintendence, in the administration of the country."*

The directors left the governor-general in council to choose the manner in which to convey to the King of Oude the welcome tidings of the annulment of a compact which, they truly observed, he regarded as inflicting not only a pecuniary penalty upon his subjects, but a disgrace upon his crown and personal dignity. They advised, however, that it should rather proceed as an act of grace from his lordship in council, "than as the consequence of the receipt of a public and unconditional instruction from England."

Lord Auckland thereupon declared, that the directors, like the resident, had much misunderstood his measure;† and his council agreed with him in the hope that, by a relaxation of the terms of the treaty, the authorities in England might be reconciled to a measure which could not be cancelled without the most serious inconvenience, and even danger:‡ and when they found that the Company were pledged to the British parliament for the annulment of the treaty, they persisted in urging the inexpediency of making any communication to the King of Oude on the subject. On the 15th of April, 1839, the directors reiterated their previous orders, and desired that no delay should take place in announcing, in such manner as the governor-general might think fit, to the King of Oude, the disallowance of the treaty of 11th of September, 1837, and the restoration of our relations with the state of Oude to the footing on which they previously stood.

On the 11th of July, 1839, they simply reverted to their previous instructions, and required their complete fulfilment.§ Yet, on the 8th of the same month, the governor-general acquainted the King of Oude that, after some months' correspondence with the Court of Directors upon the subject of the treaty, he was empowered to relieve his majesty from the payment of the annual sixteen lacs. His lordship expressed his cordial sympathy with the liberal feelings which dictated this renunciation of a sum, the raising of which he had "sometimes feared" might lead to "heavier exactions on the people of Oude than they were well able, in the present state of the country, to bear."

Then followed an exordium on the lightening of taxation, and the extension of

* Despatch, 10th April, 1838, from Secret Committee; p. 38. Signed by J. R. Carnac and J. L. Lushington.

† Minute by Governor-general Auckland, dated "Umritsir, 13th December, 1838."—Parl. Papers, pp. 43—52.

‡ Minutes by Messrs. Morison and Bird, 28th January, 1839; pp. 52; 57.

§ Parl. Papers, pp. 57—60.

useful public works, which might be effected with the aforesaid sixteen lacs; and a complacent reference to the fresh proof thus afforded, "of the friendship with which your majesty is regarded by me and by the British nation." Not one word, not the most distant hint of the abrogation of the treaty; nay, more—the newly-appointed resident, Colonel Caulfield, was specially desired "to abstain from encouraging discussion as to the treaty of 1837," except as regarded the reasons above quoted from the letter of the governor-general, for releasing the king from the pecuniary obligation of maintaining an auxiliary force.*

The above statements are taken from the returns laid before parliament on the motion of Sir Fitzroy Kelly; but it is confidently alleged that the papers therein published are, as in the case of the Nizam, fragmentary and garbled; especially that the important letter written by Lord Auckland to the King of Oude is not a correct translation of the original, but a version adapted to meet the ideas of the British public.†

No such aggravation is needed to enhance the effect of the duplicity exhibited by the Indian government, in their sifted and carefully prepared records laid before parliament, of the mode in which the king was led to believe that the treaty which the Court of Directors had disavowed, because it was essentially unjust and had been obtained by unfair means, was really in force, the pressure being temporarily mitigated by the generous intervention and paternal solicitude of the governor-general.

This is a painful specimen of Anglo-Indian diplomacy. Still more painful is it to find such a man as Lord Dalhousie characterising the deliberate concealment practised by his predecessor, as "an inadvertence." The treaty was never disallowed in India—never even suppressed. The discussion regarding its public disallowance seems to have fallen to the ground; the directors, engrossed by the cares and excitements of that monstrous compound of injustice, folly, and disaster—the Afghan war—probably taking it for granted that their reiterated injunctions regarding Oude had been obeyed by Lord Auckland and his council.

Mohammed Ali Shah died in 1842, in the full belief that the treaty which so galled and grieved him was in operative existence. His son and successor, Amjud Ali, had no reason for doubt on the subject: the British functionaries around him spoke and wrote of it as an accepted fact; and, in 1845, it was included in a volume of treaties, published in India by the authority of government. No important change, for good or for evil, appears to have taken place during the five years' sway of Amjud Ali, who died in February, 1847, and was succeeded by Wajid Ali, the last of his dynasty. The new king was not deficient in natural ability. He had considerable poetical and musical gifts; but these, precociously developed under the enervating influences of the zenana, had been fostered to the exclusion of the sterner qualities indispensable to the wielder of a despotic sceptre.

Notwithstanding the acknowledged and often sharply-exercised supremacy of the British government, the dynasty of Oude still preserved, by virtue of Lord Wellesley's treaty of 1801 (that is to say, by the portions of it not cancelled by that of 1837), a degree of independence, and of exemption from internal interference; which, rightly used by an upright, humane, and judicious sovereign, might yet have raised fertile, beautiful Oude to a state of prosperity which, by affording incontestable proofs of its efficient government, should leave no plea for its annexation. Public works, efficient courts of justice, reduced rates of assessment—these things can never be wholly misrepresented

* Deputy Secretary of Government to the Resident, 8th July, 1839.—Parl. Papers, p. 61.

† The letter published in the Parl. Papers, and the Persian and English versions sent to the king: all three differed on important points. In *Dacoitee in Excelsis* (written, according to the editor of Sleeman's *Oude*, by Major Bird), a literal translation of the Persian letter actually sent to the King of Oude is given, which differs widely and essentially from that above quoted from the Parl. Papers. In the latter there is no sentence which could fairly be rendered thus:—"From the period you ascended the throne, your majesty has, in comparison with times past, greatly improved the kingdom; and I have, in consequence, been authorised by the Court of Directors to inform you, that, *if I think it advisable, for the present, I may* relieve your majesty from part of the clause of the treaty alluded to, by which clause expense is laid upon your majesty." The writer of *Dacoitee in Excelsis*, says that the italicised words bear a different sense in the autograph English letter, in which they run thus:—*I am directed to relieve you.* The king pointed out the non-agreement of the two documents, and the governor-general forthwith issued an order, directing that the old custom of sending the original English letter as well as the Persian version, should be discontinued.—(p. 92.) See also *Oude, its Princes and its Government Vindicated:* by Moulvee Museehood-deen Khan Bahadoor; p. 75.

or overlooked; but such reforms were little likely to be effected while Wajid Ali sat at the helm.

In November, 1847, the governor-general, Lord Hardinge, visited Lucknow, held a conference with the king, and caused a memorandum, previously drawn up, to be specially read and explained to him. In this memorandum, Wajid Ali was enjoined "to take timely measures for the reformation of abuses," and for "the rescue of his people from their present miserable condition." Failing this, the governor-general stated, he would have no option but to act in the manner specified by the treaty of 1837; which not only gave the British government a right to interfere, but rendered it obligatory on them to do so whenever such interference should be needful to secure the lives and property of the people of Oude from oppression and flagrant neglect. If the king, within the following two years, should fail in "checking and eradicating the worst abuses," then the governor-general would avail himself of the powers vested in him by the aforesaid treaty.*

Two years and more passed, but the king evinced undiminished aversion for the duties of his position. His time and attention were devoted entirely to the pursuit of personal gratifications, and he associated with none but such as contributed to his pleasures—women, singers, fiddlers, and eunuchs; and could, in fact, submit to the restraints of no other society. He ceased to receive the members of the royal family, or the aristocracy; would read no reports from his local officers, civil or military—from presidents of his fiscal and judicial courts, or functionaries of any kind; and appeared to take no interest whatever in public affairs.

A change was made about this time in the mode of collecting the land revenue (from the *ijara*, or contract system, to the *amanee*, or trust-management system) in many districts; but no favourable result was produced—the same rack-rent being exacted under one as under the other; the same uncertainty continuing to exist in the rate of the government demand; and the same exactions and peculations on the part of the native officials.

Colonel (afterwards Sir William) Sleeman received the appointment of resident in 1849, and was authorised by Lord Dalhousie to make a tour throughout Oude, and report upon the general condition of the people. The letter which communicates the information of the appointment, shows that the governor-general was bent on the assumption of sovereign power over Oude, and the reconstruction of the internal administration of that "great, rich, and oppressed country."† The mission of Colonel Sleeman was evidently designed to collect a mass of evidence which should convince the home authorities of the necessity for the "great changes" which their representative had resolved upon initiating; and in this sense the new resident has been truly called "the emissary of a foregone conclusion."‡ Still, though not unprejudiced, Colonel Sleeman was an honest and earnest man, well calculated by character and long training to extract truth, and experienced in framing a plain, unvarnished statement of facts. Forty years of active Indian service had afforded him opportunities of intercourse with the natives, of which he had taken abundant advantage. Active, methodical, and rigidly abstemious, he had been invaluable in the very departments where his countrymen have usually proved least able to grapple with the enervating influences of climate, routine, and red tape.§ His successful efforts in bringing to justice, and almost eradicating the murderous fraternity of the Thugs,|| by dispersing the horrible obscurity in which their midnight deeds of assassination and theft had been so long shrouded, breaking up their gangs, and tracking them out in detail, was altogether most masterly, and conferred an incalculable amount of benefit on the peaceable and industrious, but helpless portion of the population. Colonel Sleeman's character and career, however,

* Sleeman's *Oude*, vol. ii., pp. 201—215.

† Letter from Lord Dalhousie to Colonel Sleeman.—*Journey through the Kingdom of Oude* (Introduction), vol. i., p. xviii.

‡ *Dacoitee in Excelsis*, p. 109.

§ Writing to Mr. Elliot, secretary to government in 1848, regarding the difficulty of getting dacoit prisoners tried, Colonel Sleeman said that political officers had little encouragement to undertake such duties; adding—"It is only a few choice spirits that have entered upon the duty *con amore*. General Nott prided himself upon doing nothing while he was at Lucknow; General Pollock did all he could, but it was not much; and Colonel Richmond does nothing. There the Buduk dacoits, Thugs and poisoners, remain without sentences, and will do so till Richmond goes, unless you give him a fillip. * * * Davidson was prevented from doing any thing by technical difficulties; so that out of four residents we have not got four days' work.—*Journey through the Kingdom of Oude* (Introduction), vol. i., p. xxviii.

|| See *Indian Empire*, vol. i., p. 429; for an account of the Thugs, or Phansi-gars.

naturally tended to render him a severe censor of incapacity, sensuality, and indolence—the besetting sins of the King of Oude. Consequently, his correspondence manifests a contemptuous aversion for the habits and associates of Wajid Ali, scarcely compatible with the diplomatic courtesy expected in the intercourse of a British functionary with a national ally. Personal acquaintance might have mitigated this feeling; but Colonel Sleeman does not seem to have attempted to employ the influence which his age, position, and knowledge of the world might have given him with the king, who was then a young man of about five-and-twenty. "I have not," he says, "urged his majesty to see and converse with me, because I am persuaded that nothing that I could say would induce him to alter his mode of life, or to associate and commune with any others than those who now exclusively form his society."*

The tour of inspection was made during three months of the cold season of 1850, in defiance of the tacit opposition of the native government, on whom the expenses, amounting to £30,000, were charged.† The mode of proceeding adopted to procure evidence against the King of Oude, and the complete setting aside of the authority of the native government therein involved, may be excused by circumstances, but cannot be justified. A similar proceeding in any Anglo-Indian province would unquestionably have revealed a mass of crime and suffering, of neglect and unredressed wrongs, of which no conception could have been previously formed. Under our system, however, the evils from which the people labour, lie deep, and resemble the complicated sufferings which affect the physical frame in a high state of civilisation. Under native despotism, the diseases of the body politic are comparatively few in number, and easily discernible, analogous to those common to man in a more natural state. The employment of torture, for instance, as a means of extorting revenue, is a barbarism which seems general among Asiatic governments; and it has been, if indeed it be not still, practised by our own native underlings, in consequence of imperfect supervision and excessive taxation. In Oude, this favourite engine of despotism and oppression was, as might have been expected, in full operation. It ought, long years before, to have been not simply inveighed against by residents in communications to their own government, but enacted against in treaties; for, clearly, when the British government guaranteed to a despotic ruler the means of crushing domestic rebellion, they became responsible that their troops should not be instrumental in perpetuating the infliction, on the innocent, of cruelties which the laws of England would not suffer to be perpetrated on the person of the vilest criminal.

The supreme government are accused of having contented themselves with inculcating rules of justice and mercy by vague generalities, without any attempt to take advantage of opportunities for initiating reforms. Major Bird, formerly assistant-resident at Lucknow, affirms that he has now in his custody proposals framed by the native government, with the assistance of the resident, Colonel Richmond, in 1848, for the introduction of the British system of administration in the king's dominions, to be tried in the first instance in such portions of them as adjoined the British territories. The scheme was submitted to Mr. Thomason, the lieutenant-governor of the North-Western Provinces, for correction, and was then forwarded to the governor-general, by whom it was rejected; the secretary to government stating, that "if his majesty the King of Oude would give up the whole of his dominions, the East India government would think of it; but that it was not worth while to take so much trouble about a portion."‡

Such a rebuff as this is quite indefensible. Although the worthless ministers and favourites by whom the king was surrounded, might have eventually neutralised any good results from the proposed experiment, yet, had the Calcutta authorities really felt the

* Parl. Papers relative to Oude.—Blue Book, 1856; p. 158.

† In the *Reply to the Charges against the King of Oude*, published in the name of Wajid Ali Shah himself, the following passage occurs:—"When Colonel Sleeman had, under pretence of change of air for the benefit of his health, expressed a wish to make a tour through the Oude dominion, although such a tour was quite unusual, I provided him with tents and bullock-trains, and ordered my officers to furnish him with men for clearing the road, provisions and all other necessaries; and although this cost me lacs of rupees, still I never murmured nor raised any objections." In Colonel Sleeman's very first halt, he is described as having received petitions, and wrote letters thereon to the native government, in defiance alike of treaties, of the express orders of the Court of Directors, and of the rule of neutrality previously observed by successive residents.—(Pp. 8; 13.)

‡ *Dacoitee in Excelsis; or, the Spoliation of Oude*, p. 102. Taylor: London.

earnest solicitude expressed by them for the people of Oude, they would have encouraged any scheme calculated to lessen the disorganisation of which they so loudly complained, instead of waiting, as they appear to have done, to take advantage of their own neglect.

It is not easy to decide how far the British government deserves to share the disgrace which rests on the profligate and indolent dynasty, of which Wajid Ali was the last representative, for the wretched condition of Oude. Of the fact of its misgovernment there seems no doubt; for Colonel Sleeman was a truthful and able man; and the entries in his Diary depict a state of the most barbarous anarchy. The people are described as equally oppressed by the exactions of the king's troops and collectors, and by the gangs of robbers and lawless chieftains who infested the whole territory, rendering tenure so doubtful that no good dwellings could be erected, and preventing more than a very partial cultivation of the land, besides perpetrating individual cruelties, torturings, and murders almost beyond belief.

No immediate result followed the report of the resident; for the Burmese war of 1851–'2 occupied the attention of government, and gave Wajid Ali Shah a respite, of which he was too reckless or too ill-advised to take advantage. Colonel Sleeman, writing to Lord Dalhousie in September, 1852, declared—

"The longer the king reigns the more unfit he becomes to reign, and the more the administration and the country deteriorates. The state must have become bankrupt long ere this; but the king, and the knaves by whom he is governed, have discontinued paying the stipends of all the members of the royal family, save those of his own father's family, for the last three years; and many of them are reduced to extreme distress, without the hope of ever getting their stipends again, unless our government interferes. The females of the palaces of former sovereigns ventured to clamour for their subsistence, and they were, without shame or mercy, driven into the streets to starve, beg, or earn their bread by their labour. * * * The king is surrounded by eunuchs, fiddlers, and poetasters worse than either; and the minister and his creatures, who are worse than all. They appropriate at least one-half the revenues of the country to themselves, and employ nothing [sic] but knaves of the very worst kind in all the branches of the administration. * * * The fiddlers have control over the administration of civil justice; the eunuchs over that of criminal justice, public buildings, &c; the minister has the land revenue: and all are making large fortunes."*

In the beginning of 1853, the resident writes to Sir James Weir Hogg, that the King of Oude was becoming more and more imbecile and crazy; and had, on several occasions during some recent religious ceremonies, gone along the streets beating a drum tied round his neck, to the great scandal of his family, and the amusement of his people. The minister, Ali Nukkee Khan, is described as one of the cleverest, most intriguing, and most unscrupulous villains in India;† who had obtained influence over his master by entire subservience to his vices and follies, and by praising all he did, however degrading to him as a man and a sovereign.

Notwithstanding the king's utter inattention to public affairs, and devotion to drumming, dancing, and versifying, he believed himself quite fit to reign; and Colonel Sleeman considered that nothing would ever induce Wajid Ali to abdicate, even in favour of his own son, much less consent to make over the conduct of the administration, in perpetuity, to our government. The conclusion at which the resident arrives is important:—

"If, therefore, our government does interfere, it must be in the exercise of a right arising out of the existing relations between the two states, or out of our position as the paramount power in India. These relations, under the treaty of 1837, give our government the right to take upon itself the administration under present circumstances; and, indeed, imposes upon our government the duty of taking it: but, as I have already stated, neither these relations, nor our position as the paramount power, give us any right to annex or to confiscate the territory of Oude. We may have a right to take territory from the Nizam of Hyderabad, in payment for the money he owes us; but Oude owes us no money, and we have no right to take territory from her. We have only the right to secure for the suffering people that better government which their sovereign pledged himself to secure for them, but has failed to secure.‡"

The entire reliance manifested in the above extracts, on the validity of the treaty of 1837, is equally conspicuous in other letters. It is repeatedly mentioned as giving the government ample authority to assume the whole administration; but it is added—"If we do this, we must, in order to stand well with the rest of India, honestly and distinctly disclaim all interested motives, and appropriate the whole of the revenues for the benefit of the people and royal family of Oude;" for, "were we to take advantage of the occasion to annex or confiscate Oude, or any part of it, our good name in India would inevitably suffer; and

* Sleeman's *Oude*, vol. ii., p. 369.
† *Ibid.* (Introduction), vol. i., p. xxii.
‡ *Ibid.*, vol. ii., p. 388.

that good name is more valuable to us than a dozen Oudes."

On the annexation policy in general, the resident commented in terms of severe censure. "There is a school in India," he says, "characterised by impatience at the existence of any native states, and by strong and often insane advocacy of their absorption—by honest means if possible; but still their absorption. There is no pretext, however weak, that is not sufficient, in their estimation, for the purpose; and no war, however cruel, that is not justifiable, if it has only this object in view." Such views he denounced as dangerous to our rule; for the people of India, seeing that annexations and confiscations went on, and that rewards and honorary distinctions were given for them, and for the victories which led to them, and for little else, were too apt to infer that they were systematic, and encouraged and prescribed from home. The native states he compared to breakwaters, which, when swept away, would leave us to the mercy of our native army, which might not always be under our control.*

With such opinions, he watched with deep anxiety the progress of the aggressive and absorbing policy favoured by Lord Dalhousie and his council, which, he considered, was tending to crush all the higher and middle classes connected with the land, and to excite general alarm in the native mind. He began to fear the adoption of some course towards Oude which would involve a breach of faith; but he does not seem to have suspected the possibility of any right of annexation being grounded on the repudiation by the Calcutta government, at the eleventh hour, of the treaty of 1837.

In a private letter (the latest of his correspondence), he writes—"Lord Dalhousie and I, have different views, I fear. If he wishes anything done that I do not think right and honest, I resign, and leave it to be done by others. I desire a strict adherence to solemn engagements with white faces or black. We have no right to annex or confiscate Oude; but we have a right, under the treaty of 1837, to take the management of it, but not to appropriate its revenues to ourselves. To confiscate would be dishonest and dishonourable. To annex would be to give the people a government almost as bad as their own, if we put our screw upon them."†

The last admission is a strange one from the narrator of the *Tour through Oude*. He was not spared to remonstrate, as he certainly would have done, against the adoption of measures he had denounced by anticipation; but he was spared the too probable pain of remonstrating in vain. In the summer of 1854 his health began to fail. He went to the hills in the hope of recruiting his strength and resuming his labours. At last, warned by indications of approaching paralysis, he resigned his office, and embarked for England, but died on his passage, on the 10th of February, 1856, at the age of sixty-seven. Four days before, his services had been recognised by his nomination as a K.C.B., at the express request of Lord Dalhousie, who, despite their difference in opinion, fully appreciated the qualities of his able subordinate. The mark of royal favour came in all respects too late: it would have been better bestowed at the time when it had been richly earned by the measures for the suppression of Thuggee and Dacoitee, instead of being connected with the ill-omened *Tour* which preceded the annexation of Oude.

General Outram (Napier's old opponent) was sent as officiating resident to Lucknow, in December, 1854, and desired to furnish a report with a view to determine whether public affairs continued in the state described from time to time by his predecessor. This he did, at considerable length, in February, 1855;‡ and his conclusion was, that matters were as bad, if not worse, than Colonel Sleeman had described them; and that "the very culpable apathy and gross misrule of the sovereign and his durbar," rendered it incumbent on the supreme government to have recourse to the "extreme measures" necessary for the welfare of the five millions of people who were now oppressed by an effete and incapable dynasty.

Major-general Outram added, that in the absence of any personal experience in the country, he was dependent for information on the residency records, and on the channels which supplied his predecessor. It would seem that he (like Colonel Caulfield) had been instructed to refrain from any mention of the treaty of 1837; for his report refers exclusively to that concluded in 1801: but in a paper drawn up by Captain

* Sleeman's *Oude*, vol. ii., p. 392.

† Written in 1854–'5. Published in the *Times*, November, 1857.

‡ See *Oude Blue Book* for 1856; pp. 12—46.

Fletcher Hayes (assistant-resident), on the "history of our connection with the Oude government," the Calcutta authorities are reminded, that in the absence of any intimation of the annulment of the treaty of 1837, all its articles (except that of maintaining an auxiliary force, from which the king had been relieved as an act of grace) were considered by the court of Lucknow as binding on the contracting powers.*

The supreme authorities had placed themselves in a difficult position: they had pertinaciously stood between the Court of Directors and the government of Oude, and had taken upon themselves the responsibility of maintaining the treaty repudiated by the directors as unjust and extortionate. But in 1855, the rapid march of the annexation policy had left the landmarks of 1837 so far behind, that it had become desirable to set the contract of that date aside, because its exactions and its penalties, once denounced as unfair to the king, would now, if enforced, limit and cripple the plans of the governor-general. The very instrument, obtained and retained for aggressive purposes, in defiance of the orders of the home authorities, was likely to prove a weapon of defence in the hands of the King of Oude, and to be rested upon as the charter of the rights of the dynasty and state. But the Red treaty palmed off on Omichund, with the forged signature of Admiral Watson, was not more easily set aside by Clive† than the treaty with Oude by the governor-general in council. In each case, the right of the stronger prevailed without a struggle, and left the weaker party no power of appeal. Still the authorities, in discussing the affairs of Oude, abstained, as far as possible, from any mention of the treaty of 1837, and evidently thought the less said on the subject the better. Thus, the governor-general, in his minute on the measures to be adopted for the future administration of Oude (extending over forty-three folio pages), adverts to the treaty of 1837, only in one short paragraph, in which he states that the instrument by which the mutual relations of the British and Oude governments were defined, was the treaty of 1801. "A very general impression prevails that a subsequent re-adjustment of those relations was made by the treaty concluded by Lord Auckland in 1837. But that treaty is null and void. It was wholly disallowed by the Hon. Court of Directors as soon as they received it."

In other paragraphs, repeated reference is made to the warnings given by Lord Hardinge to Wajid Ali, in 1847, of the determination of the supreme government, in the event of continued neglect, to interfere for the protection of the people of Oude; but the important fact is suppressed, that the right of interference was explicitly stated to rest, wholly and solely, "on the treaty ratified in the year 1837."‡

"It is to the treaty of 1801," said Lord Dalhousie, "that we must exclusively look:"§ and, accordingly, it was looked to, for the express purpose of proving that it had been violated by the King of Oude, and might, therefore, be likewise declared null and void. Yet Lord Dalhousie hesitated at "resorting to so extreme a measure as the annexation of the territory, and the abolition of the throne." The rulers of Oude, he admitted, had been unwavering in their adherence to the British power, and had "aided us as best they could in our hour of utmost need:" he therefore recommended that the king should be suffered to retain his title and rank, but should be required to transfer the whole civil and military administration into the hands of the E. I. Company, in perpetuity, by whom the surplus revenues were to be appropriated, a liberal stipend being allowed for the maintenance of the royal family. "The king's consent," he added, "is indispensable to the transfer of the whole, or of any part, of his sovereign power to the government of the East India Company. It would not be expedient or right to extract this consent by means of menace or compulsion." Lord Dalhousie, therefore, advised that the king should be requested to sign a treaty based on the foregoing terms, and warned that, in the event of refusal, the treaty of 1801 would be declared at an end, and the British subsidiary force entirely withdrawn. The proposal appears to have been made under the idea that the very existence of the throne of Oude depended so entirely on the presence

* *Oude Blue Book*, p. 81.

† *Indian Empire*, vol. i., pp. 276—278.

‡ Minute by Lord Dalhousie, June 18th, 1855.—*Oude Blue Book*, p. 149.

§ Any reader who doubts the illegality of Lord Dalhousie's conclusion, would do well to peruse the able opinion of Dr. Travers Twiss, dated 24th February, 1857, on the infraction of the law of nations, committed by setting aside the treaty of 1837: quoted in *Dacoitee in Excelsis*, pp. 192—199.

of a British force, that the king would accede to any conditions required from him. But the other members of council unanimously deprecated the offering of the proposed alternative, on the ground of the terrible crisis of anarchy which would be the probable consequence; and it was suggested that, "if there should be in the king's council but one person of courage and genius, though it should be but a dancing-girl (such as Indian annals show many), the king might be led to elect disconnection rather than abdication."*

Mr. Dorin minuted in favour of the entire incorporation of Oude, and objected to continuing "to the most unkingly monarch of Oude any portion of the royal position and dignity which, by nature and inclination, he is incapable of sustaining;" yet he foresaw that the king would never surrender his kingdom except on compulsion. All Mr. Dorin's sympathies were, he declared, with the people of Oude, the "fine, manly race," from whom we drew "almost the flower of the Bengal army."

Mr. Grant agreed generally with Mr. Dorin, but thought that the king might be suffered to retain his title for his lifetime. Mr. Grant took strong views of the rights and responsibilities of the British government, both in its own right, and as having "succeeded to the empire of the Mogul;" and he denied that the Oude rulers had ever stood in the position of sovereign princes. Major-general Low (who had held the position of resident at Lucknow for eleven years) minuted in favour of annexation, but desired to see more liberal provision made for the present king and his successors than the other members of council deemed necessary. He urged that the well-known habits of Mohammedans of rank afforded a guarantee for their income being expended among the people from whom it was levied, and not hoarded up, and sent off to a distant country, according to the practice of most European gentlemen on reaching the highest offices in the Indian service. The character of the last five princes of Oude, all of whom he had known personally, had, he said, been much misrepresented: they had sadly mismanaged their own affairs, but they had constantly proved active and useful allies, having again and again forwarded large supplies of grain and cattle to our armies with an alacrity that could not be exceeded by our own British chiefs of provinces, and having lent us large sums of money when we were extremely in want of it, and could not procure it elsewhere. As individual princes, their intercourse with our public functionaries had been regular, attentive, courteous, and friendly.†

Mr. Peacock minuted in favour of the assumption of sovereign power over Oude, but desired that the surplus revenue might be disposed of entirely for the benefit of the people, and no pecuniary benefit be derived by the East India Company. The suggestion deserved more notice than it appears to have received, seeing that "the benefit of the people" is declared by the directors to have been "the sole motive, as well as the sole justification," of the annexation.‡

Not one of the four members of council (not even Mr. Peacock, though an eminent lawyer) took the slightest notice of the treaty of 1837, or alluded to the frequent references concerning it made by their delegates at the court of Lucknow. They spoke freely enough of treaties in general, discussed the law of nations, and quoted Vattel; but the latest contract was tabooed as dangerous ground. The governor-general, in forwarding to the Court of Directors the minutes and other papers above quoted, alluded to his own approaching departure, but offered to remain and carry out the proposed measures regarding Oude, if the directors considered that the experience of eight years would enable him to do so with greater authority than a newly-appointed governor might probably command. The task, he added, would impose upon him very heavy additional labour and anxiety; the ripened fruit would be gathered only by those who might come after him.§ The simile is an unfortunate one, if the fruit we are now gathering in Oude is to be viewed as evidencing the character of the tree which produced it.

The Court of Directors, in announcing their decision on the subject, imitated the reserve of their representatives; and having the fear of Blue Book revelations, and India Reform Society philippics before

* Minute by Mr. Grant.—*Oude Blue Book*, p. 218.

† This last portion of Major-general Low's minute certainly does not accord with the account given by Colonel Sleeman of his intercourse with Wajid Ali; but the colonel, though just and honourable in deed, was not conciliatory in manner; and his official communication with the king would be naturally affected by this circumstance.

‡ *Oude Blue Book*, p. 234.

§ Despatch dated July 3rd, 1855.—*Ibid.*, p. 1.

their eyes (but not of mutiny and insurrection), they ignored the chief difficulty, and accepted Lord Dalhousie's offer in the most complimentary terms, leaving him unfettered by any special instructions. They suggested, however, that the officiating resident (Outram) should be instructed to ascertain whether the prospect of declaring our connection with the Oude government at an end, would be so alarming to the king as to render his acceptance of the proposed treaty a matter of virtual necessity. If this could be relied on, the alternative was to be offered; if not, the directors authorised and enjoined the attainment of the "indispensable result," in such manner as the governor-general in council should see fit. Concerning the appropriation of the surplus revenue, they made no remark whatever.*

The idea of offering the king the withdrawal of the subsidiary force as the alternative of abdication, was abandoned, and measures were taken for the assumption of the government of Oude, by issuing orders for the assembling of such a military force at Cawnpoor as, added to the troops cantoned at that station, and to those already in Oude, was considered sufficient to meet every immediate contingency. The additional troops numbered about 13,000 men, and were placed under the divisional command of (the late) Major-general Penny; but constituted a distinct field force under (the late) Colonel Wheeler, as brigadier. In the meantime, the disorganisation of Oude was clearly on the increase, and one of its marked features was a rising spirit of Moslem fanaticism. It happened that a Mohammedan fast fell on the same day as a Hindoo feast; and Ameer Ali, a moolvee, or priest, of high repute, took advantage of the circumstance to incite his co-religionists to a fierce onslaught on the Hindoos. Troops were ordered out to quell the disturbances; but Ameer Ali seized and confined two of the officers, assembled 3,000 men, and declared his intention of destroying a certain Hindoo temple, and erecting a mosque in its stead. At length the British subsidiary force was employed by the king against the moolvee. An affray ensued, in which a body of Patans fought with the recklessness of fanaticism, and were cut down, standing shoulder to shoulder round their guns, by a party of Hindoo zemindars and their retainers. In all, 200 Hindoos and 300 Patans perished. This occurred in November, 1855. About the same time the Oude government became aware that some great change was in agitation. They asked the reason for the assembling of so large a force at Cawnpoor; and were, it is alleged, solemnly assured that it was intended to keep in check the Nepaulese, who were supposed to be meditating a descent towards the district of Nanparah.†

The veil, however, was soon withdrawn. On the 30th of January, 1856, General Outram requested the attendance of Ali Nukki Khan at the residency, and after informing him of the contemplated changes, "mentioned that, in order to prevent the chance of a disturbance on the part of evil-disposed persons, a strong brigade of troops was directed to cross the Ganges, and march on the capital."‡

Having impressed the minister with the futility of resistance, the resident proceeded to seek, or rather to insist upon, an interview with the king. Remembering the discussions which had taken place between the Nizam of Hyderabad and Colonel Low, the governor-general was anxious that General Outram should not be surprised into indiscreet admissions; and warned him, that it was "very probable" that the king would refer to the treaty negotiated with his predecessor in the year 1837, of the entire abrogation of which the court of Lucknow had never been informed. "The effect of this reserve, and want of full communication, is felt to be embarrassing to-day. It is the more embarrassing that the cancelled instrument was still included in a volume of treaties which was published in 1845, by the authority of government. There is no better way of encountering this difficulty than by meeting it full in the face." This was to be done by informing the king that the communication had been inadvertently neglected; and the resident was authorised to state the regret felt by the governor-general in council, that "any such neglect should have taken place even inadvertently." Should the king observe, that although the treaty of 1837 was annulled, a similar measure, less stringent than that now proposed, might be adopted, he was to be told, that all subsequent experience had

* Despatch from the Court of Directors, dated November 21st, 1855. Signed—E. Macnaghten, W. H. Sykes, &c., &c., &c.—*Oude Blue Book*, pp. 233—236.

† *Dacoitee in Excelsis*, p. 140.

‡ *Oude Blue Book*, p. 280.

shown that the remedy then provided would be wholly inadequate to remove the evils and abuses which had long marked the condition of Oude.*

Such were the arguments put by the supreme government of India, into the mouth of General Outram. They must have been extremely unpalatable to a man whose friendly feeling towards Indian princes had been strengthened by personal and friendly intercourse, and not frozen by viceregal state, or neutralised by exclusive attention to the immediate interests and absorbing pecuniary anxieties of the East India Company. But the resident had swallowed a more bitter pill than this when negotiating with the unfortunate Ameers of Sinde, whom, in his own words, he had had to warn against resistance to our requisitions, as a measure that would bring down upon them utter and merited destruction; while he firmly believed, that every life lost in consequence of our aggressions, would be chargeable upon us as a murder.†

In the present instance he was spared the task of adding insult to injury. Neither the king nor his minister attempted to stand upon any abstract theory of justice, or fought the ground, inch by inch, as Mahratta diplomatists would have done—throwing away no chance, but, amid defeat and humiliation, making the best possible terms for themselves. Wajid Ali Shah, on the contrary, "unkingly" as he had been described to be, and unfit to reign as he certainly was, did not stoop to discussions which he knew would avail him nothing, but acted on the imperial axiom, "*aut Cæsar aut nullus.*"

When the resident proceeded, as pre-arranged, to present to the king the draft treaty now proposed, accompanied by a letter from the governor-general urging its acceptance, he found the palace courts nearly deserted, and the guns which protected the inner gates dismounted from their carriages. The guard of honour were drawn up unarmed, and saluted him with their hands only. The mere official report of the interview is very interesting. The king received the treaty with the deepest emotion, and gave it to a confidential servant, Sahib-oo-Dowlah, to read aloud; but the latter, overcome by his feelings, was unable to proceed beyond the first few lines; on which the king took the treaty into his own hands, and silently read the document, in which he was called upon to admit that he and his predecessors had, by continual maladministration, violated the treaty of 1801; and to make over the entire government of Oude to the East India Company in perpetuity, together with the free and exclusive right to "the revenues thereof." In return for signing this humiliating abdication, Wajid Ali was to retain and bequeath "to the heirs male of his body born in lawful wedlock" (not his heirs generally, according to Mohammedan law), the style of a sovereign prince, and a stipend of twelve lacs per annum.

After carefully perusing every article, the king exclaimed, in a passionate burst of grief—"Treaties are necessary between equals only; who am I now, that the British government should enter into treaties with me?" Uncovering himself (the deepest token of humiliation which a Mohammedan can give),‡ he placed his turban in the hands of the resident, declaring that, now his titles, rank, and position were all gone, he would not trouble government for any maintenance, but would seek, in Europe, for that redress which it was vain to look for in India.

General Outram begged the king to reflect, that if he persisted in withholding his signature, "he would have no security whatever for his future maintenance, or for that of his family; that the very liberal provision devised by the British government would inevitably be reconsidered and reduced; that his majesty would have no guarantee for his future provision, and *would have no claim whatever on the generosity of the government.*" The prime minister warmly supported the resident; but the king's brother exclaimed, that there was no occasion for a treaty, as his majesty was no longer in a position to be one of the contracting powers. The king reiterated his unalterable resolve not to sign the treaty: the resident intimated that no further delay than three days could be permitted; and then, with the usual ceremonies and honours, took his leave.

The government, in their anxiety to obtain the king's signature, had empowered

* Letter from secretary of government to Major-general Outram, January 23rd, 1856.—*Oude Blue Book*, p. 243.

† Outram's *Commentary on Napier's Conquest of Sinde*, p. 439. See also *Indian Empire*, vol. i., p. 451.

‡ May your father's head be uncovered! is one of the most bitter curses of the Mohammedans.

the resident to increase the proffered stipend of twelve lacs (£120,000) to fifteen, if their object could be thus attained. But the demeanour of Wajid Ali convinced General Outram that the promise of double that sum, or of any amount of money, would have no effect; and he therefore considered it unworthy of the government he represented, to make any offer to raise the proposed allowance by a lac or two per annum.

An attempt was made to gain the king's consent through his mother, a lady remarkable for good sense and intelligence,* who exercised great influence over her son; and a yearly stipend of a lac of rupees was offered her as the reward of success. The reply of the queen-mother is not stated in General Outram's account of the conference, and the circumstance itself is only incidentally mentioned; but it is evident that she rejected it, and ceased not to protest against the proposed treaty, and to beg that a further period might be allowed, during which the king might be enabled to show to the world, by the adoption of vigorous reforms, how anxious and eager he was to follow out the plans of the British government.

The three days allowed for consideration elapsed: the king persisted in his resolve; and the resident carried out his instructions by issuing a proclamation, previously prepared at Calcutta, notifying the assumption of the exclusive and permanent administration of the territories of Oude by the Hon. East India Company.

The king offered no opposition whatever to the measures adopted by the British government; but, in what the resident called "a fit of petulance," he ordered all his troops at the capital to be immediately paid-up and dismissed. General Outram thereupon informed the king, that it was incumbent on him to retain the soldiery until the arrangements of the new administration should be completed; adding, that should any disturbance take place, his majesty would be held responsible, and made answerable for the same. Upon the receipt of this threat, Wajid Ali Shah, having resolved to give no pretext for a quarrel, issued proclamations, desiring all his people, civil and military, to obey the orders issued by the British government; to become its faithful subjects; and on no account to resort to resistance or rebellion. He expressed his determination of proceeding at once to Calcutta, to bring his case to the notice of the governor-general, and thence to England, to intercede with the Queen; but he specially commanded that his subjects should not attempt to follow him. General Outram desired that this last paragraph should be omitted. It originated, he said, in the absurd idea impressed upon the king by his flatterers, that a general exodus of his people would follow his departure; or else was introduced with the intention of exciting sympathy in Europe. "Another manœuvre," he added, "has been had recourse to, with the same object doubtless. For two days past, a written declaration of satisfaction with his majesty's rule has been circulated for signature in the city, where it may probably meet with considerable success. Of course, most classes at Lucknow will suffer, more or less, from the deprivation of the national plunder which is squandered at the capital."†

There is reason to believe that very general dismay was caused at Lucknow by the annexation of the kingdom. The breaking up of a native government is always a terrible crisis to the metropolis. In the present instance, the amount of immediate and individual suffering was unusually large. The suddenness of the king's deposition, and his refusal to sign the treaty, aggravated the distress which the change from native to European hands must have occasioned, even had it happened as a so-called lapse to the paramount power, in the event of the sovereign's death without heirs. As it was, the personal rights of the deposed monarch were dealt with as summarily as the inherited ones of the royal family of Nagpoor had been. No official account has been published of these proceedings; but in the statement of the case of the King of Oude, attributed to Major Bird, the following assertions are made:—

"Since the confiscation of the Oude territory, the royal palaces, parks, gardens, menageries, plate, jewellery, household furniture, stores, wardrobes, carriages, rarities, and articles of *vertu*, together with the royal museum and library, containing 200,000 volumes of rare books, and manuscripts of immense value, have been sequestered. The king's most valuable stud of Arabian, Persian, and English horses, his fighting, riding, and baggage elephants, his camels, dogs and cattle, have all been sold by public auction at nominal prices. His majesty's armoury, including the most rare and beautifully worked arms of every description, has also

* "Note of a Conference with the queen-mother, by General Outram."—*Oude Blue Book*, p. 286.

† Major-general Outram to secretary of government, February 7th, 1856.—*Oude Blue Book*, p. 292.

been seized, and its contents disposed of by sale or otherwise. * * * The ladies of the royal household were, on the 23rd of August, 1856, forcibly ejected from the royal palace of the Chuttar Munzul, by officers who neither respected their persons nor their property, and who threw their effects into the street."*

It is to be hoped that the above statement is exaggerated; and if so, it is especially to be regretted that the British public, or their representatives, are not furnished with authentic information on so interesting and important a point as the manner in which the deposition of Wajid Ali Shah was accomplished, and in what respects it was calculated to raise or allay the ferment of the mass of the aristocratic and manufacturing classes, the interests of the latter being closely associated with the former. In the *Reply to the Charges against the King of Oude* (already quoted), Wajid Ali Shah asserts, that the usurpation of his dominion would tend to destroy the trade in embroidered silk and cotton cloths. "It is notorious, that three-fourths of the rich embroidered cloths of Benares are imported to Oude; the remainder, one-fourth, being sent to other countries. In Bengal and other provinces, people very seldom use these costly dresses." The reason implied, rather than declared, by the king is probably the true one; namely, that his subjects could afford to clothe themselves in luxurious apparel, whereas those of the East India Company could not; and he adds—"My territories have not been strictly measured with chains so as to render it impossible for the agriculturist to derive a profit, nor have I resumed the allowances of any class of people."†

The testimony of the king regarding the probable results of his deposition, is, in part, corroborated by that of an eye-witness, who will hardly be accused of exaggerating the case; and who, in speaking of the many innocent sufferers from the change of government, includes in his list, "thousands of citizens who had previously found employ in providing for the ordinary wants of the court and nobility. There were several hundreds of manufacturers of hookah snakes. The embroiderers in gold and silver thread were also reckoned by hundreds. The makers of rich dresses, fine turbans, highly ornamental shoes, and many other subordinate trades, suffered severely from the cessation of the demand for the articles which they manufactured."‡

Oude was taken possession of, very much more as if it had been obtained by force of arms than by diplomacy. Annexation on a large scale, is in either case a hazardous operation, requiring the greatest circumspection. Let any one turn to the Wellesley and Wellington despatches, or to the Indian annals of that eventful period, and see the extreme care which was taken in the settlement of Mysoor—the forethought in preparing conciliatory measures, and meeting national prejudices; the liberal consideration for individual interests—and then peruse, in the parliamentary papers, the summary manner in which the native institutions in Oude, without the least consideration or examination, were to be rooted up and superseded by a cut-and-dried system, to be administered in the higher departments exclusively by Europeans. After such a comparison of preliminary measures, the different results, in the case of Oude and Mysoor, will be deemed amply accounted for. It has been truly said of Lord Wellesley, in a leading Indian journal, that "whatever he was suffered to carry out to his premeditated conclusion, fell into its place with as few disadvantages to the political and social state of Indian society, as a radical operation could well be attended with." In the settlement of Mysoor, it is asserted, "every difficulty was foreseen, and every exigency met; and the dynasty of Tippoo was plucked up, flung aside, and replaced by a new arrangement, which fitted into its place as if it had been there, untouched, from the days of Vishnu." Regarding the occupation of Oude, a very different picture is drawn by the writer, who asserts, that its annexation was carried out in the most reckless manner, and that most important circumstances connected with it were entirely overlooked. "In Lord Dalhousie's opinion, all that was necessary was simply to march a small body of troops to Lucknow, and issue the fiat of annexation. This done, everything, it was supposed, would go on in an easy, plain-sailing manner. The inhabitants might not be satisfied; the zemindars might grumble a little in their forts; the budmashes might frown and swagger in the bazaar; but what of that? The power of the British was invincible."§

* *Dacoitee in Excelsis*, p. 145.

† *Reply to Charges, &c.*, p. 43.

‡ *Mutinies in Oudh;* by Martin Richard Gubbins, of the Bengal civil service, financial commissioner for Oudh. London: Bentley, 1858; p. 70.

§ *Bombay Athenæum.*

The minutes of the supreme council certainly tend to corroborate the foregoing opinion, by showing that the difficulties and dangers attendant on the annexation of Oude were very imperfectly appreciated. The refusal of the king to sign the proffered treaty (though previously deprecated by the governor-general as an insurmountable obstacle to direct absorption), seems to have been welcomed when it actually occurred, as an escape from an onerous engagement; and the submission of all classes—hereditary chiefs, discarded officials, unemployed tradespeople, and disbanded soldiery—was looked for as a matter of course; any concessions made by the annexators being vouchsafed as a matter of free grace, to be received with gratitude, whether it regarded the confirmation of an hereditary chiefdom, or a year's salary on dismissal from office.

The king, Lord Dalhousie considered, by refusing to enter into any new engagement with the British government, had placed himself in entire dependence upon its pleasure; and although it was desirable that "all deference and respect, and every royal honour, should be paid to his majesty Wajid Ali Shah," during his lifetime, together with a stipend of twelve lacs per annum, yet no promise ought now to be given of the continuance of the title, or of the payment of the same amount of money to his heirs. Messrs. Dorin, Grant, and Peacock concurred in this opinion; but Major-general Low minuted against "the salary of the heirs" of Wajid Ali being left to the decision of a future government, the members of which would very probably not sufficiently bear in mind the claims of the Oude family on the British government for comfortable income at least. The minute proceeded to state, that though, for many reasons, it was to be regretted that the king had not signed the treaty, yet, in a pecuniary point of view, his refusal was advantageous. To himself the loss had been great; and, as he had issued all the orders and proclamations that could be desired, and had done his utmost to prevent all risk of strife at the capital, by dismounting his artillery, guns, &c., it would be harsh, and not creditable to a great paramount state, which would "gain immense profit from the possession of the Oude territories," if, in addition to the punishment inflicted on the king, the income intended for his direct male heirs should also be curtailed.

Major-general Low was in a minority of one, as Mr. Peacock had been regarding the appropriation of the surplus revenue; and their opinions, in neither case, appear to have met with any consideration. The claims of the various classes of the population were treated in as summary and arbitrary a manner as those of their sovereign; and, owing to the peculiar constitution of Oude, the experiment was a much more dangerous one in their case than in his. The administration was to be conducted, as nearly as possible, in accordance with the system which the experience of nearly seven years had proved to be eminently successful in the provinces beyond the Sutlej; that is to say, the measures which had been matured, and gradually carried through, in the conquered Punjab, by the co-operation of some of the most earnest and philanthropic men whom India has ever seen, was now to be thrust upon Oude, without any preliminary inquiry into its adaptation. In the Punjab, the Lawrences and their staff acted as a band of pacificators on an errand of love and mercy, rather than in the usual form of a locust-cloud of collectors. Such men, invested with considerable discretionary power, could scarcely fail of success; yet one at least of them shrunk from enforcing the orders of government, and left the Punjab, because he could not bear to see the fallen state of the old officials and nobility.*

In Oude, the newly-created offices, rather than the men who were to fill them, occupy the foreground of the picture. General Outram was appointed chief commissioner, with two special military assistants, a judicial and financial commissioner, four commissioners of divisions, twelve deputy-commissioners of districts, eighteen assistant-commissioners, and eighteen extra assistants, to begin with. An inspector of gaols was to be appointed as soon as the new administration should be fairly established; and a promise was held out for the organisation of a department of public works, to aid in developing the resources of the country.

The pay of the new functionaries was to range from 3,500 rupees to 250 rupees a month (say from £4,200 to £300 a-year.) The number of native officials to be retained was, as usual, miserably small, and their remuneration proportionately low. As a body, they were of course great losers by the revolution.

* Arthur Cocks, chief assistant to the resident.—Raikes' *Revolt in the North-West Provinces*, p. 25.

The king urged, as a special ground of complaint, the manner in which "writers, clerks, and other *attachés*" of departments had been supplanted by strangers. "Is it," he asks, "consistent with justice to deprive people of the soil of situations of this nature, and bestow them on foreigners? Foreigners have no claim to support from the government of Oude, while natives of the soil are left without means of procuring their livelihood."*

Mr. Gubbins, the financial commissioner for Oude, who was sent there at the period of the annexation, speaks of the sufferings of the nobility as having been aggravated by the neglect of the British functionaries. "The nobles had received large pensions from the native government, the payment of which, never regular, ceased with the introduction of our rule. Government had made liberal provision for their support; but before this could be obtained, it was necessary to prepare careful lists of the grantees, and to investigate their claims. It must be admitted, that in effecting this there was undue delay; and that, for want of common means of support, the gentry and nobility of the city were brought to great straits and suffering. We were informed that families which had never before been outside the zunana, used to go out at night and beg their bread."†

When Sir Henry Lawrence came to Lucknow, towards the close of March, 1857, we are told that he applied himself to cause the dispatch of the necessary documents, and gave the sufferers assurance of early payment and kind consideration. But nearly fourteen months had dragged slowly away before his arrival; and a smouldering mass of disaffection had meanwhile accumulated, which no single functionary, however good and gifted, could keep from bursting into a flame.

The discharged soldiery of the native government, amounting to about 60,000 men, naturally regarded the new administration with aversion and hostility. Service was given to about 15,000 of them in newly-formed local regiments, and some found employment in the civil departments. The large proportion, for whom no permanent provision could be made, received small pensions or gratuities: for instance, those who had served from twenty-five to thirty years, received one-fourth of their emoluments as pension; and those who had served from seven to fifteen years, received three months' pay as a gratuity. Under seven years' service, no gratuity whatever appears to have been given to the unfortunates suddenly turned adrift for no fault of their own. It was further decreed, that no person whatever should be recommended for pension or gratuity, who should decline employment offered to him under the British government.‡ Of the late king's servants, civil and military, many remained without any permanent provision; and not a few refused employ—some because they hoped that the native kingdom would be restored; but the majority of the soldiery, on account of the severity of the British discipline.§

By far the greatest difficulties in which the new government became involved, regarded the settlement of titles to land. Considering the long series of years during which at least the temporary assumption of the powers of administration had been contemplated by the British government, it is not a little surprising to find the governor-general in council avowedly unprovided with "any information as to the extent and value of rent-free holdings in Oude, or as to the practice which may have prevailed under the native government in respect of these grants." Without waiting for any enlightenment on the subject, rules are laid down "for the adjudication of claims of the class under consideration;" and, as might have been reasonably expected, these rules worked badly for all parties.

The despatch above quoted is very able, but decidedly bureaucratic throughout: its arbitrary provisions and minute details remind one of the constitutions which the Abbé Sièyes kept in the pigeon-holes of his writing-table, ready for any emergency. No consideration was evinced therein for the peculiar state of society in Oude, or even for the prominent features portrayed by Colonel Sleeman in his honest but cursory investigation. The fact was, that Oude, instead of the exclusively Mohammedan kingdom, or the British dependency, which it was represented to be, was really a Hindoo confederacy, presided over by a foreign dynasty. The most powerful class were Rajpoot chiefs, claiming descent from the sun and the moon; who laughed to scorn the mushroom dynasty of Wajid Ali, and regarded, with especial contempt, his assumption of the kingly title. These men,

* *Reply to Charges*, p. 43.
† Gubbins' *Mutinies in Oudh*, p. 70.
‡ *Oude Blue Book* for 1856, p. 278.
§ Gubbins' *Mutinies in Oudh*, p. 69.

united, might at any moment have compelled the Mohammedan ruler to abdicate or govern on just principles, had not co-operation for such an object been rendered impracticable by their own intestine strife. The state of things among them resembled that which brought and kept the Rajpoot princes under partial subjection: the faggots bound up together could not have been broken; but it was easy to deal with them one by one. Thus the suzerainty of the Mogul emperor was established over Rajast'han; and thus, though somewhat more firmly, because on a smaller scale, the power of the usurping governors was fixed in Oude. But the great jungle barons were overawed rather than subjugated; and, in the time of Colonel Sleeman, the officers of the native government could not examine into their rent-rolls, or measure their lands, or make any inquiry into the value of the estates, except at the risk of open rebellion. They had always a number of armed and brave retainers, ready to support them in any enterprise; and the amount was easily increased; for in India there is seldom any lack of loose characters, ready to fight for the sake of plunder alone.*

The talookdars were mostly the hereditary representatives of Rajpoot clans; but some were the heads of new families (Hindoo or Mohammedan), sprung from government officials, whose local authority had enabled them to acquire a holding of this description. The term "talookdar" means holder of a talook, or collection of villages, and, like that of zemindar (as used in Bengal), implied no right of property in the villages on behalf of which the talookdar engaged to pay the state a certain sum, and from which he realised a somewhat larger one, which constituted his remuneration. In fact, the property in the soil was actually vested in the village communities; who "are," says Mr. Gubbins, "the only proprietors of the soil; and they value this right of property in the land above all earthly treasure."†

Over these talookdars there were government officers (with whom they have often been confounded), and who, under the title of Nazims or Chukladars, annually farmed from government the revenues of large tracts of country for a certain fixed payment; all that they could squeeze out in excess being their own profit. "These men, from the necessities of their position, were," says Carre Tucker, "the greatest tyrants and oppressors imaginable. Backed by artillery, and the armed force of government, it was their business to rack-rent the country, extracting, within the year of their lease, all that they possibly could; whilst landholders resisted their exactions by force of arms. A constant war was thus carried on, and the revenue payments varied according to the relative strength of the nazim and the landowners. To avoid such contests, and obtain the privilege of paying a fixed sum direct into the government treasury, many of the talookdars would bid for the farm of their own part of the country. Such men, while acting as lord-lieutenants, would of course use their delegated authority to consolidate their influence over their own clan and tenantry, and also to usurp rights over independent village communities." This system led to the most cruel oppression; but it was supported by the ministers and courtiers of the king at Lucknow, as leading to an annual repetition of presents and bribes, without which no candidate could hope to obtain investiture as nazim or chukladar.‡

The government, not content with abolishing this manifest evil, attempted to revolutionise, at a stroke, the whole state of society, by sweeping aside the entire class of chiefs and barons, with the incidents of their feudal tenure, and making the revenue settlement with the village communities and smaller holders. Hereditary rights, unquestioned during successive generations, were confounded with those exercised by the revenue farmers *ex officio*, and the settlement officers were desired to deal with the proprietary coparcenaries which were believed to exist in Oude, and not to suffer the interposition of middlemen, such as talookdars, farmers of the revenue, and such like. The claims of these, if they had any tenable ones, might be, it was added, more conveniently considered at a future period.

Nothing could be more disheartening to the great landowners than this indefinite adjournment of any consideration of their claims; which, in effect, acted like a decree of confiscation, with a distant and very slight chance of ultimate restitution. It was quite evident that the motive of the measure was expediency, and that the government had, as stated by the *Times*,

* Sleeman's *Oude*, vol. ii., pp. 1, 2.

† Gubbins' *Mutinies in Oudh*, p. 61.

‡ *Letter on Oudh and its Talookdars*, p. 2.

"a natural leaning in favour of the peasant cultivators, to the detriment of the warlike and turbulent chiefs," whom it was thought politic to put down; and the plan of ignoring their ancient possessions had the additional advantage of bringing their manorial dues, averaging from ten to twenty per cent. on the village assessment, into the public exchequer.

The summary settlement in Oude too far resembled that which had been previously carried through, with a high hand, in the North-West Provinces, concerning which much evidence has recently been made public. Mr. H. S. Boulderson, a Bengal civilian, engaged in establishing the revenue settlement of 1844, declares, that whether the talookdars in Oude experienced, or only anticipated, the same dealings from our government which the talookdars in the North-West Provinces received, they must have had a strong motive to dread our rule. "The 'confiscation' which has been proclaimed against them—whether it really means confiscation, or something else—could not be more effectually destructive to whatever rights they possessed, than the disgraceful injustice by which the talookdars of the North-West Provinces were extinguished." He asserts, that the settlement involved an utter inversion of the rights of property; and that the commissioners, in dealing with what they termed "the patent right of talookdaree," and which even they acknowledged to be an hereditary right which had descended for centuries, treated it as a privilege dependent on the pleasure of government, and assumed the authority of distributing at pleasure the profits arising out of the limitation of their own demand.*

The opinion of Sir William Sleeman has been already quoted concerning the treatment which the landed proprietors had received in the half of Oude annexed by the British government in 1801, and now included in the North-West Provinces. By his testimony, the measures, and the men who enforced them, were equally obnoxious to the native chiefs and talookdars; being resolved on favouring the village communities, to the exclusion of every kind of vested interest between them and the state treasury. Sir William states—

"In the matter of discourtesy to the native gentry, I can only say that Robert Martin Bird insulted them whenever he had the opportunity of doing so; and that Mr. Thomason was too apt to imitate him in this, as in other things. Of course their example was followed by too many of their followers and admirers. * * * It has always struck me that Mr. Thomason, in his system, did all he could to discourage the growth of a middle and upper class on the land—the only kind of property on which a good upper and middle class could be sustained in the present state of society in India. His village republics, and the ryotwar system of Sir Thomas Munro at Madras, had precisely the same tendency to subdivide minutely property in land, and reduce all landholders to the common level of impoverishment. * * * Mr. Thomason would have forced his village republics upon any new country or jungle that came under his charge, and thereby rendered improvement impossible. * * * He would have put the whole under our judicial courts, and have thereby created a class of pettifogging attornies, to swallow up all the surplus produce of the land. * * * Mr. Thomason, I am told, systematically set aside all the landed aristocracy of the country as a set of *middlemen*, superfluous and mischievous. The only part of India in which I have seen a middle and higher class maintained upon the land, is the moderately settled districts of the Saugor and Nerbudda territories; and there is no part of India where our government and character are so much beloved and respected."†

Mr. Gubbins makes some very important admissions regarding the revenue system pursued in the North-West Provinces, and that subsequently attempted in Oude. "The pressure of the government demand is, in many districts, greatly too high. It is too high in Alighur, in Mynpoorie, in Boolundshuhur, and throughout the greater part of Rohilcund. The principle on which that settlement was made, was to claim, as the share of government, two-thirds of the nett rental. But the fraud and chicanery opposed to our revenue officers, caused them unwittingly to fix the demand at more than this share. In Oude, after repeated and most careful examination, I came unhesitatingly to the conclusion, that the government collector appropriated, if possible, the entire rent, and never professed to relinquish any part of it."‡ Of course, under a system which grasped at the *entire rent* of the soil, there could be no landlord class: a very short period of time would suffice for their extinction; and any so-called proprietary rights must, in due course, have also been annihilated.

No arguments in favour of the village system (excellent as this was in its place and degree), could justify the suppression of

* Minute on the Talookdaree cases, recorded on 2nd of April, 1844. Printed for private circulation in June, 1858; p. 19.

† Sleeman's *Oude*, vol. ii., p. 413. Letter to Mr. Colvin, dated "Lucknow, 28th December, 1853."

‡ Gubbins' *Mutinies in Oudh*. p. 73.

every other co-existing institution. But the projected change, even had it been unexceptionable in its tendency, was altogether too sudden: the village communities were not strong enough to feel safe in occupying the vantage-ground on which they were so unexpectedly placed; and many of them considered the rough-and-ready patriarchal sway of their chiefs but ill-exchanged for our harsh and unbending revenue system, and tedious and expensive law processes. Government erred grievously "in following supposed political and financial expediency, instead of ascertaining and maintaining existing rights in possession; and in supposing, that in the course of a very hurried assessment of revenue by officers, many of whom were inexperienced, it was possible to adjudicate properly difficult claims to former rights.* Lord Dalhousie's successor admits it to be too true, "that unjust decisions were come to by some of our local officers, in investigating and judging the titles of the landholders."† The natural consequence was, as stated by General Outram, that the landholders, having been "most unjustly treated under our settlement operations," and "smarting, as they were, under the loss of their lands," with hardly a dozen exceptions, sided against us, when they saw that "our rule was virtually at an end, the whole country overrun, and the capital in the hands of the rebel soldiery."‡ The yeomanry, whom we had prematurely attempted to raise to independence, followed the lead of their natural chiefs. All this might, it is alleged, have been prevented, had a fair and moderate assessment been made with the talookdar, wherever he had had clear possession for the legal limit of twelve years, together with a sub-settlement for the protection of the village communities and cultivators.§

Very contradictory opinions are entertained regarding the manner in which the British sepoys were affected by the annexation of Oude.

Mr. Gubbins admits, that when the mutinies commenced in the Bengal army, the talookdars in Oude were discontented and aggrieved; numbers of discharged soldiers were brooding over the recollection of their former license; and the inhabitants of the cities generally were impoverished and distressed; but the sepoys, he says, had benefited by the change of government, and were rejoicing in the encouragement given to the village communities at the expense of the talookdars. Thousands of sepoy families laid complaints of usurpation before the revenue officers, and "many hundreds of villages at once passed into their hands from those of the talooqdars! Whatever the talooqdar lost, the sepoy gained. No one had so great cause for gratulation as he."

The sepoys, although an exceptional class, had their own grievance, besides sharing in the general distrust and aversion entertained by the whole people at the idea of being brought under the jurisdiction of our civil courts; as well as at the introduction of the Company's opium monopoly, and the abkaree, or excise, on the retail sale of all spirituous liquors and intoxicating drugs, the consumption of which was very large throughout Oude, and especially among the soldiery.

Under the native government, the British sepoys enjoyed special and preferential advantages, their complaints being brought to its notice by the intervention of the resident. Each family made a point of having some connection in the British army, and, through him, laid their case before his commanding officer. The sepoy's petition was countersigned by the English colonel, and forwarded to the resident, by whom it was submitted to the king.|| This privilege was not recognised or named in any treaty or other engagement with the sovereign of Oude, nor could its origin be traced in any document recorded in the resident's office;¶ but it was in full operation at the time of our occupation of Oude; and had been, for a long term of years, the subject of continued discussion between successive residents and the native durbar.

Mr. Gubbins considers that the termination of this custom could not have produced disaffection among the sepoys, because but little redress was thereby procured by them. "Some trifling alleviation of the injury complained of, might be obtained; but that was all. That a sepoy plaintiff ever succeeded in wresting his village from the grasp of the oppressor, by aid of the British

* *Letter on Oudh and its Talookdars;* by H. Carre Tucker: p. 5.

† Despatch dated 31st March, 1858.—Parl. Papers on Oude (Commons), 20th May, 1858; p. 4.

‡ Despatch dated 8th March, 1858.—Parl. Papers, p. 1.

§ Carre Tucker's *Letter*, p. 7.

|| Gubbins' *Mutinies in Oudh*, p. 64.

¶ Sleeman's *Oude*, vol. i., p. 289.

resident, I never heard; if it ever occurred, the cases must have been isolated and extraordinary."*

The evidence of Sir W. Sleeman (whose authority is very high on this subject, in his double character of officer and resident) is directly opposed to that above cited. He thought the privilege very important; but desired its abolition because it had been greatly abused, and caused intolerable annoyance to the native government. The military authorities, he said, desired its continuance; for though the honest and hard-working sepoys usually cared nothing about it, a large class of the idle and unscrupulous considered it as a lottery, in which they might sometimes draw a prize, or obtain leave of absence, as the same sepoy has been known to do repeatedly for ten months at a time, on the pretext of having a case pending in Oude. Consequently, they endeavoured to impress their superiors with the idea, "that the fidelity of the whole native army" depended upon the maintenance and extension of this right of appeal. And the privilege was gradually extended, until it included all the regular, irregular, and local corps paid by the British government, with the native officers and sepoys of contingents employed in, and paid by, native states, who were drafted into them from the regular corps of our army up to a certain time—the total number amounting to between 50,000 and 60,000. At one period, the special right of the sepoys to the resident's intervention extended to their most distant relatives; but at the earnest entreaty of the native administration, it was restricted to their wives, fathers, mothers, brothers, and sisters. "In consequence, it became a common custom with them to lend or sell their names to more remote relations, or to persons not related to them at all. A great many bad characters have, in this way, deprived men of lands which their ancestors had held in undisputed right of property for many generations or centuries; for the court, to save themselves from the importunity of the residency, has often given orders for the claimant being put in possession of the lands without due inquiry, or any inquiry at all."†

The use or abuse of the privilege depended chiefly on the character of the resident; and that it was occasionally shamefully abused, is a fact established, we are told, by the residency records.

"If the resident happens to be an impatient, overbearing man, he will often frighten the durbar and its courts, or local officers, into a hasty decision, by which the rights of others are sacrificed for the native officers and sepoys; and if he be at the same time an unscrupulous man, he will sometimes direct that the sepoy shall be put in possession of what he claims, in order to relieve himself from his importunity, or from that of his commanding officer, without taking the trouble to inform himself of the grounds on which the claim is founded. Of all such errors there are, unhappily, too many instances recorded in the resident's office."‡

Sir W. Sleeman adduces repeated instances of sepoys being put in possession of landed estates, to which they had no rightful claim, by the British government, at the cost of many lives; and quotes, as an illustration of the notorious partiality with which sepoy claims were treated, the case of a shopkeeper at Lucknow, who purchased a cavalry uniform, and by pretending to be an invalid British trooper, procured the signature of the brigadier commanding the troops in Oude, to numerous petitions, which were sent for adjustment to the durbar through the resident. This procedure he continued for fifteen years; and, to crown all, succeeded in obtaining, by the aid of government, forcible possession of a landed estate, to which he had no manner of right. Soon after, he sent in a petition stating that he had been in turn ejected, and four of his relations killed by the dispossessed proprietor. Thereupon an inquiry took place, and the whole truth came out. The King of Oude truly observed, with regard to this affair:—"If a person known to thousands in the city of Lucknow is able, for fifteen years, to carry on such a trade successfully, how much more easy must it be for people in the country, not known to any in the city, to carry it on!"§

On one occasion, no less than thirty lives were lost in attempting to enforce an award in favour of a British sepoy. On another, a sepoy came to the assistant-resident (Captain Shakespear), clamouring for justice, and complaining that no notice of his petition had been taken by the native government. On being questioned, he admitted that no less than forty persons had been seized, and were in prison, on his requisition.

* Gubbins' *Mutinies in Oudh*, p. 65.
† Sleeman's *Oude*, vol. i., pp. 288—292.
‡ *Ibid.*, p. 289.

§ Letter of the King of Oude to the resident; 16th June, 1836.—Sleeman's *Journey through Oude*, vol. i., p. 286.

As to punishing the sepoys for preferring fraudulent claims, that was next to impossible, both on account of the endless trouble which it involved, and the difficulty, if not impossibility, of procuring a conviction from a court-martial composed of native officers; the only alternative being, to lay the case before the governor-general. The natural consequence was, that the sepoys became most importunate, untruthful, and unscrupulous in stating the circumstances of their claims, or the grounds of their complaints.*

It is impossible to read the revelations of Colonel Sleeman on this subject, without feeling that the British authorities themselves aggravated the disorganisation in the native administration, which was the sole plea for annexation. At the same time, it is no less clear, that the injustice perpetrated on behalf of the sepoys, was calculated to exercise a most injurious effect on their morals and discipline. The unmerited success often obtained by fraud and collusion, was both a bad example and a cause of disgust to the honest and scrupulous, on whom the burthen of duties fell, while their comrades were enjoying themselves in their homes, on leave of absence, obtained for the purpose of prosecuting unreasonable or false claims. Of the honest petitioners, few obtained what they believed to be full justice; and where one was satisfied, four became discontented. Another cause of disaffection arose when it was found necessary to check the growing evil, by decreeing that the privilege of urging claims through the resident should cease when native officers and sepoys were transferred from active service to the invalid establishment.

Altogether, the result of making the sepoys a privileged class (in this, as in so many other ways), was equally disastrous to their native and European superiors. Colonel Sleeman says, that the British recruits were procured chiefly from the Byswara and Banoda divisions of Oude, whose inhabitants vaunt the quality of the water for *tempering* soldiers, as we talk of the water of Damascus for tempering sword-blades. "The air and water of Malwa," it is popularly said, "may produce as good trees and crops as those of Oude, but cannot produce as good soldiers." They are described as never appearing so happy as when fighting in earnest with swords, spears, and matchlocks, and consequently are not much calculated for peaceful citizens; but the British sepoys who came home on furlough to their families (as they were freely permitted to do in time of peace, not only to petition the native government, but also ostensibly to visit their families, on reduced pay and allowances), were the terror, even in the midst of this warlike population, of their non-privileged neighbours and co-sharers in the land.

The partiality shown them did not prevent "the diminished attachment felt by the sepoys for their European officers" from becoming an established fact; and officers, when passing through Oude in their travels or sporting excursions, have of late years generally complained, that they received less civility from villages in which British invalids or furlough sepoys were located, than from any others; and that if anywhere treated with actual disrespect, such sepoys were generally found to be either the perpetrators or instigators.†

The evidence collected in preceding pages, seems to place beyond dispute, that the annexation of Oude, if it did not help to light the flames of mutiny, has fanned and fed them by furnishing the mutineers with refuge and co-operation in the territories which were ever in close alliance with us when they formed an independent kingdom; but which we, by assuming dominion over them on the sole plea of rescuing the inhabitants from gross misgovernment, have changed into a turbulent and insurrectionary province.

The metamorphosis was not accomplished by the deposition of the dynasty of Wajid Ali Shah. Indian princes generally, might, and naturally would, view with alarm so flagrant a violation of treaties, and of the first principles of the law of nations; but the Hindoos of Oude could have felt little regret for the downfall of a government essentially sectarian and unjust. The kings of Oude, unlike the majority of Mohammedans in India, were Sheiahs;‡ and so bigoted and exclusive, that no Sheiah could be sentenced to death at Lucknow for the murder even of a Sonnite, much less for that of a Hindoo. According to Colonel Sleeman, it was not only the law, but the everyday practice, that if a Hindoo murdered a Hindoo, and consented to become a Mussulman, he could not be executed for

* Sleeman's *Journey through Oude*, vol. i., p. 292.
† *Ibid.*, vol. i., p. 289.
‡ See *Indian Empire*, vol. i., p. 62.

the crime, even though convicted and sentenced.*

Under such a condition of things, it is at least highly probable, that a rigidly impartial and tolerant administration would have been a welcome change to the Hindoo population. That it has proved the very reverse, is accounted for by the aggressive measures initiated by the new government, and the inefficient means by which their enforcement was attempted.

The latter evil was, to a certain extent, unavoidable. The Russian war deprived India of the European troops, which Lord Dalhousie deemed needful for the annexation of Oude: but this does not account for the grave mistake made in raising a contingent of 12,000 men, for the maintenance of the newly-annexed country, almost entirely from the disbanded native army. These levies, with half-a-dozen regular corps, formed the whole army of occupation.

Sir Henry Lawrence foresaw the danger; and in September, 1856, seven months before the commencement of the mutiny, he urged, that some portion of the Oude levies should change places with certain of the Punjab regiments then stationed on the Indus. Oude, he said, had long been the Alsatia of India—the resort of the dissipated and disaffected of every other state, and especially of deserters from the British ranks. It had been pronounced hazardous to employ the Seiks in the Punjab in 1849; and the reason assigned for the different policy now pursued in Oude was, that the former kingdom had been conquered, and the latter "fell in peace." Sir Henry pointed out the fallacy of this argument, and the materials for mischief which still remained in Oude, which he described as containing "246 forts, besides innumerable smaller strongholds, many of them sheltered within thick jungles. In these forts are 476 guns. Forts and guns should all be in the hands of government, or the forts should be razed. Many a foolish fellow has been urged on to his own ruin by the possession of a paltry fort, and many a paltry mud fort has repulsed British troops."†

The warning was unheeded. The government, though right in their desire to protect and elevate the village communities, were unjust in the sweeping and indiscriminating measures which they adopted in favour of the villagers, and for the increase in the public revenue, anticipated from the setting aside of the feudal claims of the so-called middlemen. Before attempting to revolutionise the face of society, it would have been only politic to provide unquestionable means of overawing the opposition which might naturally be expected from so warlike, not to say turbulent, a class as the Rajpoot chiefs.

Had men of the Lawrence school been sent to superintend the "absorption" of Oude, it is probable they might have seen the danger, and suggested measures of conciliation; but, on the contrary, it is asserted, that the European officials employed were almost all young and inexperienced men, and that their extreme opinions, and the corruption of their native subordinates, aggravated the unpopularity of the system they came to administer. Personal quarrels arose between the leading officers; and the result was a want of vigour and co-operation in their public proceedings.‡

Meantime, the obtainment of Oude was a matter of high-flown congratulation between the home and Indian authorities. The Company have changed their opinion since;§ but, at the time, they accepted the measure as lawful, expedient, and very cleverly carried out. Far from being disappointed at the want of enthusiasm evinced by the people in not welcoming their new rulers as deliverers, their passive submission (in accordance with the proclamations of Wajid Ali Shah) called forth, from the Court of Directors, an expression of "lively emotions of thankfulness and pleasure," at the peaceable manner in which "an expanse of territory embracing an area of nearly 25,000 square miles, and containing 5,000,000 inhabitants, has passed from its native prince to the Queen of England, without the expenditure of a drop of blood, and almost without a murmur."||

Upon the assumption of the government of Oude, a branch electric telegraph was commenced to connect Cawnpoor and Lucknow. In eighteen working days it was completed, including the laying of a cable,

* Sleeman's *Oude*, vol. i., p. 135.

† Article on "Army Reform;" by Sir H. Lawrence.—*Calcutta Review* for September, 1856.

‡ See Letter signed "Index," dated "Calcutta, December 9th, 1857."—*Times*, January 15th, 1858.

§ See Despatch of the Secret Committee of the Court of Directors, 19th April, 1858.—Parl. Papers, 7th May, 1858; p. 4.

|| Despatch dated December, 1856.—*Oude Blue Book* for 1856; p. 288.

6,000 feet in length, across the Ganges. On the morning of the 1st of March, Lord Dalhousie (who on that day resigned his office) put to General Outram the significant question—"Is all quiet in Oude?" The reply, "All is quiet in Oude," greeted Lord Canning on his arrival in Calcutta.

On the previous day, a farewell letter had been written to the King of Oude by the retiring governor-general, expressing his satisfaction that the friendship which had so long existed between the Hon. East India Company and the dynasty of Wajid Ali Shah, should have daily become more firmly established. "There is no doubt," he adds, "that Lord Canning will, in the same manner as I have done, strengthening and confirming this friendship, bear in mind and give due consideration to the treaties and engagements which are to exist for ever."*

It is difficult to understand what diplomatic purpose was to be served by this reference to the eternal duration of treaties which had been declared null and void, and engagements proffered by one party, which the other had at all hazards persisted in rejecting; or why Lord Dalhousie, so clear, practical, and upright in his general character, should seem to have acted so unlike himself in all matters connected with what may be termed his foreign policy.

It must not, however, be forgotten, that that policy, in all its circumstances, was sanctioned and approved, accepted and rewarded, by the East India Company. Lord Dalhousie's measures were consistent throughout; and he enjoyed the confidence and support of the directors during the whole eight years of his administration, in a degree to which few, if any, of his predecessors ever attained. It was the unqualified approval of the home authorities that rendered the annexation policy the prominent feature of a system which the people of India, of every creed, clime, and tongue, looked upon as framed for the express purpose of extinguishing all native sovereignty and rank. And, in fact, the measures lately pursued are scarcely explicable on any other ground. The democratic element is, no doubt, greatly on the increase in England; yet our institutions and our prejudices are monarchical and aristocratic: and nothing surprises our Eastern fellow-subjects more, than the deference and courtesy paid by all ranks in the United Kingdom, to rajahs and nawabs, who, in their hereditary principalities, had met—as many of them aver—with little civility, and less justice, at the hands of the representatives of the East India Company.

Yet, it was not so much a system as a want of system, which mainly conduced to bring about the existing state of things. The constant preponderance of expenditure above income, and an ever-present sense of precariousness, have been probably the chief reasons why the energies of the Anglo-Indian government have been, of late years, most mischievously directed to degrading kings, chiefs, nobles, gentry, priests, and landowners of various degrees, to one dead level of poverty—little above pauperism. We have rolled, by sheer brute force, an iron grinder over the face of Hindoo society—crushed every lineament into a disfigured mass—squeezed from it every rupee that even torture could extract; and lavished the money, thus obtained, on a small white oligarchy and an immense army of mercenary troops, who were believed to be ready, at any moment, to spread fire and the sword wherever any opposition should be offered to the will of the paramount power, whose salt they ate.

We thought the sepoys would always keep down the native chiefs, and, when they were destroyed, the people; and we did not anticipate the swift approach of a time when we should cry to the chiefs and people to help us to extinguish the incendiary flames of our own camp, and to wrench the sword from the hands in which we had so vauntingly placed it.

In our moment of peril, the defection of the upper classes of Hindoostan was "almost universal." But surely it is no wonder that they should have shown so little attachment to our rule, when it is admitted, even by the covenanted civil service, that they "have not much to thank us for."

Throughout British India, several native departments are declared to have been "grossly underpaid," particularly the police service, into which it has been found difficult to get natives of good family to enter at all. In revenue offices, they were formerly better paid than at present. The general result of our proceedings has been, that at the time of the mutiny, "the native

* Letter, vouched for as a true translation by Robert Wilberforce Bird, and printed in a pamphlet entitled *Case of the King of Oude;* by Mr. John Davenport: August 27th, 1856.

gentry were daily becoming more reduced, were pinched by want of means, and were therefore discontented."*

It is difficult to realise the full hardship of their position. Here were men who would have occupied, or at least have had the chance of occupying, the highest positions of the state under a native government, and who were accustomed to look to the service of the sovereign as the chief source of honourable and lucrative employment, left, frequently with no alternative but starvation or the acceptance of a position and a salary under foreign masters, that their fathers would have thought suitable only for their poorest retainers. Not one of them, however ancient his lineage, however high his attainments, could hope to be admitted within the charmed circle of the covenanted civil service, as the equal of the youngest writer, or even in the army, to take rank with a new-fledged ensign.

The expenses of an Asiatic noble are enormous. Polygamy is costly in its incidentals; and the head of a great family is looked to, not only for the maintenance of his own wives and children, in a style proportionate to their birth, but also of those of his predecessors. The misery which the levelling policy produced, was severely felt by the pensioners and dependents of the fallen aristocracy, by the aged and the sick, by women and children. And this latter fact explains a marked feature in the present rebellion; namely, the number of women who have played a leading part in the insurrection. The Ranee of Jhansi, and her sister, with other Hindoo princesses of less note, have evinced an amount of ability and resolve far beyond that of their countrymen; and the cause of disaffection with almost all of these, has been the setting aside of their hereditary rights of succession and of adoption. They have viewed the sudden refusal of the British government to sanction what they had previously encouraged, as a most faithless and arbitrary procedure; and many chiefs, whose hostility is otherwise unaccountable, will probably, like the chief of Nargoond, prove to have been incited to join the mutineers chiefly, if not exclusively, by this particular grievance.

A branch of the annexation question, in which the violation of rights of succession is also a prominent feature, yet remains to be noticed—namely, the

Resumption of Rent-free Lands; whereby serious disaffection has been produced in the minds of a large class of dispossessed proprietors. All rightful tenure of this kind is described, in the regulations of the East India Company, as based upon a well-known provision "of the ancient law of India, by which the ruling power is entitled to a certain proportion of the annual produce of every beegah (acre) of land, excepting in cases in which that power shall have made a temporary or permanent alienation of its right to such proportion of the produce, or shall have agreed to receive, instead of that proportion, a specific sum annually, or for a term of years, or in perpetuity."†

Both Hindoo and Mohammedan sovereigns frequently made over part, or the whole, of the public revenue of a village, or even of a district, to one of their officers; they often assigned it in jaghire for the maintenance of a certain number of troops, or gratuitously for life, as a reward for service done; and sometimes in perpetuity. In the latter case, the alienation was more complete than that practised in the United Kingdom;‡ for here titles and estate escheat to the state on the death of the last legal representative of a family; but, among the Hindoos, such lapse never, or most rarely occurs, since all the males marry, in childhood generally, several wives; and their law vests rights of succession and adoption in the widows of the deceased. These rights were acknowledged equally by Hindoo and Moslem rulers—by the Peishwa of Poona, and the Nawab-vizier of Oude; the only difference being, that in the event of adoption, a larger nuzzurana, or tributary offering, was expected on accession, than if the heir had been a son by birth: in other words, the legacy duty was higher in the one case than the other.

"Enam," or "gift," is the term commonly given to all gratuitous grants, whether temporary or in perpetuity—whether to individuals, or for religious, charitable, or educational purposes: but it is more strictly applicable to endowments of the latter description; in which case, the amount of state-tribute transferred was frequently very considerable, and always in perpetuity. "A large proportion of the grants to individuals," Mountstuart Elphinstone writes,

* Gubbins' *Mutinies in Oudh*, pp. 56, 57.

† Regulation xxxi., of 1803.

‡ For instance, in the alienation of a part of the revenues of the post-office, and other public departments; enacted in the case of certain noble families.

"are also in perpetuity, and are regarded as among the most secure forms of private property; but the gradual increase of such instances of liberality, combined with the frequency of forged deeds of gift, sometimes induces the ruler to resume the grants of his predecessors, and to burden them with heavy taxes. When these are laid on transfers by sales, or even by succession, they are not thought unjust; but total resumption, or the permanent levy of a fixed rate, is regarded as oppressive."*

During the early years of the Company's rule, the perpetual enam tenures were sedulously respected; but as the supreme government grew richer in sovereignty, and poorer in purse (for the increase of expenditure always distanced that of revenue), the collectors began to look with a covetous eye on the freeholders. They argued, truly enough, that a great many of the titles to land were fraudulent, or had been fraudulently obtained; and in such cases, where grounds of suspicion existed, any government would have been in duty bound to make inquiry into the circumstances of the original acquisition.

But instead of investigating certain cases, a general inquiry was instituted into the whole of them; the principle of which was, to cast on every enamdar the burthen of proving his right—a demand which, of course, many of the ancient holders must have found it impossible to fulfil. The lapse of centuries, war, fire, or negligence might, doubtless, have occasioned the destruction of the deeds. Some of the oldest were, we know, engraven on stone and copper, in long-forgotten characters; and few of the commissioners could question the witnesses in the modern Bengalee or Hindoostani, much less decipher Pali or Sanscrit.

A commission of inquiry was instituted in Bengal in 1836, "to ascertain the grounds on which claims to exemption from the payment of revenue were founded, to confirm those for which valid titles were produced, and to bring under assessment those which were held without authority."† In theory, this sounds moderate, if not just; in practice, it is said to have proved the very reverse, and to have cast a blight over the whole of Lower Bengal. The expense of the commission was, of course, enormous; and even in a pecuniary sense, the profit reaped by government could not compensate for the ruin and distress caused by proceedings which are asserted to have been so notoriously unjust, that "some distinguished civil servants" refused to take any part in them.‡

Mr. Edmonstone, Mr. Tucker, and a few of the ablest directors at the East India House, protested, but in vain, against the resumption laws, which were acted upon for many years. The venerable Marquess Wellesley, a few weeks before his decease (July 30th, 1842), wrote earnestly to the Earl of Ellenborough (then governor-general), as follows:—

"I am concerned to hear that some inquiry has been commenced respecting the validity of some of the tenures under the permanent settlement of the land revenue. This is a most vexatious, and, surely, not a prudent measure. Here the maxim of sound ancient wisdom applies most forcibly—'*Quieta non movere.*' We ancient English settlers in Ireland have felt too severely the hand of Strafford, in a similar act of oppression, not to dread any similar proceeding."

Strafford, however, never attempted anything in Ireland that could be compared with the sweeping confiscation which is described as having been carried on in Bengal, where "little respect was paid to the principles of law, either as recognised in England or in India;" and where, "it is said, one commissioner dispossessed, in a single morning, no less than two hundred proprietors."§

In the Chittagong district, an insurrection was nearly caused by "the wholesale sweeping away of the rights of the whole population;" and in the Dacca district, the commission likewise operated very injuriously.||

The general alarm and disaffection excited by these proceedings, so materially affected the public tranquillity, that the Court of Directors was at length compelled to interfere, and the labours of the Bengal commission were fortunately brought to a close some years before the mutiny.¶

The enam commission appointed for the Deccan, was no less harsh and summary in

* Quoted in evidence before Colonization Committee of House of Commons, of 1858.—Fourth Report, published 28th July, 1858; p. 36.

† Statement of the East India Company.

‡ Fourth Report of Colonization Committee, p. 47.

§ *Quarterly Review*, 1858.—Article on "British India;" attributed to Mr. Layard: p. 257.

|| See Second Report of Colonization Committee of 1858; p. 60.

¶ *Quarterly Review*, 1858; p. 257.

its proceedings, the results of which are now stated to afford the people their "first and gravest cause of complaint against the government."*

Due investigation ought to have been made in 1818, when the dominions of the Peishwa first became British territory, into the nature of the grants, whether hereditary or for life; and also to discover whether, as was highly probable, many fraudulent claims might not have been established under the weak and corrupt administration of the last native ruler, Bajee Rao. All this might have been done in perfect conformity with the assurance given by the tranquilliser of the Deccan (Mountstuart Elphinstone), that "all wuttuns and enams (birthrights and rent-free lands), annual stipends, religious and charitable establishments, would be protected. The proprietors were, however, warned that they would be called upon to show their sunnuds (deeds of grant), or otherwise prove their title."†

Instead of doing this, the government suffered thirty years to elapse—thus giving the proprietors something of a prescriptive right to their holdings, however acquired; and the Court of Directors, as late as September, 1846, expressly declared, that the principle on which they acted, was to allow enams (or perpetual alienations of public revenue, as contradistinguished from surinjams, or temporary ones) to pass to heirs, as of right, without need of the assent of the paramount power, provided the adoption were regular according to Hindoo law.‡

The rights of widows were likewise distinctly recognised, until the "absorption" policy came into operation; and then investigations into certain tenures were instituted, which paved the way for a general enam commission for the whole Bombay presidency; by which all enamdars were compelled to prove possession for a hundred years, as an indispensable preliminary to being confirmed in the right to transmit their estates to lineal descendants—the future claims of widows and adopted sons being quietly ignored.

The commission was composed, not of judicial officers, but of youths of the civil service, and of captains and subalterns taken from their regiments, and selected principally on account of their knowledge of the Mahratta languages; while, at the head of the commission, was placed a captain of native infantry, thirty-five years of age.§

These inexperienced youths were, besides, naturally prejudiced in deciding upon cases in which they represented at once the plaintiff and the judge. The greater the ingenuity they displayed in upsetting claims, the greater their chance of future advancement. Every title disallowed, was so much revenue gained. Powers of search, such as were exercised by the French revolutionary committees, and by few others, were entrusted to them; and their agents, accompanied by the police, might at any time of the night or day, enter the houses of persons in the receipt of alienated revenue, or examine and seize documents, without giving either a receipt or list of those taken. The decisions of previous authorities were freely reversed; and titles admitted by Mr. Brown in 1847, were re-inquired into, and disallowed by Captain Cowper in 1855.||

An appeal against a resumptive decree might be laid before the privy council in London; and the rajah of Burdwan succeeded in obtaining the restoration of his lands by this means.¶ But to the poorer class of ousted proprietors, a revised verdict was unattainable. Few could afford to risk from five to ten thousand pounds in litigation against the East India Company. But, whatever their resources, it was making the evils of absentee sovereigntyship most severely and unwisely felt, to require persons, whose families had occupied Indian estates fifty to a hundred years and upwards, to produce their title-deeds in England; and to make little or no allowance for the various kinds of proof, which, duly weighed, were really more trustworthy, because less easily counterfeited, than any written documents.

The commissioners on whom so onerous a duty as the inquiry into rent-free tenures was imposed, ought at least to have been tried and approved men of high public character, who would neither hurry over cases by the score, nor suffer them to linger on in needless and most harassing delays; as the actual functionaries are accused of

* *Quarterly Review*, p. 259.

† Proclamation of Mr. Elphinstone; and instructions issued to collectors in 1818.

‡ Fourth Report of Colonization Committee, p. 35.

§ *Ibid.*

|| *Quarterly Review*, p. 258. Stated on the authority of "Correspondence relating to the Scrutiny of the revised Surinjam and Pension Lists." Printed for government. Bombay, 1856.

¶ Second Report of Colonization Committee, p. 9.

having done, according to their peculiar propensities. Perhaps it would have been better to have acted on altogether a different system, and acknowledged the claim established by many years of that undisturbed possession which is everywhere popularly looked upon as nine-tenths of the law; and, while recognising all in the positions in which we found them on the assumption of sovereignty, to have claimed from all, either a yearly subsidy or (in pursuance of the practice of native sovereigns) a succession duty. At least, we should thereby have avoided the expense and odium incurred by the institution of a tribunal, to which Lieutenant-governor Halliday's description of our criminal jurisdiction would seem to apply—viz., that it was "a lottery, in which, however, the best chances were with the criminal." On the outbreak of the rebellion, the resumption commission was brought suddenly to a close; its introduction into Guzerat (which had been previously contemplated) was entirely abandoned, and some of the confiscated estates were restored. But the distrust inspired by past proceedings will not easily be removed, especially as the feeling of ill-usage is aggravated by the fact, that in border villages belonging jointly to the Company and to Indian princes, the rent-free lands, on the side belonging to the former, have been resumed, while those on the latter remain intact.*

In the North-West Provinces, the government avoided incurring the stigma of allowing a prescriptive right of possession and transmission to take root through their neglect, by immediately making a very summary settlement. The writings of Sleeman, Raikes, Gubbins and others, together with the evidence brought before the colonization committee, tend to prove the now scarcely disputed fact, that the attempted revenue settlement of the North-West Provinces, and the sweeping away of the proprietary class as middlemen, has proved a failure. With few exceptions, the ancient proprietors, dispossessed of their estates by the revenue collectors, or by sales under decrees of civil courts, have taken advantage of the recent troubles to return, and have been suffered, and even encouraged, to do so by the ryots and small tenants, to whom their dispossession would have appeared most advantageous.†

A number of cases of alleged individual injustice towards the rajahs and talookdars, were collected, and stated, in circumstantial detail, in a minute laid before Mr. Thomason (the lieutenant-governor of Agra in 1844), by Mr. Boulderson, a member of the Board of Revenue; who eventually resigned his position, sooner than be associated in proceedings which he believed to be essentially unjust. His chief ground of complaint was, that the board, instead of instituting a preliminary inquiry into what the rights of talookdars and other proprietors really were, acted upon *à priori* arguments of what they must be; and never, in any one of the many hundred resumptions made at their recommendation, deemed the proofs on which the proceedings rested, worthy of a moment's inquiry.

After reciting numerous instances of dispossession of proprietors who had held estates for many years, and laid out a large amount of capital in their improvement, the writer adds:—

"I have in vain endeavoured, hitherto, to rouse the attention of my colleague and government to this virtual abolition of all law. * * * The respect of the native public I know to have been shaken to an inexpressible degree: they can see facts; and are not blinded by the fallacious reasonings and misrepresentations with which the board have clothed these subjects; and they wonder with amazement at the motives which can prompt the British government to allow their own laws—all laws which give security to property—to be thus belied and set aside. All confidence in property or its rights is shaken; and the villany which has been taught the people they will execute, and reward the government tenfold into their own bosom."‡

In a Preface, dated "London, 8th June, 1858," Mr. Boulderson states, that his minute "produced no effect in modifying or staying the proceedings" of the revenue board; and if "forwarded to England, as in due official course it should have been, it must have had as little effect upon the Hon. Court of Directors."

Even in the Punjab, the system pursued was a levelling one. Notwithstanding all that the Lawrences and their disciples did to mitigate its severity, and especially to conciliate the more powerful and aggrieved chiefs, the result is asserted to have been, to a great extent, the same there as in the Deccan: "the aristocracy and landed gentry who have escaped destruction by the settlement, have been ruined by the resumption of alienated land."§

Thus annexation and resumption, confiscation and absorption, have gone hand-in-

* *Quarterly Review*, p. 259. † *Ibid.*, p. 251.
‡ Minute on Talookdaree cases; by Mr. Boulderson.
§ *Quarterly Review* (July, 1858), p. 260.

hand, with a rapidity which would have been dangerous even had the end in view and the means of attainment been both unexceptionable. However justly acquired, the entire reorganisation of extensive, widely scattered, and, above all, densely populated territories, must always present difficulties which abstract rules arbitrarily enforced can never satisfactorily overcome.

The fifteen million inhabitants brought by Lord Dalhousie under the immediate government of the British Crown, were to be, from the moment of annexation, ruled on a totally different system: native institutions and native administrators were expected to give place, without a murmur, to the British commissioner and his subordinates; and the newly absorbed territory, whatever its history, the character of its population, its languages and customs, was to be "settled," without any references to these important antecedents, on the theory which found favour with the Calcutta council for the time being.

Many able officials, with much ready money, and a thoroughly efficient army to support them, were indispensable to carry through such a system. In the Punjab, these requisites were obtained at the expense of other provinces; and the picked men sent there, were even then so few in number and so overworked, that they scarcely had time for sleep or food. Their private purse often supplied a public want. Thus, James Abbott was sent by Sir Henry Lawrence to settle the Huzara district, which he did most effectually; going from valley to valley, gaining the confidence of all the tribes, and administering justice in the open air under the trees—looking, with his long grey beard on his breast, and his grey locks far down his shoulders, much more like an ancient patriarch than a deputy-commissioner. "Kâkâ," or "Uncle" Abbott, as the children called him (in return for the sweetmeats which he carried in readiness for them), took leave of the people in a very characteristic fashion, by inviting the entire population to a feast on the Nara hill, which lasted three nights and days; and he left Huzara with only a month's pay in his pocket, "having literally spent all his substance on the people." His successor, John Becher, ably fills his place, "living in a house with twelve doors, and all open to the people. * * * The result is, that the Huzara district, once famous for turbulence, is now about the quietest, happiest, and most loyal in the Punjab."* Of course, Kâkâ Abbott and his successor, much less their lamented head (Sir Henry Lawrence), cannot be taken as average specimens of their class. Such self-devotion is the exception, not the rule: it would be asking too much of human nature, to expect the entire civil service to adopt what Colonel Herbert Edwardes calls the Bahaduree (summer-house) system of administration, and keep their cutcherries open, not "from ten till four" by the regulation clock, but all day, and at any hour of the night that anybody chooses.† Neither can chief commissioners be expected, or even wished, to sacrifice their health as Sir Henry Lawrence did in the Punjab, where, amid all his anxieties for the welfare of the mass, he preserved his peculiar character of being pre-eminently the friend of the man that was down; battling with government for better terms for the deposed officials and depressed aristocracy, and caring even for thieves and convicts. He originated gaol reform; abolished the "night-chain," and other abominations; introduced in-door labour; and himself superintended the new measures—going from gaol to gaol, and rising even at midnight to visit the prisoners' barracks.‡

The manner in which the Punjab was settled is altogether exceptional: the men employed certainly were; so also was the large discretionary power entrusted to them. Elsewhere matters went on very differently. The civil service could not furnish an efficient magistracy for the old provinces, much less for the new; the public treasury could not satisfy the urgent and long reiterated demand for public works, canals to irrigate the land, roads to convey produce, and avert the scourge of famine, even from Bengal: how, then, could it spare ready money to build court-houses and gaols in its new possessions?

Like Aurungzebe, in the Deccan, we swept away existing institutions without being prepared to replace them, and thereby became the occasion of sufferings which we had assumed the responsibility of preventing. Thus, in territories under British government, the want of proper places of

* See the graphic description given by Colonel Herbert Edwardes, of Sir Henry Lawrence's old staff in the Punjab, previous to annexation.—Quoted in Raikes' *Revolt in the North-West Provinces*, p. 25.

† *Ibid.*, p. 29. ‡ *Ibid.*, p. 34.

confinement is alleged to be so great, that "prisoners of all classes are crammed together into a dungeon so small, that, when the sun goes down, they fight for the little space upon which only a few can lie during the weary night. Within one month, forty die of disease, produced by neglect, want of air, and filth. The rest, driven to despair, attempt an escape; twenty are shot down dead. Such is a picture—and not an imaginary picture—of the results of one of the most recent cases of annexation!"*

Even supposing the above to be an extreme, and, in its degree, an isolated case, yet one such narrative, circulated among the rebel ranks, would serve as a reason for a general breaking open of gaols, and as an incitement and excuse for any excesses on the part of the convicts, to whom, it will be remembered, some of the worst atrocities committed during the rebellion are now generally attributed.

In fact, the increase of territory, of late years, has been (as the Duke of Wellington predicted it would be) greatly in excess of our resources. Annex we might, govern we could not; for, in the words of Prince Metternich, we had not "the material."† That is, we had not the material on which alone we choose to rely. Native agency we cannot indeed dispense with: we could not hold India, or even Calcutta, a week without it; but we keep it down on the lowest steps of the ladder so effectually, that men of birth, talent, or susceptibility, will serve us only when constrained by absolute poverty. They shun the hopeless dead-level which the service of their country is now made to offer them.

Our predecessors in power acted upon a totally different principle. Their title was avowedly that of the sword; yet they delegated authority to the conquered race, with a generosity which puts to shame our exclusiveness and distrust; the more so because it does not appear that their confidence was ever betrayed.

Many of the ablest and most faithful servants of the Great Moguls were Hindoos. The Moslem knew the *prestige* of ancient lineage, and the value of native ability and acquaintance with the resources of the country too well, to let even bigotry stand in the way of their employment.

* *Quarterly Review* (July, 1858), p. 273.

† Quoted by Mr. Layard, in a Lecture delivered at St. James's Hall, Piccadilly, on his return from India, May 11th, 1858.

The command of the imperial armies was repeatedly intrusted to Rajpoot generals; and the dewans (chancellors of the exchequer) were usually Brahmins: the famous territorial arrangements of Akber are inseparably associated with the name of Rajah Todar Mul; and probably, if we had availed ourselves of the aid of native financiers, and made it worth their while to serve us well, our revenue settlements might have been ere now satisfactorily arranged. If Hindoos were found faithful to a Moslem government, why should they not be so to a Christian one, which has the peculiar advantage of being able to balance the two great antagonistic races, by employing each, so as to keep the other in check? Of late, we seem to have been trying to unite them, by giving them a common cause of complaint, and by marking the subordinate position of native officials more offensively than ever. They are accused of corruption—so were the Europeans: let the remedy employed in the latter case be tried in the former, and the result will be probably the same. The need of increased salary is much greater in the case of the native official. Let the government give him the means of supporting himself and his family, and add a prospect of promotion: it will then be well served.

By the present system we proscribe the higher class, and miserably underpay the lower. The result is unsatisfactory to all parties, even to the government; which, though it has become aware of the necessity of paying Europeans with liberality, still withholds from the native "the fair day's wage for the fair day's work." Latterly, the Europeans may have been in some cases overpaid; but the general error seems to have lain, in expecting too much from them; the amount of writing required by the Company's system, being a heavy addition to their labours, especially in the newly annexed territories. The natural consequence has been, that while a certain portion of the civilians, with the late governor-general at their head, lived most laboriously, and devoted themselves wholly to the duties before them; others, less zealous, or less capable, shrunk back in alarm at the prospect before them, and, yielding to the influences of climate and of luxury, fell into the hands of interested subordinates—signed the papers presented by their clerks, and, in the words of their severest censor, "amused themselves, and kept a servant to wash each separate toe."*

Under cover of their names, corruption and extortion has been practised to an almost incredible extent. Witness the exposure of the proceedings of provincial courts, published in 1849, by a Bengal civilian, of twenty-one years' standing, under the title of *Revelations of an Orderly*.

An attempt has been made to remedy the insufficient number of civilians, by taking military men from their regiments, and employing them in diplomatic and administrative positions; that is to say, the Indian authorities have tried the Irishman's plan of lengthening the blanket, by cutting off one end and adding it to the other.

The injurious effect which this practice is said to have exercised on the army, is noticed in the succeeding section.

The State of the Indian Army, and the alleged Causes of the Disorganisation and Disaffection of the Bengal Sepoys, remain to be considered. The origin of the native army, and the various phases of its progress, have been described in the earlier chapters of this work. We have seen how the restless Frenchman, Dupleix, raised native levies, and disciplined them in the European fashion at Pondicherry;† and how these were called sepoys (from *sipahi*, Portuguese for soldier), in contradistinction to the *topasses* (or hat-wearers); that is to say, to the natives of Portuguese descent, and the Eurasians, or half-castes, of whom small numbers, disciplined and dressed in the European style, were entertained by the East India Company, to guard their factories. Up to this period, the policy of the Merchant Adventurers had been essentially commercial and defensive; but the French early manifested a political and aggressive spirit. Dupleix read with remarkable accuracy the signs of the times, and understood the opportunity for the aggrandisement of his nation, offered by the rapidly increasing disorganisation of the Mogul empire, and the intestine strife which attended the assertion of independence by usurping governors and tributary princes. He began to take part in the quarrels of neighbouring potentates; and the English levied a native soldiery, and followed his example.

The first engagement of note in which the British sepoys took part, was at the capture of Devicotta, in 1748, when they made an orderly advance with a platoon of Europeans, as a storming party, under Robert Clive. Three years later, under the same leader, a force of 200 Europeans and 300 sepoys, marched on, regardless of the superstitions of their countrymen, amid thunder and lightning, to besiege Arcot; and having succeeded in taking the place, they gallantly and successfully defended it against an almost overwhelming native force, supported by French auxiliaries.

The augmentation in the number of the sepoys became very rapid in proportion to that of the European troops. The expedition with which Clive and Watson sailed from Madras in 1756, to recapture Calcutta from Surajah Dowlah, consisted of 900 Europeans and 1,500 natives.

The total military force maintained by the English and French on the Madras coast was at this time nearly equal, each comprising about 2,000 Europeans and 10,000 natives. The British European force was composed of H. M.'s 39th foot, with a small detail of Royal Artillery attached to serve the regimental field-pieces; the Madras European regiment, and a strong company of artillery. The sepoys were supplied with arms and ammunition from the public stores, but were clothed in the native fashion, commanded by native officers, and very rudely disciplined.

At the commencement of the year 1757, Clive organised a battalion of sepoys, consisting of some three or four hundred men, carefully selected; and he not only furnished them with arms and ammunition, but clothed, drilled, and disciplined them like the Europeans, appointing a European officer to command, and non-commissioned officers to instruct them. Such was the origin of the first regiment of Bengal native infantry, called, from its equipment, the "Lall Pultun," or "Red regiment" (pultun being a corruption of the English term "platoon," which latter is derived from the French word "peloton.") It was placed under the direction of Lieutenant Knox, who proved a most admirable sepoy leader. There was no difficulty in raising men for this and other corps; for during the perpetually-recurring warfare which marked the Mussulman occupation of Bengal, adventurers had been accustomed to flock thither from Bahar, Oude, the Dooab, Rohilcund, and even from beyond the Indus;

* Sir Charles Napier.—*Life and Opinions.*

† See *Indian Empire,* vol. i., pp. 114; 258; 304; 533.

engaging themselves for particular services, and being dismissed when these were performed. It was from such men and their immediate descendants that the British ranks were filled. The majority were Mussulmans; but Patans, Rohillas, a few Jats, some Rajpoots, and even Brahmins were to be found in the early corps raised in and about Calcutta.*

The Madras sepoys, and the newly-raised Bengal battalion, amounting together to 2,100, formed two-thirds of the force with which Clive took the field against Surajah Dowlah at Plassy, in June, 1757. Of these, six Europeans and sixteen Natives perished in the so-called battle, against an army estimated by the lowest calculation at 58,000 men.† Of course, not even Clive, "the daring in war," would have been so mad as to risk an engagement which he might have safely avoided, with such an overwhelming force; but he acted in reliance on the contract previously made with the nawab's ambitious relative and commander-in-chief, Meer Jaffier, who had promised to desert to the British with all the troops under his orders at the commencement of the action, on condition of being recognised as Nawab of Bengal. The compact was fulfilled; and Meer Jaffier's treachery was rewarded by his elevation to the musnud, which the East India Company allowed him to occupy for some years. Meanwhile, the cessions obtained through him having greatly increased their territorial and pecuniary resources, they began to form a standing army for each of the three presidencies, organising the natives into a regular force, on the plan introduced by Clive.

The first instance on record of a Native court-martial occurred in July, 1757. A sepoy was accused of having connived at the attempted escape of a Swiss who had deserted the British ranks, and acted as a spy in the service of the French. The Swiss was hanged. The sepoy was tried by a court composed of the subahdars and jemadars (Native captains and lieutenants) of his detachment, found guilty, and sentenced to receive 500 lashes, and be dismissed from the service—which was accordingly done.

The hostilities carried on against the French, subjected the East India Company's troops to great hardships. The Europeans had been much injured in health and discipline by repeated accessions of prize-money, and by the habits of drinking and debauchery into which they had fallen. Numbers died; and the remainder had neither ability nor inclination to endure long marches and exposure to the climate. During an expedition in pursuit of a detachment under M. Law, they positively refused to proceed beyond Patna: Major Eyre Coote declared that he would advance with the sepoys alone; which, they rejoined, was "the most desirable event that could happen to them." Major Coote marched on with the sepoys only; but the French succeeded in effecting their escape. The recreants got drunk, and behaved in a very disorderly manner; whereupon thirty of the worst of them were brought before a court-martial, and, by its decree, publicly flogged for mutiny and insubordination.

The sentence was pronounced and executed on the 28th of July, 1757. On the following day, the sepoys, undeterred by the penalty exacted from their European comrades, laid down their arms in a body, and refused to proceed farther. The Madrassees especially complained, that although they had embarked only for service in Calcutta, they had been taken on to Chandernagore, Moorshedabad, and Patna; and that now they were again required to advance, to remove still farther from their families, and endure additional fatigues and privations. They alleged that their pay was in arrears, and that they had not received the amount to which they were entitled. Major Coote warned them of the danger which would accrue from the want of unanimity and discipline among a small force surrounded with enemies, and the hazard to which, by laying down their arms, they exposed the savings they had already accumulated, and the large amount of prize-money then due to them. These considerations prevailed; the men resumed their arms, and marched at once with the artillery to Bankipoor, the European infantry proceeding thither by water.

When Clive first left India, in 1760, the Bengal force consisted of one European battalion of infantry and two companies of artillery (1,000 men in all), and five Native battalions (1,000 men in each.) The number of European officers was at the same time increased: one captain as commandant, one lieutenant and one ensign as staff, with four sergeants, being allowed to each Native

* *Rise and Progress of the Bengal Army;* by Captain Arthur Broome, Bengal Artillery; 1850: vol. i., p. 93.

† See *Indian Empire*, "Table of Battles," vol. i., pp. 460, 461.

battalion. There was likewise a Native commandant, who took post in front with the captain, and a Native adjutant, who remained in the rear with the subalterns.

In 1764, very general disaffection was manifested throughout the army, in consequence of the non-payment of a gratuity promised by the nawab, Meer Jaffier. The European battalion, which was, unfortunately, chiefly composed of foreigners (Dutch, Germans, Hessians, and French), when assembled under arms for a parade on the 30th of January, refused to obey the word of command, declaring, that until the promised donation should be given, they would not perform any further service. The battalion marched off under the leadership of an Englishman named Straw, declaring their intention of joining their comrades then stationed on the Caramnassa, and with them proceeding to Calcutta, and compelling the governor and council to do them justice. This appears to have been really the design of the English mutineers; but the foreigners, who were double their number, secretly intended to join Shuja Dowlah, the nawab-vizier of Oude; and went off with that intention.

The sepoys were at first inclined to follow the example of the Europeans, whose cause of complaint they shared; but the officers succeeded in keeping them quiet in their lines, until the Mogul horse (two troops of which had been recently raised) spread themselves among the Native battalions, and induced about 600 sepoys to accompany the treacherous foreigners.

The European officers rode after the mutineers, and induced their leader Straw, and the greater part of them, to return. Probaby they would have done so in a body but for the influence exercised over them by a sergeant named Delamarr, who had been distinguished by intelligence and good conduct in the previous campaign, but who had a private grievance to avenge, having, as he alleged, been promised a commission on leaving the King's and entering the Company's service; which promise had been broken to him, though kept to others similarly circumstanced. This man was born in England of French parents, and spoke both languages with equal facility; on which account he was employed by the officers as a medium of communication with the foreign troops. As long as any of the officers remained with the mutineers, he affected fidelity; but when the last officer, Lieutenant Eyre, was compelled to relinquish the hope of reclaiming his men, by their threatening to carry him off by force, Delamarr put himself at the head of the party, and gave out an order that any one who should attempt to turn back, should be hanged on the first tree. The order appears to have had a contrary effect to that which it was intended to produce; for the Germans thought the French were carrying the matter too far; and they, with all but three of the few remaining English, returned on the following day, to the number of seventy, accompanied by several sepoys.

Thus the original deserters were diminished to little more than 250, of whom 157 were of the European battalion (almost all Frenchmen), sixteen were of the European cavalry, and about 100 were Natives, including some of the Mogul horse. They proceeded to join the army of Shuja Dowlah of Oude; and some of them entered his service, and that of other Indian potentates; but the majority enlisted in Sumroo's brigade.*

On the 12th of February (the day following the mutiny), a dividend of the nawab's donation was declared as about to be paid to the army, in the proportion of forty rupees to each European soldier, and six to each sepoy. The sepoys were extremely indignant at the rate of allotment: they unanimously refused to receive the proffered sum, and assembled under arms on the 13th of February, at nine in the forenoon. The Europeans were very much excited; and it became difficult "to restrain their violence, and prevent their falling upon the sepoys, for presuming to follow the example they themselves had afforded."†

Suddenly the sepoys set up a shout, and rushed down, in an irregular body, towards the Europeans, who had been drawn up in separate companies across the parade, with the park of artillery on their left, and two 6-pounders on their right.

Captain Jennings, the officer in command, perceiving that the sepoys were moving with shouldered arms, directed that they should be suffered to pass through the intervals of the battalion, if they would do so quietly. Several officers urged resistance; but Captain Jennings felt that the discharge of a single musket would be the signal for a fearful struggle, which must end either in the extermination of the Europeans, or in the total dissolution of the

* *Indian Empire*, vol. i., p. 297.

† Broome's *Bengal Army*, vol. i., p. 420.

Native force, on which the government were deeply dependent. He rode along the ranks, urging the men to be quiet; and arrived at the right of the line just in time to snatch the match out of the hand of a subaltern of artillery, as he was putting it to a 6-pounder, loaded with grape.

The result justified his decision. Two corps (the late 2nd grenadiers and 8th Native infantry) went off towards the Caramnassa river. The other two Native battalions present (the late 1st and 3rd Native infantry), remained behind—the one perfectly steady, the other clamorous and excited. The remaining three detached battalions all exhibited signs of disaffection. Captain Jennings, with the officers of the mutinous corps, followed them, and induced every man of them to return, by consenting to their own stipulation, that their share of the donation should be raised to half that of the corresponding ranks of the European battalion. This concession being made generally known, tranquillity was at once re-established.

The question of the better adaptation of the natives of India to serve as regular or irregular cavalry, was discussed. The council considered that a body of regular Native cavalry might be raised on the European system, under English officers. Major Carnac objected on the following grounds:—"The Moguls," he said, "who are the only good horsemen in the country, can never be brought to submit to the ill-treatment they receive from gentlemen wholly unacquainted with their language and customs. We clearly see the ill effects of this among our sepoys, and it will be much more so among horsemen, who deem themselves of a far superior class; nor have we a sufficiency of officers for the purpose: I am sorry to say, not a single one qualified to afford a prospect of success to such a project." These arguments prevailed. The Mogul horse was increased, during the year (1764), to 1,200 men each risallah (or troop) under Native officers, with a few Europeans to the whole.

The number of the Native infantry was also rapidly on the increase; but their position and rights remained on a very indefinite footing, when Major Hector Munro succeeded to the command of the Bengal army in August, 1764. In the following month a serious outbreak occurred. The oldest corps in the service, then known as the 9th, or Captain Galliez' battalion, but afterwards the 1st Native infantry, while stationed at Manjee (near Chupra), instigated by some of their Native officers, assembled on parade, and declared themselves resolved to serve no longer, as certain promises made to them (apparently regarding the remainder of the donation money) had been broken. They retained their arms, and imprisoned their European officers for a night; but released them on the following morning.

There did not then exist, nor has there since been framed, any law decreeing gradations of punishment in a case which clearly admits of many gradations of crime. It has been left to the discretion of the military authorities for the time being, to punish what Sir Charles Napier calls "passive, respectful mutinies," with sweeping severity, or to let attempted desertion to the enemy, and sanguinary treachery, escape almost unpunished.

The present proceeding resembled the outbreak of spoilt children, rather than of concerted mutiny.* No intention to desert was shown, much less to join the enemy. Such conduct had been before met with perhaps undue concessions. Major Munro now resolved to attempt stopping it by measures of extreme severity. Accordingly he held a general court-martial; and on receiving its verdict for the execution of twenty-four of the sepoys, he ordered it to be carried out immediately. The sentence was, "to be blown away from the guns"—the horrible mode of inflicting capital punishment so extensively practised of late.

Four grenadiers claimed the privilege of being fastened to the right-hand guns. They had always occupied the post of honour in the field, they said; and Major Munro admitted the force of the argument by granting their request. The whole army were much affected by the bearing of the doomed men. "I am sure," says Captain Williams, who then belonged to the Royal Marines employed in Bengal, and who was an eye-witness of this touching episode, "there was not a dry eye among the Marines, although they had been long accustomed to hard service, and two of them had actually been on the execution party which shot Admiral Byng, in the year 1757."† Yet Major Munro gave the signal, and the explosion followed. When the loathsome results became apparent—the mangled limbs scattered far and wide, the strange burning

* Broome's *Bengal Army*, vol. i., p. 459.

† Captain Williams' *Bengal Native Infantry*, p. 170.

smell, the fragments of human flesh, the trickling streams of blood, constituted a scene almost intolerable to those who witnessed it for the first time. The officers commanding the sepoy battalions came forward, and represented that their men would not suffer any further executions; but Major Munro persevered. The other convicted mutineers attempted no appeal to their comrades, but met their deaths with the utmost composure.

This was the first example, on a large scale, of the infliction of the penalty of death for mutiny. Heretofore there had been no plan, and no bloodshed in the numerous outbreaks. Subsequently they assumed an increasingly systematic and sanguinary character.

On the return of Clive to India in 1765 (as Lord Clive, Baron of Plassy), the Bengal army was reorganised, and divided into three brigades—respectively stationed at Monghyr, Allahabad, and Bankipoor. Each brigade consisted of one company of artillery, one regiment of European infantry, one risallah, or troop, of Native cavalry, and seven battalions of sepoys.

Each regiment of European infantry was constituted of the following strength:—

1 Colonel commanding the whole Brigade.
1 Lieutenant-colonel commanding the Regiment.

1 Major.	36 Sergeants.
6 Captains.	36 Corporals.
1 Captain Lieutenant.	27 Drummers.
9 Lieutenants.	630 Privates.
18 Ensigns.	

The artillery comprised four companies, each of which contained—

1 Captain.	4 Corporals.
1 Captain Lieutenant.	2 Drummers.
1 First Lieutenant.	2 Fifers.
1 Second Lieutenant.	10 Bombardiers.
3 Lieut. Fireworkers.	20 Gunners.
4 Sergeants.	60 Matrosses.

Each risallah of Native cavalry consisted of—

1 European Subaltern in command.

1 Sergeant-major.	3 Jemadars.
4 Sergeants.	2 Naggers.
1 Risaldar.	6 Duffadars.
	100 Privates.

A Native battalion consisted of—

1 Captain.	30 Jemadars.
2 Lieutenants.	1 Native Adjutant.
2 Ensigns.	10 Trumpeters.
3 Sergeants.	30 Tom-toms.*
3 Drummers.	80 Havildars.
1 Native Commandant.	50 Naiks.
10 Native Subahdars.	690 Sepoys.

Captain Broome, from whom the above details are derived, remarks, "that the proportion of officers, except to the sepoy battalions, was very much more liberal than in the present day; and it is most important to remember, that every officer on the list was effective—all officers on other than regimental employ, being immediately struck off the roll of the corps; although, as there was but one roster for promotion in the whole infantry, no loss in that respect was sustained thereby. The artillery and engineers rose in a separate body, and were frequently transferred from one to the other."†

The pay of the sepoy was early fixed at seven rupees per month in all stationary situations, and eight rupees and a-half when marching, or in the field; exclusive of half a rupee per month, allotted to the off-reckoning fund, for which they received one coat, and nothing more, annually. From that allowance they not only fed and clothed themselves, but also erected cantonments in all stationary situations, at their own expense, and remitted to their wives and families, often to aged parents and more distant relatives, a considerable proportion of their pay; in fact, so considerable, that the authorities have been obliged to interfere to check their extreme self-denial.‡

In 1766, the mass of the British officers of the Bengal army entered into a very formidable confederacy against the government, on account of the withdrawal of certain extra allowances, known as "double batta." The manner in which Lord Clive then used the sepoys to coerce the Europeans, has been already narrated.§

The first epoch in the history of the Bengal army may be said to end with the final departure of Clive (its founder) from India, in 1767. Up to this time, no question of caste appears to have been mooted, as interfering with the requirements of military duty, whether ordinary or incidental; but as the numbers of the sepoys increased, and the proportion of Hindoos began to exceed that of Mussulmans, a gradual change took place. A sea voyage is a forbidden thing to a Brahminist; it is a violation of his religious code, under any circumstances: he must neglect the frequent ablutions which his creed enjoins, and to which he has been accustomed from childhood; and if he do not irrecoverably forfeit his caste, it must be by enduring severe privations in regard to food

* That is, Tom-tom (native drum) players.
† Broome's *Bengal Army*, vol. i., p. 540.
‡ Williams' *Bengal Native Infantry*, p. 263.
§ See *Indian Empire*, vol. i., p. 305.

while on board ship. The influence of the officers, however, generally sufficed to overcome the scruples of the men; and, in 1769, three Bengal battalions prepared to return by sea from the Madras presidency to Bengal. Two grenadier companies embarked for the purpose, and are supposed to have perished; for the ship which they entered was never heard of afterwards. This event made a deep impression on the minds of the Hindoos, confirmed their superstitious dread of the sea, and aggravated the mingled fear and loathing, which few Englishmen, except when actually rounding the "Cape of Storms," or becalmed in a crowded vessel in the Red Sea, can understand sufficiently to make allowance for.

In 1782, a mutiny occurred at Barrackpoor, in consequence of the troops stationed there being ordered to prepare for foreign service, which it was rumoured would entail a sea voyage. No violence was attempted; no turbulence was evinced; the men quietly combined, under their Native officers, in refusing to obey the orders, which the government had no means of enforcing. After the lapse of several weeks, a general court-martial was held. Two Native officers, and one or two sepoys, were blown from the guns. The whole of the four corps concerned (then known as the 4th, 15th, 17th, and 31st) were broken up, and the men drafted into other battalions.

In 1787, Lord Cornwallis arrived in India, as governor-general and commander-in-chief. He earnestly desired to dissipate, by gentle means, the prejudices which marred the efficiency of the Native army; and he offered a bounty of ten rupees per man, with other advantages, to such as would volunteer for service on an expedition to Sumatra. The required four companies were obtained; the promised bounty was paid previous to embarkation; every care was taken to ensure abundant supplies of food and water for sustenance and ablution; the detachment was conveyed on board a regular Indiaman at the end of February; and was recalled in the following October. Unfortunately the return voyage was tedious and boisterous: the resolute abstinence of the Hindoos from all nutriment save dry peas and rice, and the exposure consequent on the refusal of the majority to quit the deck night or day, on account of the number of sick below, occasioned many to be afflicted with *nyctalopia*, or night-blindness; and deaths were numerous. Notwithstanding this, the care and tact of the officers, and the praise and gratuities which awaited the volunteers on relanding, appear to have done much to reconcile them to the past trial, and even to its repetition if need were.

The government thought the difficulty overcome, and were confirmed in their opinion by the offers of proceeding by sea made during the Mysoor war. In 1795, it became desirable to send an expedition to Malacca, whereupon a proposition was made to the 15th battalion (a corps of very high character), through its commanding officer, Captain Ludovick Grant, to volunteer for the purpose. The influence of the officers apparently prevailed; the men were reported as willing to embark; but, at the last moment, a determined mutiny broke out, and the 29th battalion was called out, with its field-pieces, to disperse the mutineers. The colours of the 15th were burnt; and the number ordered to be left a blank in the list of Native corps.* Warned by this occurrence, the government proceeded to raise a "Marine battalion,"† consisting of twelve companies of a hundred privates each; and it became generally understood, if not indeed officially stated, that the ordinary Bengal troops were not to be sent on sea voyages.

A corps of Native militia was raised for Calcutta and the adjacent districts, and placed, in the first instance, under the town major. It consisted of eighty companies of ninety privates; but was subsequently augmented to sixteen or more companies of one hundred privates each. Captain Williams, writing in 1816, says—"It is now commanded by an officer of any rank, who may be favoured with the patronage of the governor-general, with one other European officer, who performs the duty of adjutant to the corps."‡ Several local corps were formed about the same time.

Some important changes were made in the constitution of the Bengal army in 1796; one effect of which was to diminish the authority and influence of the Native officers. The staff appointment of Native adjutants was abolished, and a European adjutant was appointed to each battalion. The principle of regimental rank and promotion (to the rank of major, inclusive), was

* A regiment was raised in Bahar, in 1798, and numbered the 15th.

† Formed into the 20th, or Marine regiment, in 1801.

‡ *Bengal Native Infantry*, p. 243.

adopted throughout the E. I. Company's forces; and, contrary to the former arrangement, the whole of the staff of the government and of the army, inclusive of a heavy commissariat, with the numerous officers on furlough in Europe, and those employed with local corps, and even in diplomatic situations, were thenceforth borne on the strength as component parts of companies and corps. Thus, even at this early period, the complaint (so frequently reiterated since) is made by Captain Williams, that the charge of companies often devolved on subalterns utterly unqualified, by professional or local acquirements, for a situation of such authority over men to whose character, language, and habits they are strangers.*

The rise, and gradual increase, of the armies of the Madras and Bombay presidencies, did not essentially differ from that of the Bengal troops, excepting that the total number of the former was much smaller, and the proportion of Mohammedans and high-caste Brahmins considerably lower than in the latter. The three armies were kept separate, each under its own commander-in-chief. Many inconveniences attend this division of the forces of one ruling power. It has been a barrier to the centralisation which the bureaucratic spirit of the Supreme government of Calcutta has habitually fostered; and attempts have been made, more or less directly, for an amalgamation of the three armies. The Duke of Wellington thoroughly understood the bearing of the question, and his decided opinion probably contributed largely to the maintenance of the chief of the barriers which have prevented the contagion of Bengal mutiny from extending to Bombay and Madras, and hindered the fraternisation which we may reasonably suspect would otherwise have been general, at least among the Hindoos. The more united the British are, the better, no doubt; but the more distinct nationalities are kept up in India, the safer for us: every ancient landmark we remove, renders the danger of combination against us more imminent.

The Madras and Bombay sepoys, throughout their career, have had, like those of Bengal, occasional outbreaks of mutiny, the usual cause being an attempt to send them on expeditions which necessitated a sea voyage. Thus, in 1779, or 1780, a mutiny occurred in the 9th Madras battalion when ordered to embark for Bombay; which, however, was quelled by the presence of mind and decision of the commandant, Captain Kelly. A fatal result followed the issue of a similar order for the embarkation of some companies of a corps in the Northern Circars. The men, on arriving at Vizagapatam (the port where they were to take shipping), rose upon their European officers, and shot all save one or two, who escaped to the ship.†

One motive was strong enough to overcome this rooted dislike to the sea; and that was, affection for the person, and confidence in the skill and fortune, of their commanding officer. Throughout the Native forces, the fact was ever manifest, that their discipline or insubordination, their fidelity or faithlessness, depended materially on the influence exercised by their European leaders. Sir John Malcolm, in his various writings, affords much evidence to this effect. Among many other instances, he cites that of a battalion of the 22nd Madras regiment, then distinguished for the high state of discipline to which they had been brought by their commanding officer, Lieutenant-colonel James Oram. In 1797, he proposed to his corps, on parade, to volunteer for an expedition then preparing against Manilla. "Will he go with us?" was the question which went through the ranks. "Yes!" "Will he stay with us?" Again, "yes!" and the whole corps exclaimed, "To Europe, to Europe!" They were ready to follow Colonel Oram anywhere—to the shores of the Atlantic as cheerfully as to an island of the Eastern Ocean. Such was the contagion of their enthusiasm, that several sepoys, who were missing from one of the battalions in garrison at Madras, were found to have deserted to join the expedition.‡

The personal character of Lord Lake contributed greatly to the good service rendered by the Bengal sepoys (both Hindoo and Mohammedan) in the arduous Mahratta war of 1803-'4. He humoured their prejudices, flattered their pride, and praised their valour; and they repaid him by unbounded attachment to his person, and the zealous fulfilment of their public duty. Victorious or defeated, the sepoys knew their efforts were equally sure of appreciation by the commander-in-chief. His conduct to the shattered corps of Colonel Monson's detachment, after their

* Williams' *Bengal Native Infantry*, p. 253.

† Parliamentary evidence of Sir J. Malcolm in 1832.

‡ *Ibid.*

gallant but disastrous retreat before Holcar,* was very remarkable. He formed them into a reserve, and promised them every opportunity of signalising themselves. No confidence was ever more merited. Throughout the service that ensued, these corps were uniformly distinguished.

The pay of the forces in the last century was frequently heavily in arrears, and both Europeans and Natives were driven, by actual want, to the verge of mutiny. The Bombay troops, in the early wars with Mysoor, suffered greatly from this cause; and yet none ever showed warmer devotion to the English. When, on the capture of Bednore, General Matthews and his whole force surrendered to Tippoo, every inducement was offered to tempt the sepoys to enter the sultan's service; but in vain. During the march, they were carefully separated from the European prisoners at each place of encampment, by a tank or other obstacle, supposed to be insurmountable. It did not prove so, however; for one of the captive officers subsequently declared, that not a night elapsed but some of the sepoys contrived to elude the vigilance of the guards by swimming the tanks (frequently some miles in circumference), or eluding the sentries; bringing with them such small sums as they could save from the pittance allowed by the sultan, for their own support, in return for hard daily labour, to eke out the scanty food of the Europeans. "We can live upon anything," they said; "but you require mutton and beef." At the peace of 1783, 1,500 of the released captives marched 500 miles to Madras, and there embarked on a voyage of six or eight weeks, to rejoin the army to which they belonged at Bombay.†

Similar manifestations of attachment were given by the various Native troops of the three presidencies; their number, and proportion to the Europeans, increasing with the extension of the Anglo-Indian empire. In 1800, the total force comprised 22,832 Europeans, and 115,300 Natives of all denominations; the Europeans being chiefly Royal troops belonging to the regular cavalry and infantry regiments, which were sent to India for periods varying from twelve to twenty years. As the requirements of government augmented with every addition of territory, the restrictions of caste became daily more obnoxious; and attempts, for the most part very ill-judged, were made to break through them. Certain regulations, trivial in themselves, excited the angry suspicions of the sepoys, as to the latent intentions of government; and the sons of Tippoo Sultan (then state-prisoners at Vellore), through their partisans, fomented the disaffection, which issued in the mutiny of 1806, in which thirteen European officers and eighty-two privates were killed, and ninety-two wounded.‡

In 1809, another serious outbreak occurred in the Madras presidency, in which the Native troops played only a secondary part, standing by their officers against the government. The injudicious manner in which Sir George Barlow had suppressed an allowance known as "tent-contract," previously made to Europeans in command of Native regiments, spread disaffection throughout the Madras force. Auber, the annalist of the East India Company, gives very few particulars of this unsatisfactory and discreditable affair; but he mentions the remarkable fidelity displayed by Purneah, the Dewan of Mysoor (chosen, and earnestly supported, by Colonel Wellesley, after the conquest of that country.) The field-officer in charge of the fortress of Seringapatam, tried to corrupt Purneah, and even held out a threat regarding his property, and that belonging to the boy-rajah in the fort. The dignified rejoinder was, that the British government was the protector of the rajah and his minister; and that, let what would happen, he (Purneah) would always remain faithful to his engagements.§

A skirmish actually took place between the mutineers and the king's troops. Lord Minto (the governor-general) hastened to Madras, and, by a mixture of firmness and conciliation, restored order, having first obtained the unconditional submission of all concerned in the late proceedings; that is to say, the great majority of the Madras officers in the Company's service.

The refusal of the 47th Bengal regiment to march from Barrackpoor in 1825, on the expedition to Burmah, is fully accounted for by the repugnance of the sepoys to embarkation having been aggravated by the insufficient arrangements made for them by the commissariat department. The authorities punished, in a most sanguinary man-

* *Indian Empire*, vol. i., p. 400.

† Sir John Malcolm's *Government of India*. London: John Murray, 1833; p. 210.

‡ See *Indian Empire*, vol. i., p. 407.

§ Auber's *British Power in India*, vol. ii., pp. 476, 477.

ner, conduct which their own negligence had provoked.*

An important change was introduced into the Native army, under the administration of Lord William Bentinck (who was appointed commander-in-chief as well as governor-general in 1833), by the abolition of flogging, which had previously been inflicted with extreme frequency and severity. Sir Charles Napier subsequently complained of this measure, on the ground of its leaving no punishment available when the army was before the enemy. The limited authority vested in the officers, increased the difficulty of maintaining discipline, by making expulsion from the service the sole punishment of offenders who deserved perhaps a day's hard labour. Sir Charles adds—"But I have been in situations where I could not turn them out, for they would either starve or have their throats cut; so I did all my work by the provost-martial." His favourite pupil, "the war-bred Sir Colin Campbell," appears to have been driven to the same alternative to check looting.

The change which has come over the habits of both military men and civilians during the present century, has been already shown. Europeans have gradually ceased to take either wives or concubines from among the natives: they have become, in all points, more exclusive; and as their own number has increased, so also has their regard for conventionalities, which, while yet strangers in the land—few and feeble—they had been content to leave in abeyance. The effect on Indian society, and especially on the army, is evident. The intercourse between the European and Native officers has become yearly less frequent and less cordial. The acquisition of Native languages is neglected; or striven for, not as a means of obtaining the confidence of the sepoys, but simply as a stepping-stone to distinction in the numerous civil positions which the rapid extension of territory, the paucity of the civil service, and the rejection of Native agency, has thrown open to their ambition. There is, inevitably, a great deal of sheer drudgery in the ordinary routine of regimental duty; but it surely was not wise to aggravate the distaste which its performance is calculated to produce, by adopting a system which makes long continuance in a regiment a mark of incapacity.

The military and civil line of promotion is, to a great extent, the same. An Indian military man is always supposed to be fit for anything that offers. He can be "an inspector of schools, an examiner in political economy, an engineer, a surveyor, an architect, an auditor, a commissary, a resident, or a governor."† Political, judicial, and scientific appointments are all open to him; and the result, no doubt, is, that Indian officers, in many instances, show a versatility of talent unknown elsewhere.

But through teaching officers to look to staff appointments and civil employ for advancement, the military profession is described as having fallen into a state of disparagement. Officers who have not acquitted themselves well in the civil service are "remanded to their regiments," as if they were penal corps; and those who remain with their regiments, suffer under a sense of disappointment and wounded self-esteem, which makes it impossible for them to have their heart in the work.‡

The employment of the army to do the civil work, was declared by Napier to be "the great military evil of India;" the officers occupying various diplomatic situations, the sepoys acting as policemen, gaolers, and being incessantly employed in detachments for the escort of treasure from the local treasuries, to the manifest injury of their discipline. "Sir Thomas Munro," he adds, "thought three officers were sufficient for regiments. This is high authority; yet I confess to thinking him wrong; or else, which is very possible, the state of the army and the style of the officer have changed, not altogether better nor altogether worse, but become different."

There is, probably, much truth in this suggestion. The character of the Native officers and sepoys, as well as that of the Europeans, had changed since the days of Munro. The Bengal army had grown, with the Bengal presidency, into an exclusively high-caste institution. The men were chiefly Brahmins and Rajpoots, or Mussulmans—handsome, stately men, higher by the head and shoulders than the Madrassees or Mahrattas; immeasurably higher in caste. Great care was taken to avoid low-caste recruits; still more, outcasts and Christians. In this respect, most exaggerated deference was paid to religious prejudices which, in

* *Indian Empire*, vol. i., p. 424. Thornton's *India*, vol. iv., p. 113.

† *Times*, 15th July, 1857. Letter from Bombay correspondent.

‡ Indophilus' *Letters to the Times*, p. 15.

other points, were recklessly infringed. In Bombay and Madras, no such distinctions were made. Recruits were enlisted without regard to caste; and the result was, a mixture much less adapted to combine for the removal of common grievances. A Native army, under foreign rule, can hardly have been without these: but so flattering a description was given of the Indian troops, that, until their rejection of our service, and subsequent deadly hostility, raised suspicions of "a long-continued course of mismanagement,"* little attention was paid to those who suggested the necessity of radical reforms.

Yet Sir John Malcolm pointed out, as early as 1799, the injustice of a system which allowed no Native soldier the most distant prospect of rising to rank, distinction, or affluence; and this "extraordinary fact" he believed to be "a subject of daily comment among the Native troops."†

The evil felt while the Indian army was comparatively small, could not but increase in severity in proportion to the augmentation of the sepoys, who, in 1851, amounted to 240,121, out of 289,529 men; the remainder being Europeans. Meanwhile, the extinction of Indian states and of national armies had been rapidly progressing. The disbanded privates (at least such of them as entered the British ranks) may have benefited by the change; regular pay and a retiring pension compensating them for the possibility of promotion and the certainty of laxer discipline, with license in the way of loot (plunder.) But the officers were heavy losers by the change. In treating of the causes of the mutiny, Mr. Martin Gubbins says, that in the Punjab, "the father may have received 1,000 rupees per mensem, as commandant of cavalry, under Runjeet Sing; the son draws a pay of eighty rupees as sub-commander, in the service of the British government. The difference is probably thought by themselves to be too great." In support of this guarded admission, he proceeds to adduce evidence of the existence of the feeling suggested by him as probable, by citing the reproachful exclamation of a Seik risaldar, conspicuous for good conduct during the insurrection—"My father used to receive 500 rupees a-month in command of a party of Runjeet Sing's horse; I receive but fifty."‡

Sir Charles Napier returned to India, as commander-in-chief of the Anglo-Indian armies, on the 6th of May, 1849. He was sent out for the express purpose of carrying on the war in the Punjab; but it had been successfully terminated before his arrival. He made a tour of inspection, and furnished reports to government on the condition of the troops; which contained statements calculated to excite grave anxiety, and prophecies of evil which have been since fulfilled.

He pointed out excessive luxury among the officers, and alienation from the Native soldiery, as fostering the disaffection occasioned among the latter by sudden reductions of pay, accompanied by the increased burthen of civil duties, consequent on the rapid extension of territory.

It was, however, not until after positive mutiny had been developed, that he recognised the full extent of the evils, which he then searched out, and found to be sapping the very foundation of the Indian army.

Writing to General Caulfield (one of his few friends in the East India direction) in November, 1849, he calls the sepoy "a glorious soldier, not to be corrupted by gold, or appalled by danger;" and he adds—"I would not be afraid to go into action with Native troops, and without Europeans, provided I had the training of them first."§

In a report addressed to the governor-general in the same month, the following passage occurs:—

"I have heard that Lord Hardinge objected to the assembling of the Indian troops, for fear they should conspire. I confess I cannot see the weight of such an opinion. I have never met with an Indian officer who held it, and I certainly do not hold it myself; and few men have had more opportunities of judging of the armies of all three presidencies than I have. Lord Hardinge saw but the Bengal army, and that only as governor-general, and for a short time; I have studied them for nearly eight years, constantly at the head of Bengal and Bombay sepoys, and I can see nothing to fear from them, *except when ill-used*; and even then they are less dangerous than British troops would be in similar circumstances. I see no danger in their being massed, and very great danger in their being spread over a country as they now are: on the contrary, I believe that, by concentrating the Indian army as I propose, its spirit, its devotion, and its powers will all be increased."‖

The above extract tends to confirm the general belief, that the private opinion of Lord Hardinge, regarding the condition of

* Speech of Lord Ellenborough: Indian debate, July 13th, 1857. The Duke of Argyll, and others, said, that "there could be no doubt there had been some mismanagement."—*Ibid.*, July 27th, 1858.

† Kaye's *Life of Malcolm*, vol i., p. 96.

‡ Gubbins' *Mutinies in Oudh*, p. 98.

§ Sir Charles Napier's *Life*, vol. iv., pp. 212, 213.

‖ Parl. Paper (Commons), 30th July, 1857.

the army, was less satisfactory than he chose to avow in public. Lord Melville has given conclusive evidence on the subject by stating, from his personal acquaintance with the ex-commander-in-chief, that—"Entertaining the worst opinion privately, Lord Hardinge never would express it publicly, trying thereby to bolster up a bad system, on the ground of the impolicy of making public the slight thread by which we held our tenure of that empire."* Napier, who never kept back or qualified his views, soon saw reason to declare, that "we were sitting on a mine, and nobody could tell when it might explode."† The circumstances which led him to this unsatisfactory conclusion were these. After the annexation of the Punjab, the extra allowance formerly given to the troops on service there, was summarily withdrawn, on the ground that the country was no longer a foreign one. The 22nd Native infantry stationed at Rawul Pindee refused the reduced pay. The 13th regiment followed the example; and an active correspondence took place between these corps, and doubtless extended through the Bengal army; for there are news-writers in every regiment, who communicate all intelligence to their comrades at head-quarters.‡

Colonel Benson, of the military board, proposed to Lord Dalhousie to disband the two regiments; but the commander-in-chief opposed the measure, as harsh and impolitic. Many other regiments were, he said, certainly involved: the government could not disband an army; it was, therefore, best to treat the cases as isolated ones, while that was possible; for, he added, "if we attempt to bully large bodies, they will do the same by us, and a fight must ensue."§ The governor-general concurred in this opinion. The insubordination at Rawul Pindee was repressed without bloodshed, by the officer in command, Sir Colin Campbell; and the matter was treated as one of accidental restricted criminality, not affecting the mass.

Sir Charles Napier visited Delhi, which he considered the proper place for our great magazines, and well fitted, from its central position, to be the head-quarters of the artillery—the best point from whence to send forth troops and reinforcements. Here, too, the spirit of mutiny manifested itself; the 41st Native infantry refusing to enter the Punjab without additional allowances as heretofore; and twenty-four other regiments, then under orders for the same province, were rumoured to be in league with the 41st. The latter regiment was, however, tranquillised, and induced to march, by what Sir William Napier terms "dexterous management, and the obtaining of furloughs, which had been unfairly and recklessly withheld."

At Vizierabad the sepoys were very sullen, and were heard to say they only waited the arrival of the relieving regiments, and would then act together. Soon after this, the 66th, a relief regiment on the march from Lucknow (800 miles from Vizierabad), broke into open mutiny near Amritsir, insulted their officers, and attempted to seize the strong fortress of Govindghur, which then contained about £100,000 in specie. The 1st Native cavalry were fortunately on the spot; and being on their return to India, were not interested in the extra-allowance question. They took part with the Europeans; and, dismounting, seized the gates, which the strength and daring of a single officer (Captain M'Donald) had alone prevented from being closed, and which the mutineers, with fixed bayonets, vainly sought to hold. This occurred in February, 1850. Lord Dalhousie was not taken by surprise. Writing to Sir Charles Napier, he had declared himself "prepared for discontent among the Native troops, on coming into the Punjab under diminished allowances; and well satisfied to have got so far through without violence." "The sepoy," he added, "has been over-petted and overpaid of late, and has been led on, by the government itself, into the entertainment of an expectation, and the manifestation of a feeling, which he never held in former times."‖

This was written before the affair at Govindghur; and in the meantime, Sir Charles had seen "strong ground to suppose the mutinous spirit general in the Bengal army."¶ He believed that the Brahmins

* Letter to General Sir William Gomm, July 15th, 1857.—*Times*, July 21st, 1857. † *Ibid.*

‡ Evidence of Colonel Greenhill.—Parl. Committee, 1832-'3.

§ Sir Charles Napier's *Life*, vol. iv., p. 227.

‖ *Ibid.*, pp. 216; 269; 427.

¶ Two great explosions of ammunition have been mentioned in connexion with the mutinous feeling of the period; one at Benares, of 3,000 barrels of powder, in no less than thirty boats, which killed upwards of 1,200 people: by the other, of 1,800 barrels, no life was lost.

were exerting their influence over the Hindoos most injuriously; and learned, with alarm, a significant circumstance which had occurred during the Seik war. Major Neville Chamberlaine, hearing some sepoys grumbling about a temporary hardship, exclaimed, "Were I the general, I would disband you all." A Brahmin havildar replied, "If you did, we would all go to our villages, and you should not get any more to replace us." Napier viewed this remark as the distinct promulgation of a principle upon which the sepoys were even then prepared to act. The Brahmins he believed to be secretly nourishing the spirit of insubordination; and unless a counterpoise could be found to their influence, it would be hazardous in the extreme to disband the 66th regiment, at the risk of inciting other corps to declare, "They are martyrs for us; we, too, will refuse;" and of producing a bayonet struggle with caste for mastery. "Nor was the stake for which the sepoy contended a small one—exclusive of the principle of an army dictating to the government: they struck for twelve rupees instead of seven—nearly double! When those in the Punjab got twelve by meeting, those in India Proper would not long have served on seven."*

The remedy adopted by Napier, was to replace the mutinous 66th with one of the irregular Goorka battalions;† and he expressed his intention of extensively following up this plan, in the event of the disbandment of further regiments becoming necessary. "I would if I could," he says, "have 25,000 of them; which, added to our own Europeans, would form an army of 50,000 men, and, well handled, would neutralise any combination amongst the sepoys."

The Goorkas themselves he describes as of small stature, with huge limbs, resembling Attila's Huns; "brave as men can be, but horrid little savages, accustomed to use a weapon called a *kookery*, like a straightened reaping-hook, with which they made three cuts—one across the shoulders, the next across the forehead, the third a ripping-up one."

The Nusseeree battalion, chosen to replace the 66th, welcomed, with frantic shouts of joy, the proposal of entering the regular army, and receiving seven rupees a month, instead of four rupees eight annas; which sum, according to their commanding officer, had been actually insufficient for their support. What the European officers of the 66th thought of the substitution does not appear; but Lord Dalhousie, while approving the disbandment of the mutineers, disapproved of the introduction of the Goorkas. The commander-in-chief was at the same time reprimanded for having, in January, 1850 (pending a reference to the Supreme government), suspended the operation of a regulation regarding compensation for rations; which he considered, in the critical state of affairs, likely to produce mutiny. This regulation, says Sir W. Napier, "affected the usual allowance to the sepoys for purchasing their food, according to the market prices of the countries in which they served: it was recent; was but partially known; was in itself unjust; and became suddenly applicable at Vizierabad, where it was entirely unknown." General Hearsey, commander at Vizierabad, and Generals Gilbert and Colin Campbell, deprecated its enforcement as most impolitic, and calculated, in the sullen temper of the sepoys, to produce a mutiny; and, in fact, only twelve days elapsed before the Govindghur outbreak occurred. The amount of money involved in the temporary suspension was only £10; but even had it been much greater, if a commander-in-chief could not, in what he believed to be a crisis, and what there is little doubt really was one, be allowed to use his discretion on a subject so immediately within his cognizance, he had, indeed, a heavy weight of responsibility to bear, without any commensurate authority. A less impetuous spirit than that of the "fiery Napier," would have felt no better than a "huge adjutant-general," when informed that he "would not again be permitted, *under any circumstances*, to issue orders which should change the pay and allowances of the troops in India, and thus practically to exercise an authority which had been reserved, and most properly reserved, for the Supreme government alone."‡

The general at once sent in his resignation (May 22nd, 1850) through Lord Fitzroy Somerset; stating the rebuke he had received, and probably hoping that the

* Sir C. Napier's *Life and Correspondence*, vol. iv., pp. 261, 262.

† See *Indian Empire*, vol. i., p. 445.

‡ After Sir Charles left India, a minute was drawn up by the Supreme Council, which stated, "that the ration and mutiny question, which led to Sir Charles Napier's resignation, was not the real cause for the reprimand; but the style of the commander-in-chief's correspondence had become offensive."—*Life*, vol. iv., p. 411.

British commander-in-chief, the Duke of Wellington, would urge its withdrawal. The Duke, on the contrary, decided, after examining the statements sent home by the Calcutta authorities (which, judging by subsequent events, were founded on a mistaken view of the temper of the troops), that no sufficient reason had existed for the suspension of the regulation, and that the governor-general in council was right in expressing his disapprobation of the act. The resignation was consequently accepted; and Sir Charles's statements regarding the condition of the army, were treated as the prejudiced views of a disappointed man.

Yet the report addressed by him to the Duke in June, while ignorant, and probably not expectant, of the acceptance of his resignation, contains assertions which ought then to have been investigated, and which are now of primary importance as regards the causes of our sudden calamity, and the system to be adopted for the prevention of its recurrence.

"The Bengal Native army," Sir Charles writes, "is said to have much fallen off from what it was in former days. Of this I am not a judge; but I must say that it is a very noble army, and with very few defects. The greatest, as far as I am capable of judging, is a deficiency of discipline among the European officers, especially those of the higher ranks. I will give your grace an instance.

"The important order issued by the governor-general and the commander-in-chief, to prepare the sepoys for a reduction in their pay, I ordered to be read, and explained with care to every regiment. With the exception of three or four commanders of regiments, none obeyed the order; some gave it to pay-sergeants to read, and others altogether neglected to do so—such is the slackness of discipline among officers of high rank, and on an occasion of such vast importance. This want of discipline arises from more than one cause: a little sharpness with officers who disobey orders will soon correct much of this; but much of it originates in the great demand made upon the troops for civil duties, which so breaks up whole regiments, that their commanding officers lose that zeal for the service which they ought to feel, and so do the younger officers. The demand also made for guards is immense. * * * I cannot believe that the discipline of the Bengal army will be restored till it is relieved from civil duties, and those duties performed by police battalions, as was intended by Lord Ellenborough.

"The next evil which I see in the Native army is, that so many of the senior officers of regiments are placed on the staff or in civil situations; and very old, worn-out officers command regiments: these carry on their duties with the adjutant and some favoured Native officer. Not above one or two captains are with the regiment; and the subalterns being all young, form a society among themselves, and neglect the Native officers altogether. Nothing is therefore known as to what is passing in a Native regiment. * * * The last, and most important thing which I reckon injurious to the Indian army, is the immense influence given to "caste;" instead of being discouraged, it has been encouraged in the Bengal army. In the Bombay army it is discouraged, and that army is in better order than the Bengal army. In this latter the Brahmins have been leaders in every mutiny." *

The manner in which courts-martial were conducted, excited his indignation throughout his Indian career. Drunkenness and gambling were, in his eyes, unsoldierly and ungentlemanly vices, and he drew no distinction between the officer and the private. "Indian courts-martial are my plagues," he writes; "they are farces. If a private is to be tried, the courts are sharp enough; but an officer is quite another thing." He mentions a case of notorious drunkenness, in which the accused was "honourably acquitted;" and he adds—"Discipline is so rapidly decaying, that in a few years my belief is, no commander-in-chief will dare to bring an officer to trial: the press will put an end to all trials, except in law courts. In courts-martial now, all is quibbling and disputes about what is legal; the members being all profoundly ignorant on the subject: those who judge fairly, in a military spirit, are afraid of being brought up afterwards, and the trials end by an acquittal in the face of all evidence!" This state of things was not one in which he was likely to acquiesce; and in six months he had to decide forty-six cases of courts-martial on officers (some for gambling, some for drunkenness), in which only two were honourably acquitted, and not less than fourteen cashiered. In the celebrated address in which he took leave of the officers of the Indian army (9th December, 1850), he blamed them severely for getting into debt, and having to be brought before the Court of Requests. "A vulgar man," he wrote, "who enjoys a champagne tiffin [luncheon], and swindles his servants, may be a pleasant companion to those who do not hold him in contempt as a vulgar knave; but he is not a gentleman: his commission makes him an officer, but he is not a gentleman."

The luxury of the Indian system was, as might be expected, severely criticised by a warrior who is popularly said to have entered on a campaign with a piece of soap and a couple of towels, and dined off a hunch of bread and a cup of water. Previous commanders-in-chief, when moving on

* Sir C. Napier to the Duke of Wellington, 15th June, 1850.—Parl. Paper, August 6th, 1857.

a military inspection, used, at the public expense, eighty or ninety elephants, three or four hundred camels, and nearly as many bullocks, with all their attendants: they had also 332 tent-pitchers, including fifty men solely employed to carry glass doors for a pavilion. This enormous establishment was reduced by Napier to thirty elephants, 334 camels, 222 tent-pitchers; by which a saving was effected for the treasury of £750 a-month. "Canvas palaces," he said, "were not necessary for a general on military inspection, even admitting the favourite idea of some 'old Indians'—that pomp and show produce respect with Indian people. But there is no truth in that notion: the respect is paid to military strength; and the astute natives secretly deride the ostentation of temporary authority."*

"Among the modern military changes," he says, "there is one which has been gradually introduced in a number of regiments by gentlemen who are usually called 'martinets'—not soldiers, only martinets. No soldier can now go up to his officer without a non-commissioned officer gives him leave, and accompanies him! * * * This is a very dangerous innovation; it is digging a ditch between the officers and their men! How are Company's officers to study men's characters, when no man dare address them but in full dress, and in presence of a non-commissioned officer?"†

Sir Charles deplored "the caste and luxury which pervaded the army," as calculated to diminish their influence equally over European soldiers and Indian sepoys.

"His [the soldier's] captain is no longer his friend and chief: he receives him with upstart condescension; is very dignified, and very insolent, nine [times?] out of ten; and as often the private goes away with disgust or contempt, instead of good, respectful, comrade feelings. Then the soldier goes daily to school, or to his library, now always at hand; while his dignified officer goes to the billiard-room or the smoking-room; or, strutting about with a forage-cap on the side of an empty pate, and clothed in a shooting-jacket, or other deformity of dress, fancies himself a great character, because he is fast, and belongs to a fast regiment—*i.e.*, a regiment unfit for service, commanded by the adjutant, and having a mess in debt!"‡

It is, of course, exclusively to the sepoys that Sir Charles refers in the following passages, in which he upholds the necessity for discipline and kindly intercourse being maintained by the European officers:—

"They are admirable soldiers, and only give way when badly led by brave but idle officers, who let discipline and drill grow slack, and do not mix with them: being ignorant themselves, they cannot teach the sepoy. * * * I could do anything I like with these natives. Our officers generally do not know how to deal with them. They have not, with some exceptions, the natural turn and soldierlike feelings necessary to deal with them. Well, it matters little to me; India and I will soon be separate: I see the system will not last fifty years. The moment these brave and able natives learn how to combine, they will rush on us simultaneously, and the game will be up. A bad commander-in-chief and a bad governor-general will clench the business.§ * * * I am disposed to believe, that we might, with advantage, appoint natives to cadetships, discharge all our Native officers on the pensions of their present rank, and so give the natives common chance of command with ourselves—before they take it!

"Every European boy, aye, even sergeants, now command all Native officers! When the native saw the English ensign live with him and cherish him, and by daily communication was made aware of his superior energy, strength, daring, and mental acquirements, all went smooth. Now things have changed. The young cadet learns nothing: he drinks, he lives exclusively with his own countrymen; the older officers are on the staff, or on civil employ, which they ought not to be; and high-caste—that is to say, mutiny—is encouraged. I have just gotten this army through a very dangerous one; and the Company had better take care what they are at, or some great mischief will yet happen!

"I think that Native ensigns, lieutenants, and captains, aye, and commanders of corps too, will assimilate with our officers, and, in course of time,

* *Life*, vol. iv., p. 206. The ostentatious parade with which the progresses of Indian functionaries, both civil and military, was usually attended, not only aggravated, by contrast, the hardships endured by their inferiors, but inflicted most cruel sufferings on the natives of the countries through which they passed, thousands being pressed for palanquin or dooly (litter) bearers, and for porters of luggage, and paid very poorly, and often very irregularly. "The coolies," says Sir C. Napier, "who are summoned to carry the governor-general's baggage when he moves, are assembled at, or rather driven by force to, Simla from immense distances, and are paid about twopence a-day, under circumstances of great cruelty. Now, I happen to know, that from the delays of offices, and without, perhaps, any tangible act of knavery in any especial officer or individual, some 8,000 or 10,000 coolies employed to take Lord —— down into the plains when he left India, were not paid this miserable pittance for three years!" It is scarcely possible to believe that Englishmen could be either so ungenerous or so short-sighted as wantonly to outrage the feelings of the natives; but, on this point, the testimony of various authorities is corroborated by the special correspondent of the *Times*, whose sympathies naturally lay with his countrymen, and who would not, without strong evidence, venture to bring such a heavy charge against them. Seeing a native badly wounded on a charpoy (movable bed), with a woman sitting beside him in deep affliction, he asked for an explanation, and was told that an officer "had been licking two of his bearers, and had nearly murdered them." Mr. Russell probably did not disguise his disgust on this or other occasions; for he was often told, "Oh, wait till you are another month in India, and you'll think nothing of licking a nigger."—*The Times*, June 17th, 1858.

† *Life and Correspondence*, vol. iv., p. 325.

‡ *Ibid.*, vol. iv., pp. 306; 326. § *Ibid.*, pp. 185; 212.

gradually throw caste to the dogs, and be like ourselves in all but colour. I have no belief in the power of caste resisting the Christian faith for any great length of time, because reason is too strong for nonsense in the long run; and I believe if the Indians were made officers, on the same footing as ourselves, they would be perfectly faithful, and in time become Christians: not that I want to convert them; but so it will be."*

So far from any idea being entertained of elevating the Native officers according to the plan propounded by the commander-in-chief, their absolute extinction was discussed in public journals and periodicals; a fact which supplies a very clear reason for general disaffection.

Sir Charles Napier, in the year in which he died (1853), writes to his brother, Sir William:—

"The Edinburgh article you mentioned says, that if the Native officers were gradually gotten rid of, the operation would be safe, though not economical or generous. But however gradually it might be done, 300,000 armed men would at once see that all their hopes of rising to be lieutenants, captains, and majors, and when no longer able to serve, the getting pensions, would, for those ranks, be blasted for ever. The writer would soon find his plan unsafe; it would end all Indian questions at once. There is no sepoy in that great army but expects to retire, in age, with a major's pension, as certainly as every ensign expects to become a major or a colonel in our army. There is but one thing to be done: give the Native officers rank with our own, reducing the number of ours. This may endanger; but it will not do so more than the present system does; and my own opinion is pretty well made up, that our power there is crumbling very fast."†

The above statements have been given at length, not simply because they were formed by the commander-in-chief of the Indian army, but because they are the grounds on which he based his assertion, that the mutiny of the sepoys was "the most formidable danger menacing our Indian empire." Certainly Sir William Napier has done good service in his unreserved exposition of his brother's opinions; and though many individuals of high position and character, may, with justice, complain of the language applied to them, yet the sarcasms of the testy old general lose half their bitterness when viewed as the ebullitions of an irascible temper, aggravated by extreme and almost constant bodily pain. When he descends to personalities, his own comparison describes him best—"a hedgehog fighting about nothing:" but his criticisms on the discipline of the Indian army, its commissariat, ordnance, and transport departments, bear witness of an extraordinary amount of judgment and shrewdness. If, as "Indophilus" asserts, "Sir Charles Napier had not the gift of foresight beyond other men," it is the more to be regretted that other men, and especially Indian statesmen, should have allowed his assertions to remain on record, neither confirmed nor refuted, until the mutinies of 1857 brought them into general notice.

Sir Charles Napier was not quite alone in his condemnation of the lax discipline of the Bengal army. Viscount Melville, who commanded the Punjab division of the Bombay forces at the time of the mutiny of the two Bengal regiments under Sir Colin Campbell, in 1849, was astonished at the irregularity which he witnessed in the Bengal army. When questioned concerning its condition, on his return to England in 1850, he did not disguise his strong disapprobation; upon which he was told that, however true his opinion might be, it would be imprudent to express it.‡

Sir Colin Campbell kept silence on the same principle; but now says, that if he had uttered his feelings regarding the sepoys ten years ago, he would have been shot.§

Major John Jacob wrote a pamphlet‖ in 1854, in which he pointed out various defects in the system; but the home authorities were evidently unwilling to listen to any unpleasant information. The reports of the commander-in-chief who succeeded Sir Charles Napier, and of the governor-general, were both exceedingly favourable; but then the efforts of both Sir William Gomm¶ and of Lord Dalhousie, seem to have been directed exclusively to the furtherance of very necessary measures for the welfare of the European troops. Indeed, in his lordship's own summary of his administration, the condition of the immense mass of the Indian army, amounting to nearly 300,000 men, is

* Letter written May 31st, 1850; published by Lieutenant-general Sir William Napier, in the *Times* of August 17th, 1857.

† *Life and Opinions*, vol. iv., p. 383.

‡ Speech in the House of Lords, July 15th, 1857.

§ *Times*, 15th January, 1858.

‖ *Native Troops of the Indian Army.*

¶ *Indian Empire*, vol. i., p. 537.

dismissed in the following brief, and, if accurate, very satisfactory sentence:—

"The position of the Native soldier in India has long been such as to leave hardly any circumstance of his position in need of improvement."*

This statement is hardly consistent with that made by the chairman of the East India Company (Mr. R. D. Mangles) to the cadets at Addiscombe, in June, 1857. He adverted to the "marked alteration in the tone and bearing of the younger officers of the Indian army, towards the natives of all ranks," as a fact which "all joined in lamenting;" and he added, that if the "estrangement of officers from men, and especially of English from Native officers, was allowed to continue and grow, it was impossible to calculate the fatal consequences that might ensue."†

Here, at least, was one point in which the treatment of the Native soldiery was susceptible of improvement. But there were others in which the peculiar advantages they had once enjoyed had sensibly diminished: their work had increased; their pay, at least in the matter of extra allowances, had decreased. Sinde, for instance, was just as unhealthy—just as far from the homes of the sepoys; under British as under Native government; yet the premium previously given for foreign service was withdrawn on annexation. So also in the Punjab, and elsewhere.

The orders for distant service came round more rapidly as territory increased. The sepoys became involved in debt by change of station, and the Madras troops could ill afford the travelling expenses of their families, from whom they never willingly separate, and whose presence has probably been a chief cause of their fidelity during the crisis. One regiment, for instance, has had, within the last few years, to build houses and huts at three different stations; and on their late return from Burmah, the men had to pay sixty rupees per cart, to bring their wives and children from Burhampoor to Vellore, a distance of 700 miles. This is said to be a fair average specimen of what is going on everywhere. "The result is, that the men are deeply embarrassed. A sepoy on seven rupees a-month, who has to pay fifty or sixty rupees for his wife's cart once in every two or three years, is unavoidably plunged in debt. He must borrow at exorbitant interest from the money-lender; and before he can reclaim the past, the 'route' comes for a fresh march to far-distant cantonments, and hurries him into fresh difficulties."‡

The Bengal sepoys do not carry their families with them on a campaign, but leave them in their native villages, visiting them every year. The furloughs granted for this purpose, have been diminished in consequence of the growing necessities of the service; and another infringement of a prerogative, which their separation from their wives and children rendered very valuable, was committed by the withdrawal of their privilege of franking letters to their homes. Several late regulations regarding the payment of pensions, and increasing strictness on the part of the general invaliding committee, are asserted to have been viewed by the sepoys as involving breach of faith on the part of the government. They are said to have felt with the old Scotchwoman, "I ken ye're cheating me, but I dinna ken exactly hoo."§ Any alteration in the rules of the retiring pension-list, was watched by the sepoy with jealous care. The terms which secured to him a fixed monthly stipend in the event of becoming incapacitated for further duty after a service of fifteen years, and which, if he died in battle, or from sickness while on foreign service, made some provision for his family, could not of course be altered, even slightly, without exciting alarm as to what further changes might follow. The Bengal sepoys were largely drawn from Oude; and not from Oude generally, but from certain limited districts. Naturally there existed among them the feeling observable in British soldiers born in the same county, when associated in a regiment on foreign service; and possibly it was clanship, quite as much as caste, which bound them together: but whatever it was, a strong tie of union, and consequent power of combination, existed among them, which rendered them efficient for good or evil. Sir John Malcolm had given a memorable warning regarding them. Neither the Hindoo nor the Mohammedan soldier were, he said, revengeful, but both were prone to acts of extreme violence in points where they deemed their honour slighted. The absence of any fear of death was common to them all. Such an instru-

* Minute, dated 28th February, 1856; p. 41.

† See *Daily News*, July 13th, 1857, p.p. 26, 27.

‡ Norton's *Rebellion in India*.

§ Letter signed "Caubulee."—*Daily News*, July 17th, 1857.

ment as an army constituted of men like these afforded, had need be managed with care and wisdom, or our strength would become our danger. The minds of the sepoys were alive to every impulse, and would all vibrate to the same touch. Kindness, liberality, and justice would preserve their attachment: besides this, Malcolm adds, "we must attend to the most trifling of their prejudices, and avoid rash innovations; but, above all, those that are calculated to convey to their minds the most distant alarm in points connected with their usages or religion."* This policy found little favour among the Europeans in 1856.

The exclusive payment of the troops in such an inconveniently heavy coin as the silver rupee (two-shilling) piece, obliges them to resort frequently to money-changers; and thus to lose a per-centage on their small stipend. Unfortunately, the governor-general, whose practical ability might have been so beneficially exercised in this and other matters, appears to have listened to only one set of statements regarding the Native army, and to have acted upon the principle that the sepoy had been "overpetted," and required sterner discipline.

General Anson, who succeeded Sir William Gomm in command of the army, took the same view of the case, only a more exaggerated one. When the cartridge agitation first commenced, he set at nought the feelings of the sepoys, by declaring that "he would never give in to their beastly prejudices." This speech sufficiently reveals the character of the commander-in-chief to whom it could be even attributed with any show of probability; and it certainly deserves a place among the immediate causes of the mutiny.† The European officers appear to have too generally adopted the same tone, especially as regarded the Bengalees; and it was commonly said, that whereas the leading feeling with the Bombay and Madras sepoys was the honour of their regiment, that of the Bengal sepoy was the pride of caste. But, in fact, all the Hindoos, except the outcastes, maintain more or less strongly, certain religious prejudices which interfere with their efficiency as soldiers; especially their invariable dislike to sea voyages, and to passing certain recognised boundaries.

The Afghan war was very unpopular for this reason; and the calamities and sore discomfiture endured there, deepened the unfavourable impression which it made upon the whole Native army, and generally upon the people of India. An insurrection in the Saugor and Nerbudda districts broke out in 1842. The wild barons of the hills and jungles swept down over the valleys and cultivated plains; yet the pillaged inhabitants yielded little support to the officers of the government, and would furnish no information with regard to the movements of the insurrectionists. Colonel Sleeman was sent by Lord Ellenborough to inquire into the cause of this inconsistency. He assembled a party of about fifty of the low-landers in his tent; and there, seated on the carpet, each man freely spoke his mind. Umrao Sing, a sturdy, honest farmer, spoke of the conduct of the chiefs as quite natural. The sudden withdrawal of the troops for objects of distant conquest, and the tidings of disaster and defeat, awakened their hopes of regaining their former position, for they thought the British raj at an end. Colonel Sleeman said, that the farmers and cultivators of the disturbed districts, having been more favoured, in regard to life and property, than in any other part of India, ought to have been stanch to their protectors: "but," he added, "there are some men who never can be satisfied; give them what you will, they will always be craving after more." "True, sir," replied Umrao Sing, with the utmost gravity, "there are some people who can never be satisfied, give them what you will; give them the whole of Hindoostan, and they will go off to Cabool to take more."‡

Hedayut Ali, a subahdar of the Bengal Seik battalion, a man of excellent character, whose father and grandfather had occupied the highest positions attainable to natives in the British service, has furnished some important evidence on the causes of disaffection among the sepoys. He lays much stress on the sufferings endured by the sepoys in Afghanistan in 1838-'9, and the violations of caste which they were compelled to commit by the extreme cold, especially in the matter of eating without first bathing, and of wearing sheepskin jackets; whereas no Hindoo, except of the lowest caste, likes to touch the skin of a dead animal.

The annexation of Oude is cited by this witness as having, in addition to other real

* Malcolm on the Government of India, p. 219.

† Cooper's *Crisis in the Punjab*, p. 37.

‡ Sleeman's *Journey through Oude*, vol. ii., p. 95.

or imaginary grievances, caused universal disaffection throughout the army, which from that time determined upon mutinying. The grounds upon which this opinion is based, are very clearly stated. On the 14th of March, 1856, the King of Oude reached Cawnpoor, on his way to Calcutta. Hedayut Ali reached that city on the same day. He remained there six days, and had frequent interviews with the king's vakeels, courtiers, and servants; as did also the principal people of Cawnpoor, and many of the Native officers and sepoys of the regiments stationed there; all of whom were indignant at the king's dispossession. The vakeel of Nana Sahib was among the visitors, and took pains to increase the excitement, by saying how displeased and grieved his master was by the conduct of the English. Shortly after, Hedayut Ali proceeded to join his corps at Lahore, and marched thence to Bengal. On the way, he learnt that the Native infantry at Barrackpoor were showing symptoms of mutiny; and this, with other intelligence, he, from time to time, communicated to his commanding officer.

The King of Oude again visited Cawnpoor in December, 1856, and stayed about a fortnight; during which time much mischief is said to have been concocted. Meanwhile the commander-in-chief and the governor-general were initiating measures very displeasing to various classes of natives. The Madras sepoys had shown, at Vellore, how dangerous it was to interfere with the marks on their foreheads, or the fashion of their turbans. The Seiks and Mohammedans are scarcely less susceptible on the subject of their beards and moustachios. Consequently, in the extensive enlistments of these races, carried on after the annexation of the Punjab, a pledge was given that no interference should be attempted in the matter of hair-dressing. General Anson, however, issued an order, directing the Mohammedans to cut their beards after a prescribed fashion. They refused, pleading the condition of their enlistment. The general insisted on their obeying the order, or quitting the service; and many of them, sooner than suffer what, in their view, was a disgrace, took their discharge, and went to their homes. Sir Charles Napier understood the native character far too well to have so needlessly played the martinet, independently of the sympathy which he would naturally have felt for the recusants, by reason of having himself "a beard like a Cashmere goat." The discharged sepoys "bitterly complained of the commanding officers having broken faith with them; and several of them, who afterwards re-enlisted in the same regiment as Hedayut Ali, frequently spoke of the manner in which they had been deprived of the benefit of several years' service. But the crowning act of innovation enacted by Lord Canning and General Anson, was the general service order of 1856, by which all recruits were to be compelled to swear that they would go, by sea or land, wherever their services were required. The refusal of the 38th Bengal infantry to march to Burmah, was severely punished by Lord Dalhousie's sending the regiment by land to Dacca, where the cantonments were very bad, and the loss of life among the troops extremely heavy."* He did not, however, attempt to strike such a blow as that now aimed at caste; for the unqualified aversion to the sea entertained by the Bengal sepoys, would, it was well known, prevent many from bringing up their children to a profession which they had learned to look upon as an hereditary means of obtaining an honourable maintenance. They feared also for themselves. Hedayut Ali says—"When the old sepoys heard of this order, they were much frightened and displeased. 'Up to this day, those men who went to Afghanistan have not been readmitted to their caste; how are we to know where the English may force us to go? They will be ordering us next to go to London.' Any new order is looked upon with much suspicion by the Native army, and is much canvassed in every regiment."

This latter remark is unquestionably a just one; the intercourse maintained throughout the Bengal army, and the rapid and correct transmission of intelligence, having been one of the most marked features of the mutinies. The following observations are also painfully correct:—

"Of late years the sepoys have not confided in their officers. * * * A native of Hindoostan seldom opens his mind to his officer; he only says what he thinks would please his officer. The sepoys reserve their real opinion until they return to their lines and to their comrades. * * * The government must be aware, that when a soldier has once or twice shown a disposition to mutiny, he is useless as a soldier: one mutinous sepoy infects a whole company; and gradually, one man after another, from fear or sympathy, joins the mutineers.

"Many commanding officers, to my knowledge, reported that regiments were all right, when they

* Norton's *Rebellion in India*, p. 21.

knew that there were discontent and bad feeling in the ranks; and, to my belief, for the sake of the name of their respective regiments, concealed the real state of their regiments, until at length the sepoys took to murdering their officers. * * * Another reason (and, in my opinion, a very serious one) why the army became mutinous and disaffected is this. Promotion all went by seniority, and not, as it ought, according to merit and proficiency. All the old men, from length of service worth nothing as commissioned or non-commissioned officers, received promotion; while younger men, in every way fit, languished in their lines: saying, 'What use is there in us exerting ourselves; we cannot get promotion until our turn comes, and that time can't come until our heads are gray and our mouths toothless.' For this reason, the sepoys for the most part drew their pay, and were careless with regard to their duty. The higher ranks of the Native army, from old age alone, were quite incapacitated from doing their duty, even had they the will to do it. I state confidently, that the generality of Native officers were an encumbrance to the state: instead of commanding sepoys, the sepoys commanded them; and instead of the commissioned and non-commissioned ranks preventing the men from mutinying, they rather persuaded them to do so."*

The above opinion of a Native officer on the effect of the Bengal military system upon his countrymen, reads like the echo of that of Indophilus, regarding its operation on the Europeans. The arguments urged in the two cases are so nearly identical, that it may well be asked whether justice and common sense do not prompt to the same course of general legislation.

"Under a pure seniority system, an officer's promotion goes on precisely in the same manner whether he exerts himself or takes his ease; and as few love exertion for its own sake, the majority take their ease. Under a system of selection according to qualification and service, promotion is dependent upon exertion, and the majority consequently exert themselves. Those only who know the Bengal army can form some estimate of the amount of idleness and bad habit engendered by the seniority system co-operating with the enervating influences of the climate, which would be converted into active interest in professional duty, by the substitution of a well-considered system of promotion according to qualification and good service."†

Lord Melville‡ had also urged, so far as he was allowed to do, the evils of the seniority system. Other authorities, more or less directly, assert, that it was the defective character, rather than the insufficient number, of the officers left to do regimental duty as "the refuse of the army," which weakened their hold on their men. Brigadier-general Jacob remarks, that "qualifications, not numbers, are necessary for the leaders of the native Indian soldiers;" and his opinion is corroborated by the fact, that the irregular and local force, which was officered entirely by a few but picked men, was—allowing for discrepancies of pay and dates of enlistment—generally held to be in an equally, if not more, efficient condition than the regular regiments.

A well-informed, but not unprejudiced witness says, that the conduct of irregular regiments, which possess only three European officers, has always contrasted so favourably with that of line regiments, with their fourteen or fifteen, that the natural conclusion one would arrive at is, that the latter are over-officered. He also deprecates the seniority system, by which a sepoy who may enter the service at the age of sixteen, cannot count on finding himself a naik (corporal) before he attains the age of thirty-six; a havildar (sergeant) before forty-five; a jemadar (lieutenant) before fifty-four; or a subahdar (captain) before sixty; while, "after fifty, most natives are utterly useless."§

The full complement of European officers to each regular regiment is twenty-six; but of these half are generally absent, either on service or on furlough. The commander is usually a lieutenant-colonel; then there is an adjutant, to superintend the drill; a quartermaster, whose duty it is to look after the clothing of the men; and, lastly, an interpreter. The necessity for this last functionary lies at the root of our late sudden calamity; for the officers, if they had been able and willing to hold close intercourse with their men, and explain to them the reasons for the various unpopular orders recently issued, would, if they could not remove disaffection, at least have become acquainted with its existence. An infantry regiment on the Bengal establishment comprises ten companies, each containing a hundred privates, two native commissioned, and twelve non-commissioned officers.

The great increase of the irregular regiments has been in itself a source of jealousy and heartburning to the regular troops, who

* Translated by Captain T. Rattray, from the original Oordoo; and published in the *Times*, April 1st, 1858.

† *Letters of Indophilus*, p. 18.

‡ The directors are said to defend themselves for neglecting Lord Melville's representations, on the ground that his "evidence was contradicted most strongly, in every particular, by that of Sir Patrick Grant, who assured us, that the Bengal army (of which he had been long adjutant-general) was all that it should be."—Letter, signed "H. C."—*Daily News*, July 25th, 1857.

§ *Mutiny of the Bengal Army* by one who has served under Sir Charles Napier; pp. 1; 7.

expected that their numbers would be largely augmented on the recent annexations, and that extensive promotions would take place. This expectation was wholly disappointed. The enormous expenses of the army rendered the comparative cheapness of irregular troops an irresistible advantage. According to the Army List for 1857, the irregular and local force of Bengal numbered forty-two infantry, and twenty-seven cavalry regiments; and the so-called contingents of Native States, comprised sixteen of cavalry and nineteen of infantry: in all, ninety-four regiments; the whole officered by picked men from the twenty-four regiments of the regular army. The relative numbers of the three armies need not be given here, as their proportions and distribution are immediately connected with the history about to be entered on. The question of the greased cartridges has been already noticed under the head of "Caste;" and will frequently recur in the ensuing narrative.

A Mohammedan Conspiracy, widely ramified and deeply rooted, is urged by some authorities as in itself the great motive power of the late political convulsion; others, on the contrary, deny its existence, on the ground of no sufficient evidence having been adduced thereof.

Dr. Alexander Duff, the eloquent Presbyterian preacher of Calcutta, writing in August, 1857, says—"It is a long-concocted Mohammedan conspiracy now come to a head. The main object is the destruction of British power, and the reascendancy of Mohammedan. Even the cartridge affair was only a casual incident, of which the conspirators adroitly took advantage."*

In his published *Letters on the Indian Rebellion*, the Doctor throughout insists on Mussulman intrigues as being continually developed and exposed; but he wrote in a season of excitement, when rumours abounded of dangers and atrocities, many of which have happily proved unfounded, but which naturally served to confirm his preconceived opinion. The truth is terrible enough; and for the sake of our national honour, for the sake of human nature, and, above all, for the sake of truth itself, we should strive to strip this fearful episode of the obscurity in which conflicting exaggerations have wrapped its origin and progress. Beyond question, the Mohammedan princes of India have strong reason for combining to restore the green flag of Islam to its former supremacy in Hindoostan. If an opportunity offered, it is at least highly probable that the orthodox Sonnites of Delhi, and the heterodox Sheiahs of Oude, would be content to forget for a time the rival claims of Caliphs and Imaums to apostolic succession, and make common cause against the power which treats both with indifference.

The whole Mussulman body would of necessity be drawn closer together by the danger which threatened all alike. They had still something to lose; that is, something to fight for. Submission had not succeeded in preserving the independence of Oude; and even Hyderabad, much more the titular principality of Delhi, seemed tottering to a close. Still the Mohammedans were as a handful amid a heap; and the chief point to solve was, whether the recent innovations had sufficiently disgusted the leading Hindoos to render them willing to forget past usurpations, and join with their former subjugators in attempting the overthrow of the British raj.

Tippoo Sultan had made an effort of the kind, but without success; and it now appears, by his own proclamation, that Prince Mirza Feroze Shah, on his return from a pilgrimage to Mecca, "persuaded many at Delhi to raise a religious war;" being incited thereto by observing that "the English were in a bad and precarious state."†

Great anxiety had been felt at Delhi, throughout the period of Lord Dalhousie's administration, regarding the manner in which his annexation policy would be brought to bear upon the family who, fallen as they were, still represented, in the minds of the Indian people, the mighty Mogul emperors of old, and whose restoration to power had been prayed for daily in the mosques throughout India for nearly a hundred years.‡

In 1849, the heir-apparent died, and the Indian government recommended the Court of Directors to "terminate the dynasty of Timour whenever the reigning king should die." The court consented; but so reluctantly, that the governor-general did not care to avail himself of their permission, and therefore recognised the grandson of

* Speech of the Hon. A. Kinnaird, 11th June, 1857: second edition; p. 35.

† Proclamation issued by Prince Mirza Mohammed Feroze Shah, 17th February, 1858.

‡ See *Times*, September 1st, 1857.

the king as heir-apparent; "but only on condition that he should quit the palace in Delhi, in order to reside in the palace at the Kootub; and that he should, as king, receive the governor-general of India, at all times, on terms of perfect equality."

These conditions show that something of external pomp and circumstance still lingered around Delhi, of which the representatives of the East India Company were anxious to be rid, and the royal family as anxious to retain. True, the power had long vanished; but even the tarnished pageantry was clung to, naturally enough, by those who had no other birthright, and no prospect of being able to win their way to wealth and honour as warriors; the profession of arms being the only one in which a Mohammedan prince of the blood could engage without forfeiting caste. The sullateen (plural for sultan)—as the various branches of the family are termed—are probably a very idle and dissolute race. It is in the nature of things that they should have become so. Certainly we never did anything to hinder their debasement; and have, while acting as their political and pecuniary trustees, been lamentably indifferent to their moral and physical welfare. We never evinced the slightest interest in them; and have no right to wonder at their degradation.

With the downfall of the dynasty we had no concern. In dealing generously with Shah Alum, we acted with sound policy. All India respected us for it. Even in Leadenhall-street, sufficient memory of the bygone feelings and events lingered in 1849, to make the application of the new absorption laws seem peculiarly harsh in the case of Delhi. The scruples of the Court of Directors induced Lord Dalhousie to draw back his hand, at least as far as the titular sovereignty was concerned; but his proposal for its extinction having been once mooted, and even sanctioned, it may be considered that the sentence was rather deferred than reversed. This, at least, was the public opinion. It is a singular fact, that the same accounts from India, which have been already quoted as describing the unbroken tranquillity of the entire peninsula at the close of 1856, state that the palace of Delhi was "in a ferment," owing to the recent death of the heir-apparent from cholera, and the renewed discussion regarding the succession. "We have (it is added) no treaty, agreement, or stipulation with Delhi. The king's privileges and pension were all granted as of free grace; and the former will probably be withdrawn. The palace is a sink of iniquity; and the family, on the death of its present head, will probably be compelled to move."*

The same paper contains the announcement that the anticipated declaration of war against Persia had appeared in a proclamation published at Calcutta on the 1st of November, 1856. The *casus belli* was the breach of the treaty of 1853, by which the Persian government promised to abstain from all interference with Herat; the independence of that city, under its brave chief, Esa Khan, being deemed essential to the security of the British frontier. On the pretence that Dost Mohammed had been instigated to seize Candahar and advance upon Herat, a Persian army crossed into the Herat territory (which was declared to be Persian soil), and laid siege to the city. Under instructions from the home government, a force was assembled at Bombay for service in the Persian Gulf. The *Times'* correspondent describes the departure of the force, in three divisions, as taking place in the middle of November. The first, consisting of H.M.'s 64th regiment and the 20th Native infantry, embarked from Vingorla in two steamers, each with its transport in tow. The second, comprising a European regiment, the 2nd Belooch cavalry, and two squadrons of the 3rd cavalry, sailed from Poorbunder and Kurrachee. The third embarked from Kurrachee a few days later, and consisted of the 4th Rifles (a very strong and well-appointed regiment), two troops of the Poona horse, a field battery, a troop of horse artillery, a third-class siege-train, and two companies of sappers and miners. The rendezvous was fixed at Bunder Abbas, a place near the entrance of the gulf, in the occupation of our Arab ally, the Imaum of Muscat.†

At the time the above facts were recorded, no idea appears to have been entertained of any connection existing between the Persian war and the ferment in the palace of Delhi. The declaration of war had been long expected; and, according to the *Times'* correspondent, created little excitement at Bombay. The Persians, who are numerous there, as also in other large Indian cities, relied on the promise of protection given them, and remained quiescent. "Even

* Calcutta correspondent, November 8th, 1856.—*Times*, December 9th, 1856.

† Bombay correspondent, November 17th, 1856.—*Times*, December 9th, 1856.

the Mussulman population, who sympathise with Persia," he adds, "sympathise still more with Afghanistan;* and the fact that we are fighting with, and not against, Dost Mohammed, is thoroughly understood. The European public accepts the war with a feeling of quiet resignation. The idea that it is our destiny to advance—that we cannot help ourselves, has obtained a control over the public mind; and every war breaks the monotony of Indian life, which is the curse of India, as of all aristocratic life."

It seems probable that the Persian war materially, though indirectly, contributed to break up the aristocratic monotony of high-caste European life, by denuding India of her most reliable troops. The number sent, of men of all arms, to the Persian Gulf, in November, 1856, amounted to 5,820, of whom 2,270 were Europeans. In the following February a still larger force was dispatched, under Brigadier-general Havelock, consisting of 5,340 men, of whom about 1,770 were Europeans; and 800 cavalry were subsequently dispatched at an enormous cost. Thus the "army of Persia" deprived India of about 12,000 men, of whom one-third were Europeans. Lord Canning considered this force quite sufficient for any operations which Major-general Outram could undertake before the hot season; but, he adds, "it is certain that very large reinforcements will be needed before a second campaign, commencing with the autumn of 1857, can be entered upon."

Man proposes—God disposes. Long before the autumn set in, an Indian campaign had commenced, which, whether the Persians had or had not withdrawn their claims on Herat, must have equally relieved the governor-general from the task of providing a third armament for the Persian Gulf, "to include not less than six European regiments of infantry and one of cavalry." The Persians were overcome, and the independence of Herat was secured, at a cost to Britain of about £500,000 in money.† Meanwhile, intimations of Persian intrigues were given to the authorities by various persons, but set at nought as idle rumours. The trial of the King of Delhi furnishes evidence that inducements to revolt were held forth by the Shah of Persia, who promised money and troops. His proclamation to that effect was posted over the mosque gate, and was taken down by order of Sir Theophilus Metcalfe, who, moreover, was informed by John Everett, a Christian risaldar very popular with the natives, that he had been warned to fly, as the Persians were coming, and the Mussulmans were greatly excited. Sir T. Metcalfe thought the information of no importance.‡ A statement of a Mohammedan plot was laid before Mr. Colvin; but he also suffered the warning to pass unheeded, and did not even report it to government.

At this very time Delhi was absolutely devoid of European troops, yet strongly fortified, and stored with the munitions of war. Its palace-fort was still tenanted by the representative of the *rois fainéants* of the East, whose persons had formerly been fought for by opposing factions as a tower of strength; their compulsory signature being used notoriously to legitimatise usurpation, and influence the populace.

Extreme insalubrity is given by Lord Ellenborough as the reason why no European regiment had ever yet been stationed there, sickness prevailing to such an extent, that, after the rains, two-thirds of the strength even of the Native troops were in hospital.§ Sanitary measures would probably have prevented, or greatly mitigated this evil (as at Seringapatam); nor does it appear that any cause but neglect existed to render Delhi less habitable than of old.

Sir Charles Napier's prediction was one which any chance traveller might have reasonably made; and there is, therefore, the less excuse for the absence of obviously necessary precautions. "Men," he said, "of all parts of Asia meet in Delhi; and, some day or other, much mischief will be hatched within those city walls, and no European troops at hand."‖ He knew also, and officially urged upon the governor-general, "that the powder-magazine was defended only by a guard of fifty natives, and the gates so weak that a mob could push them

* This assertion may be reasonably questioned, since the Sheiahs of Oude looked up to the Shah of Persia as the head of their sect. Mr. Ludlow says that the Persian war caused great excitement in Northern India, where many of the Moslems were of the Sheiah sect; and he adds, that one of his relatives had himself, within the last two or three years, read placards on the walls of Delhi, calling true believers to the holy war in the name of the Shah of Persia.—*Lectures on British India*, vol. ii., p. 219.

† Speech of Lord Claude Hamilton: Indian debate, July 20th, 1857.

‡ Calcutta correspondent.—*Times*, March 29, 1858.

§ Indian debate, July 13th, 1857.

‖ Letter to a lieutenant-colonel in the Bengal artillery: published in the *Times*, 20th August, 1857.

in; whereas the place ought to be garrisoned by 12,000 picked men."*

The absence of a European garrison in Delhi is the most unpardonable of our blunders; and—what does not always follow—it is the one for which we have most dearly paid, not in money only, but in the life-blood of our best and bravest soldiers. One cannot think of Nicholson and his gallant companions without bitterly denouncing the neglect which suffered Delhi to fall defenceless at the feet of a few rebels, put at once a sword and shield into their hands, and gave them the ancient Mussulman metropolis of India as a nucleus for every aggrieved chief, every disaffected soldier, every reckless adventurer, escaped convict, pindarree, thug, dacoit, to rally round, for the destruction of the British raj—at least for a long carnival of war and loot. The very heroism of the troops who regained Delhi embitters the recollection of the neglect by which it was lost. *Dulce et decorum est pro patria mori!* as one of them (Captain Battye) said when mortally wounded; but, to their country, their very devotion only renders it more painful that the necessity for such sacrifices should have been so culpably occasioned. This is, however, anticipating events, the progress of which will best evidence how far Persian intrigues may have been connected with the mutiny. At present, many assertions are made, the truth of which yet remains in dispute. It would seem, however, that the efforts of the King of Persia had been chiefly directed to Delhi; and that if communications were entered into with leading Mohammedans in other parts of India, these had not had time to ripen; and, consequently, when the mutinies broke forth, heralded by incendiary fires in every British camp, the conspirators must have been taken by surprise almost as much as the Europeans themselves.†

Shett Nowmull, "a native merchant of Kurrachee, for many years favourably known to government on account of his great intelligence, his extensive influence and connexions throughout the countries on our western frontier, and his true attachment to the British government," communicated, to Mr. Freere, commissioner of Sinde, in June, 1857, his reasons for believing that "Persian influence was at the bottom of the mutiny." He declared that cossids (messengers), under different disguises, with letters secreted in the soles of their shoes or otherwise, had, for the last two years, been regularly passing between Delhi and the Persian court, *viâ* Candahar; that a great spread of the Sheiah tenets of Islamism had been observable during the same period; and also that a very perceptible decrease had taken place in the rancour usually existing between the Sheiahs and Sonnites. The new cartridges had been used "through the same influence," to excite the feelings of the Hindoo portion of the army, and lead them to mutiny. Dost Mohammed, he said, thought more of Persia than of England, for a very pertinent reason—"Persia is on the Dost's head; Peshawur is under his feet:"‡ in other words, a man placed between two fires, would especially dread the more immediate one.

Prophecies of various kinds were current—always are current, in India; but when the mutiny broke out, more heed was given to them by the natives; and the Europeans also lent an ear, knowing that a pretended prophecy might disguise an actual plot, and, in more ways than one, work out its own fulfilment. The alleged prediction which limited the duration of the British raj to a hundred years, was repeated far and wide;§

* *Memoir on the Defence of India;* addressed by Sir C. Napier to Lord Dalhousie. See Indian debate of 23rd July, 1857.

† In the captured tent of the Shahzada commander, after the rout of the Persians at Mohumrah, there was found a royal proclamation addressed "to all the people of Heran;" but which also called on "the Afghan tribes, and the inhabitants of that country who are co-religionists of the Persians, and who possess the same Koran and Kebla, and laws of the prophet, to take part in the *Jahâd.*" It expressly invited the followers of Islam in India and Sinde to unite and wreak vengeance on the British for all the injuries which the holy faith had suffered from them, and not to withhold any sacrifice in the holy cause. "The old and the young, the small and the great, the wise and the ignorant, the ryot and the sepoy, all without exception," are summoned by the Shah-in-Shah to arise in defence of the orthodox faith of the prophet; and having girt up the waist of valour, adorn their persons with arms and weapons; and let the Ullema and preachers call on the people in the mosques and public assemblies, and in the pulpits, to join in a *Jahâd*, in the cause of God; and thus shall the Ghazis in the cause of faith have a just title to the promises contained in the words of the prophet, "Verily we are of those who fought in the cause of God."—Blackwood's *Edinburgh Magazine* for 1857: article entitled "The Poorbeah Mutiny."

‡ Letter from H. B. B. Freere, commissioner of Sinde, to Lord Elphinstone, governor of Bombay, 11th June, 1857.—Parl. Papers (253), 4th May, 1858; p. 48.

§ Dr. A. Duff's *Letters:* London, 1858; p. 26.

and the Europeans in Calcutta and many of the leading cities, watched the approach of the centenary of Plassy with a feverish anxiety bordering on panic.

But prophecies such as these, are usually the consequence or the sign, rather than the cause, of popular tumults. In health we can smile at language which, in sickness, excites a fevered imagination to frenzy. For years the natives had been allowed to speculate on the future destiny, and comment on the present policy, of their rulers, without any restraint whatever; now, every third word seemed treason. Such of the English functionaries as understood Indian languages, began to examine the literature of the day; and were exceedingly puzzled to decide what was, and what was not, written with a sinister intent.

A Persian paper, for instance, was brought to Mr. Freere about the commencement of hostilities, which described the signs preceding the day of judgment, in language strikingly applicable to existing circumstances, and calculated to unsettle and excite men's minds, and prepare them for some sudden disturbance; but it read so like a free translation of a sermon by a popular English preacher on the same subject, as to render it difficult to decide how to act with regard to it.*

The struggle which has taken place between the Christians and the Mussulmans, in various distinct parts of Europe as well as Asia, and which has been cotemporaneous with the Indian mutiny, is viewed as indicating a desire on the part of the present representatives of Islam to regain something of their former dominancy. The Indo-Mohammedans are, however, very unlike their co-religionists in other countries, and the anti-idolatrous doctrines of their founder have been so corrupted by intermixture of the superstitious practices of modern Brahminism, that it is not possible to judge their feelings by any test applicable to Mohammedans in general.

The English naturally viewed, with great alarm, the fanatical outbreaks at Jaffa, Marash, and Belgrade, and still more so the alarming one at Jeddah; but the government have wisely striven to repress the suspicious distrust and aversion manifested by the Europeans to the Mohammedans as a class, fearing to see them driven to revolt by conduct equally unjust and impolitic.†

* Letter from H. B. B. Freere.—Parl. Papers (253), 4th May, 1858; p. 48.

This possible source of mutiny has been as yet but very partially explored, and the present heat of prejudice and excitement must be allowed to subside before any satisfactory conclusion can be formed on the subject.

Foreign intrigues are alleged to have been practised against us, and attempts made to undermine our position in India, in various ways, by a Christian as well as by a Mohammedan power; by Russia as well as Persia. It is difficult to say how far the vague expectation of Russian invasion (which certainly exists in India) has been occasioned by exaggerated rumours, and perverted reports gleaned from European journals, and circulated by the native press during the period of the Crimean war, or how much of it may be attributed to the deliberate machinations of Russia.

In England, both sources of danger were equally disregarded; and, amid the miserable inconsistencies which marked the war from beginning to end, not the least was the fact, that one of the arguments used to reconcile the people to heavy additional taxation, was the necessity of maintaining and restoring effete and incapable Mohammedan Turkey, as a means of checking the inordinate increase of the power of Russia, and making the battle-field in the Crimea, rather than on the frontier of our Indian empire. The Russian government intimated, that to roll back their European boundary would but lead them to advance their Asiatic one; and some years before the campaign of 1853, their organ at St. Petersburg declared that, in the event of war, the czar would dictate the terms of peace at Calcutta. In the teeth of this defiant warning, the British ministry, accustomed to treat India as a sort of peculiarly circumstanced colony, and to neglect colonies as a matter of course, paid no heed whatever to the strange excitement manifested throughout India at the first tidings of the Crimean conflict. No pains were taken to ascertain the tone adopted by the natives, or to guard against rumours circulated and schemes set afoot by foreign emissaries, in a country where a passport system would have been a common measure of prudence. Ministers concentrated all their energies on the conduct of the European struggle (though not with any very satisfactory result), and acted as if on the understanding that, "during the Russian war, the

† See letter of Lord Hobart.—*Times*, December 3rd, 1857.

government had too much to do, to be expected to attend to India."*

The ill effects which the tidings of the Russian and Persian wars were calculated to produce in India, were aggravated by the drain of European troops thereby occasioned. The government demand for two regiments of infantry for the Crimean war, was earnestly deprecated by Lord Dalhousie.

"Although the war with Russia," observes his lordship, "does not directly affect our Indian dominions, yet it is unquestionably exercising at this moment a most material influence upon the minds of the people over whom we rule, and upon the feelings of the nations by which we are surrounded; and thus it is tending indirectly to affect the strength and the stability of our power.

"The authorities in England cannot, I think, be aware of the exaggerated estimate of the power of Russia which has been formed by the people of India. I was myself unaware of it until the events of the past year have forced it upon my convictions. Letters from various parts of India have shown me, that the present contest is regarded by them with the deepest interest, and that its issue is by no means considered so certain as we might desire. However mortifying to our pride it may be to know it, and however unaccountable such a belief may appear in people living amidst the visible evidences of our might, it is an unquestionable fact, that it is widely believed in India, that Russia is pressing us hard, and that she will be more than a match for us at last.

"We know by our correspondence in the East, that the King of Ava has declaredly been acting on this feeling; and that, influenced by it, he has been delaying the dispatch of the mission which many months ago he spoke of sending to Calcutta. * * *

"India is now in perfect tranquillity from end to end. I entertain no apprehension whatever of danger or disturbance. We are perfectly secure so long as we are strong, and are believed to be so: but if European troops shall be now withdrawn from India to Europe; if countenance shall thus be given to the belief already prevalent, that we have grappled with an antagonist whose strength will prove equal to overpower us; if, by consenting to withdrawal, we shall weaken that essential element of our military strength, which has already been declared to be no more than adequate for ordinary times; and if, further, we should be called upon to dispatch an army to the Persian Gulf—an event which, unlooked-for now, may any day be brought about by the thraldom in which Persia is held, and by the feeble and fickle character of the Shah; then, indeed, I shall no longer feel, and can no longer express the same confidence as before, that the security and stability of our position in the East will remain unassailed. * * * In a country where the entire English community is but a handful of scattered strangers, I feel it to be a public duty to record, that in my deliberate judgment, the European infantry force in India, ought in no case to be weakened by a single man, so long as England shall be engaged in her present struggle with Russia."†

The regiments were nevertheless withdrawn, and were not even returned at the close of the Russian war. Then came the Persian war, and the requisition upon Lord Canning, who complied less reluctantly than Lord Dalhousie had done; but still under protest. Lord Canning reminded the home authorities, that, for all Indian purposes, the strength of the army would be equally reduced, whether the regiments were sent to Persia or to the Crimea. He spoke of the excitement which even a distant war raised in the minds of the natives, and insisted on the necessity of an increase of European troops, as necessary to the safety of India during the continuance of hostile operations against Persia.‡

It is at least possible that the Russian government should have retaliated on us our invasion of its territory, by striving to sow discord in India. The course of the rebellion has afforded many incidents calculated to produce a conviction of their having done so: for instance, the assertion of one of the Delhi princes, that when the mutineers marched on that city, the royal family believed them to be the advanced guard of the Russian army. Another far more significant fact, which was communicated to me on the authority of a naval officer in a high position on the Indus, was the extraordinary amount of silver roubles seen in the bazaars in the North-West Provinces, immediately before the mutiny, and supposed to have passed to the tables of the money-changers from the notoriously well-filled pockets of Russian spies. The extent and mode in which this agency may have been employed, will probably never be revealed; but it can hardly be doubted that it is an active and recognised mode of obtaining the accurate and comprehensive information possessed by the government of St. Petersburg, regarding the condition of the domestic and foreign affairs of every other nation. Spies, in time of peace, may easily become political incendiaries in time of war, in countries hostile to the authority which they serve. As to detecting them, that is next to impossible: a charge of this nature is always difficult to prove; but, to an Englishman, the difficulty is insur-

* Speeches of Mr. Disraeli and Mr. Vernon Smith, president of the India Board.—Indian debate, July 26th, 1857.

† Minute by the governor-general: 13th September, 1854.—Parl Papers, 12th February, 1858; pp. 7; 9.

‡ Minutes dated 7th and 8th February, 1857.—Parl. Papers, 20th July, 1857; pp. 8, 9.

mountable. Clever thieves, clever forgers, England has produced in abundance: unscrupulous politicians are not quite unknown among us; but our secret service department has, on the whole, been singularly free from subterranean and systematised "dirty work." The secret opening of a letter is scouted at, in a political functionary, as listening at a keyhole would be in a private individual; and, even while quite uncertain as to the extent of the mutiny in 1849, Sir Charles Napier would not entertain the idea of examining the correspondence of the sepoys, then passing to an unusual extent through the government post-offices. The Russian language has probably many words which, like the French one *fin, finesse,* and others, have no equivalent in English; nor has America—sharp, shrewd, and slick as some of her children are—annexed to the mother-tongue any words which serve as fit exponents for that peculiar branch of continental diplomacy which renders trained spies a regular governmental department. We have no political detectives among us. Our aristocracy, whether of rank or letters, may indeed be occasionally annoyed by the indiscretion of caterers for the public press, in the shape of newspaper reporters and gossiping memoir writers; but, at our tables, the host speaks his mind in the plainest terms regarding the most powerful personages of the moment, without fearing that one of his servants may be taking notes behind his chair, which may procure his exile or imprisonment; and the hostess is equally certain that none of her guests will drive from her roof to lodge information of some enthusiastic ebullition which has escaped her lips, and for which neither youth nor beauty, character nor station, would save her from personal chastisement under the orders of a Russian Usher of the Black Rod. What we call grumbling in Great Britain, folks abroad call treason; and that is an offence for which Britons have so little temptation, that they are slow to note its existence, or provide against it even when themselves exercising those despotic powers which, if men dare not openly oppose, they secretly strive against. To what extent Russian emissaries have fomented Indian disaffection, will probably never be proved: the natives can, perhaps, give information on the subject, if they will; and if that evidence be obtained, and thoroughly sifted, by men possessing intimate acquaintance with the Indian languages and character, united to sound judgment, some light may yet be thrown on a subject every branch of which is most interesting as regards the past, most important as regards the future.

No Englishman, except under very peculiar circumstances, would ever detect spies amid a multitude of foreigners. I speak strongly on this point, because, in China, several Russians were pointed out to me by the experienced Dr. Gutzlaff; dressed in the costume of the country, speaking the language, adopting the habits of the people, and appearing, to the casual observer, to all intents native born.

It is notorious that a Captain Vikovitch played a conspicuous part in inciting the unjust and disastrous expedition to Afghanistan against Dost Mohammed. This and many other instances, leave little doubt that Russia maintains, in Central Asia, agents to watch and, if possible, influence the proceedings of England, and probably receives from some of the Greek or Armenian merchants settled at Calcutta or Bombay, accounts about the state finances, the army, and affairs in general; but, besides this, disclosures are said to have been made which prove that Russian emissaries, under various guises, have been successfully at work in inflaming the bigotry of the Mussulman, and the prejudices of the high-caste Hindoo.* It is possible, however, that information on this subject obtained by the government, may, for obvious reasons, be withheld from the public.

This introductory chapter has extended to a greater length than the writer anticipated at its commencement. His design was simply to state the alleged causes of the mutiny, as far as practicable, in the words of those who were their chief exponents, and to refrain from mingling therewith his own views. But the future welfare of India and of England is so manifestly connected with the policy now evolving from the crucible of heated and conflicting public and party feeling, that it is barely possible for any one really interested in the result, to look on, and describe the struggle, without revealing his own convictions on points where right and wrong, truth and fallacy, justice and oppression, are clearly at issue.

In the foregoing summary, some alleged causes are noted which appear to be scarcely compatible with one another. The incom-

* Dr. Duff's *Indian Rebellion*, p. 93.

patibility is perhaps less real than apparent. What we call BRITISH INDIA, is, in fact, a congeries of nations, differing in language, creed, and customs, as do European states, and with even less points of union, excepting only their involuntary association under a foreign government.

It follows, that in striving to trace the origin of wide-spread disaffection, and the connection between seemingly distinct insurrectionary movements, we must be prepared to find great variety of motive—general, local, and temporary—affecting scattered masses, and manifesting itself sometimes in active hostility, sometimes in sullen discontent.

Under a despotic government, with an enormous army of native mercenaries, the outbreak of rebellion would naturally occur among the soldiery. While they were contented, the people would almost necessarily remain in complete subjection; but if the soldiery had grievances, however slight compared with those of the people, the two classes would coalesce; the separate discontent of each party reacting upon the other, the army would initiate rebellion, the people would maintain it. According to Mr. Disraeli, this has actually been the case; the conduct of the Bengal troops, in revolting, having been that of men "who were not so much the avengers of professional grievances, as the exponents of general discontent."*

It is difficult to understand what the reason can have been for keeping up such an enormous Native army as a peace establishment. Soldiers were used to perform police duties in the older provinces, where war had been unknown for years, simply because there were not policemen to do them; and this confounding of civil and military duties lies at the bottom of much misgovernment, extortion, and unnecessary expense. The troops so variously engaged were trained only for arms, yet employed mainly in duties which officers and men looked upon as derogatory to them as soldiers, and which, in fact, they had no business with at all. It was at once deteriorating their efficiency, and putting power unnecessarily in their hands, to employ them in functions which should have been, as a mere matter of policy, kept perfectly distinct.

There is much justice in Lord John Russell's remark, that we have had altogether too large an army, and that 50,000 Europeans, with 100,000 Natives, would be a much better security, as far as force is concerned, than a Native army of 300,000.†

At this moment, the total amount of troops in our service is scarcely less than before the mutiny, so rapidly have new corps replaced the old ones, and new sources of supply become available to meet an urgent demand.‡

There is need of care, lest our new auxiliaries prove equally, if not more dangerous than the old ones. There is more need than ever of moderation, or rather of justice and charity, being urged by the British public on their countrymen in India, lest we lose for ever our hold on the confidence of its vast population.

It is most true that "the time is really come for the people of England and for the government of the country to meet the manifestations of a spirit which would render our rule in India not only a crime but an impossibility, by an active and resolute policy. Outrages on natives must be punished, unless we would willingly and knowingly accept the hostility of India, and, with our eyes open, justify the assertions of the intriguers, who tell the people that nothing will content us but their utter extermination."

The growing alienation of the Europeans from the natives has been already noticed as a cause of disaffection; but since that section was written, the free, fearless, graphic representations of Mr. Russell have thrown new light on the subject, and shown but too plainly a sufficient reason for "the rift, bottomless and apparently causeless, which, even before the mutiny, was observed as separating the European from the native, and increasing in breadth every day."§

Unhappily, it is no new thing to be told

* Debate (Commons), July 28th, 1857. † *Ibid.*

‡ The new recruits are, however, very different men from the tall, well-formed Brahmin or Rajpoot sepoys of the old Bengal army. These were six feet in height, and forty inches round the chest; docile, polite, doing credit to their officers on parade, smart at drill, neat and clean on duty. Already the reaction has commenced; and Indian officers in general appear disposed to recollect (what the best and wisest of them have never forgotten), that "Pandy, until he went mad in 1857, was a good orderly soldier." "For myself," an officer writes in a recent Indian journal, "I would rather serve with them than with the dirty, unworthy, ungentlemanly (Pandy was a gentleman) set of strange bedfellows with whom misfortune has made us acquainted."—Mr. Russell—*Times*, Nov. 8th, 1858.

§ *Ibid.*, October 20th, 1858.

that Englishmen in India are arrogant and exclusive. In the last century, West Indian proprietors and East Indian nabobs were chosen by essayists, novelists, and play-writers, as representing a peculiar class of domestic tyrants, wealthy and assumptious; whose presence, Lord Macaulay said, raised the price of everything in their neighbourhood, from a rotten borough to a rotten egg. The habits they had acquired indicated the life they had led; and all who knew India, and had the intelligence to form, and the moral courage to express, an opinion on the subject, sorrowfully agreed with Bishop Heber in deprecating the "foolish, surly, national pride," of which he daily saw but too many instances, and which he was convinced did us much harm in India. "We are not guilty," he said, "of wilful injustice or oppression; but we shut out the natives from our society, and a bullying, insolent manner is continually assumed in speaking to them."

Some went still further than this, and echoed Lord Byron's emphatic warning,* of the sure retribution that would attend us, if, instead of striving to elevate India, by safe and sure degrees, to our own height of freedom, we tried, with selfish blindness, to get and keep her down beneath the iron heel of despotism, using the energy our own dear-bought freedom sustains in us, not to loosen, but to rivet the chains of a feebler race, for whose welfare we have made ourselves responsible before God and man.

Nothing can be more incompatible with the dignity of our position, than the "vulgar bahaudering" which disgusted Sir Charles Napier in 1850. It appeared then as if Mr. Thackeray's lash were needed to keep within bounds the vagaries of the Anglo-Indian variety of the *genus* "Snob." Now the evil seems to have passed dealing with by such means; it is the provost-marshal or the police-magistrate, not the accomplished satirist, who can alone cope with men whose insolent cruelty needs corporeal rather than mental discipline.

The Duke of Wellington always listened with impatience to commendations of the mere courage of officers. "Brave!" he would say, "of course they are; all Englishmen are brave; but it is the spirit of the gentleman that makes a British officer." Yet, at this very time, when Englishmen and Englishwomen have passed all former traditions of valour and steadfastness in extremest peril, when once again India has proved, in Canning's words, "fertile in heroes"—a class, it would appear not inconsiderable in number, are acting in such a manner as to disgrace the British army, and even the British nation, in the eyes of Europe, and to render the restoration of peace in India as difficult as they possibly can.

The excessive timidity of the Hindoos (of which their reckless daring, or passive submission when hopeless, is the natural counterpart) encourages, in coarse natures, the very arrogance it disarms in higher ones. The wretched manner in which our law-courts are conducted, and the shilling necessary to procure the stamped paper on which to draw up a petition to the court,† operate, in the extreme poverty and depression of the sufferers, in deterring them from bringing any formal complaint, even to obtain justice for a ferocious assault; and so the "sahibs" (European *gentlemen*) ride through the bazaars (markets), and lay open the heads of natives with the butt of their whips, just to clear the way; or, when summoned to court for debt, lay the lash across the shoulders of the presumptuous summonser in the open street, as an expression of opinion. A young gentleman in his cups shoots one of his servants with his revolver; an officer kicks a servant down-stairs because he has entered without leaving his shoes outside the door; and now, daily at the mess-tables, "every man of the mute white-turbaned file, who with crossed hands, glistening eyes, and quick ears, stand motionless in attendance," hears the word "nigger" used every time a native is named, and knows well that it is an expression of contempt. In India, the ears of Europeans become familiarised with the term, which soon ceases to excite surprise or disgust. In England, it is felt to be painfully significant of the state of opinion among those who use it, and cannot be disassociated with the idea of slaves and slave-drivers. It seems the very last word whereby British officers (even in the "griffin" stage) would

* "Look to the East, where Ganges' swarthy race
Shall shake your tyrant empire to the base;
Lo! there rebellion rears her ghastly head,
And glares the Nemesis of native dead;
Till Indus rolls a deep purpureal flood,
And claims his long arrear of Northern blood;
So may ye perish! Pallas, when she gave
Your free-born rights, forbade ye to enslave."
The Curse of Minerva.

† The number of petitions rejected because not written on stamped paper, is said to be enormous. The fact has been repeatedly alluded to in parliament.

choose to denote the men they commanded, or even the people among whom they lived, and who, whatever their colour, are not the less British subjects. But what is to be said for the example given to the European soldiery* by British officers, of Christian parentage and education, one of whom "takes his syce (native groom), because he has put a wrong saddle on his horse, and fastens him on a pole placed out in the full sun of May?"—or by another, who "fastens down his syce in the sun by heel-ropes and foot-ropes, as if he were a horse, and spreads grain before him in mockery?" These instances Mr. Russell gives publicly. Privately, he offers to send the editor of the *Times* evidence of still greater significance.

It is a mockery to talk of equal laws, and yet suffer such outrages as these to pass unpunished. It is difficult to understand why the senior regimental officers do not bring the offenders to justice, unless, indeed, the courts-martial are becoming, as Sir Charles Napier prophesied, mere forms, and the most undoubted offenders certain of "honourable acquittal." Some of the old officers are said to watch the state of affairs with great dissatisfaction; and Sir Frederick Currie (the late chairman of the Court of Directors), with Colonel Sykes and some other leading men, have expressed their opinions with a plainness which has exposed them to the invectives of a certain portion of the Anglo-Indian press.†

"That most vindictive, unchristian, and cruel spirit which the dreadful contest and the crimes of the mutineers have evoked," is not, however, confined to the army and the press; it extends to the counting-house, and even to the pulpit. "One reverend divine has written a book, in which, forgetting that the heart of man is deceitful and desperately wicked, he takes the cheerful view that the Oriental nature is utterly diabolical and hopelessly depraved, as contradistinguished from his own nature and that of his fellows. * * * An excellent clergyman at Simla, recently took occasion, in his sermon, to rebuke the disposition on the part of certain of his hearers to ill-use the natives; but generally, the voice from the pulpit has been mute on this matter, or it has called aloud, 'Go forth and spare not.'"‡

The plain speaking of Mr. Russell himself, is of the first importance to the best interests of England and of India. Nothing but the strongest and most genuine love of justice and hatred of oppression, could give him courage to write as he does, circumstanced as he is. Among the deeds of heroism he so eloquently chronicles, none can surpass that which he is himself enacting, in pleading even now for the rights of the wretched and despised native population, while living in the midst of the class to whom that very wretchedness furnishes food for cruel tyranny, or idle, heartless, senseless jests. On this point, as indeed some other leading features of the rebellion, the public journals, with the *Times* at their head, and the fragmentary but deeply interesting accounts of individual sufferers, are almost the exclusive sources of information. The government have, it is true, furnished the House of Commons with reams of Blue Books and other parliamentary papers; but not one of these contains anything approaching a connected statement of the view taken by the home or Indian authorities of the cause, origin, or progress of the mutiny, which has now lasted fully eighteen months. Each department appears to have sent in its own papers, duly sifted, weeded, and garbled; but no person appears to have revised them as a whole. The omissions of one set are partially supplied by the admissions of another; decided assertions made in ignorance by one functionary, are qualified in the next page by the statement of a colleague. This is the case throughout the whole series yet published, beginning with the various and contradictory allegations made regarding the greased cartridges. To enter into discussion on each point would be endless; and therefore, in subsequent pages, facts, so far as they can be ascertained, will be simply stated, with the authority on which they rest; the counter-statements being left unnoticed, unless they happen to be of peculiar importance or interest.

* The European soldiery are unhappily not slow to follow the example. It is alleged, that very recently a convoy, under a party of the 97th and 20th regiments, were on their way to Lucknow. Darkness fell upon them; there were confusion and delay on the road; probably there were apathy, neglect, and laziness on the part of the garrewans, or native drivers, who are usually a most harmless, inoffensive, and honest race. Some ruffians among the soldiery took advantage of the obscurity to wreak their brutal ferocity on the drivers, and pricked them with their bayonets so severely that one man died of his wounds almost immediately, and the others were removed to the hospital in litters.—*Times*, Nov. 8th, 1858.

† *Ibid.*, Oct. 20th, 1858.

‡ *Ibid.*, November 8th, 1858.